MACHIAVELLI

MACHIAVELLI

J. H. Whitfield

NEW YORK / RUSSELL & RUSSELL

1965

FIRST PUBLISHED IN 1947

REISSUED, 1966, BY RUSSELL & RUSSELL

BY ARRANGEMENT WITH BASIL BLACKWELL, LTD., OXFORD

L.C. CATALOG CARD NO: 66—13175

PRINTED IN THE UNITED STATES OF AMERICA

PREFACE

A CLOUD of English names cling round the progress of Machiavelli. John Wolfe pirated his works in the reign of Queen Elizabeth, and was not found out in doing so till nearly our own day. But Bacon may perhaps have read them in his printing for some justly famous judgments to emerge from his reading. Bedingfield translated the *Florentine Histories*, Edward Dacres the *Prince* and the *Discourses*. Cardinal Reginald Pole uttered the first stern moral rebuke, Marlowe dragged his Machiavel upon the stage to set up there an Elizabethan bogey. Yet, succeeding to Dacres' separate translations, there began to appear towards the end of the seventeenth century, continuing on into the next, a whole series of translations in folio of Machiavelli's collected works. Then was it not an Englishman who played Maecenas to the edition in quarto of 1782 which supplanted finally the old Testina editions, and from which the modern interest in Machiavelli may be said to date? The same Lord Nassau Clavering, Earl Cowper, was the patron whose munificence made possible the monument in Santa Croce on which there was inscribed, for Machiavelli long dead, that motto as brief and proud as the one which was about the same time dedicated in France to Buffon living: TANTO NOMINI NULLUM PAR ELOGIUM.[1] Macaulay wrote a famous essay on Machiavelli, and Lord Morley followed him. And was there not in the nineteenth century that Mr. Philipps who possessed, or was reputed to possess, many manuscript volumes of Machiavelli's letters that had passed by the fraudulent action of a priest out of the hands of the Vettori family into those of Lord Guilford? Mr. Philipps was so jealous of the treasure that he owned as to allow nobody to examine it, not even the editors of the Tuscan edition decreed in 1859, who would have liked to have his letters copied. Finally, in our own times, how many have read the *Prince* under the guidance of L. A. Burd, and after the stimulus of Lord Acton's preface? Despite this widespread interest in him, which can be paralleled in Italy and in Europe generally, or even maybe because of it, Machiavelli has usually been presented garbled. This is an attempt to make him plain.

---

[1] With Buffon's statue outside the Cabinet du Roi was the inscription MAJESTATI NATURAE PAR INGENIUM.

v

CONTENTS

MACHIAVELLI

I

THE NATURE OF HIS GENIUS

NO name in Italian literature is quite as familiar to English ears as that of Machiavel. Even Dante, now that something of the fashion and the fervour of nineteenth-century study has evaporated, is less easily apprehensible than Machiavelli. It is not that respect for Dante as Poet has disappeared, but knowledge of him through personal contact and reverent study has grown rarer. Call something 'dantesque', and you will risk being misunderstood: call something else 'machiavellian', and nobody will doubt, though few will like, your meaning. But it is apparent that those who take the sense of the adjective 'dantesque' do so through some acquaintance with Dante, while the adjective 'machiavellian' is unattached, for the most part, to any knowledge of Machiavelli's works, even by name. That divorce between the common legend of the man and the actual writing on which it is based is quite traditional. When Marlowe claimed, in introducing Machiavel as a Prologue to the *Jew of Malta* in 1592,

> Though some speak openly against my books,
> Yet will they read me,

he nevertheless proved sufficiently by the sentiments he attributed to his puppet in this same prologue that he had not drawn them from his own reading of Machiavelli's books.

> Might first made kings, and laws were then most sure
> When, like the Draco's, they were writ in blood.
> Hence comes it that a strong built citadel
> Commands much more than letters can import.

Alas! Marlowe is the mere opposite of those men who read in secret, and openly deny their reading. His is the opposite hypocrisy: that of not reading, and of claiming to have read. For Machiavelli would have very little of your citadels, as more than one text plainly states; and Marlowe was merely echoing Gentillet, whose primary object was to show that Machiavelli should be held responsible for the massacre of St. Bartholomew.

All that interpretation at second-hand, and at less than second-hand, was enough to produce the concept of 'machiavellianism'; and it is obvious from my title that I do not propose to study this. Few will disagree now (in theory at least) with the statement that it leads away from, and not to, Machiavelli. And, for instance, the development from Marlowe's Prologue to the 'matchless villains' and 'macharetines' of the Elizabethan stage tradition was sufficiently shown by Meyer well before the close of last century. Yet criticism has never quite managed to throw off the shadow of this excrescence. From Cardinal Pole, who was convinced that Satan held the pen, to the author of the *Anti-Machiavel ou Examen du Prince*, with his emphatic hatred of 'le Docteur de la scélératesse', there were few authors who did not curse him. Those who were ready to excuse him did so by the side-step which Macaulay was later to accept, perhaps, from the pages of Bayle, and in the terms of Boccalini, or in those of Seneca's anticipation. For how did Machiavelli himself defend his ways when he was accused in the court of Apollo? Only by handing the moral responsibility on to those who had invented in action what he put down on paper. 'I intend not to defend my writings, I publickly accuse them, and condemn them as wicked and execrable documents for the Government of a State. So if that which I have printed be a doctrine invented by me, or be any new Precepts, I desire that the Sentence given against me by the Judges, be put in execution. But if my writings contain nothing, but such Politick precepts, such rules of State, as I have taken out of the actions of Princes, which (if your Majestie will give me leave) I am ready to name, whose lives are nothing but doing and saying of evil things; what reason is there that they who have invented the mad desperate policies written by me should be held for holy, and that I who am only the publisher of them should be esteemed a Knave and an Atheist?'[1] It is not certain that to codify, to make accessible as recipes, a wickedness that already exists in fact is more excusable, or less dangerous, than to act it. But Machiavelli could have at least the benefit of Seneca's sad remark, *Ut nemo doceat fraudem et scelerum vias regnum docebit*. Needless to say, this fact did not at any time prevent abuse from being directed against Machiavelli, as though he held the chief responsibility.

It was an exception for someone (as Alberigo Gentile) to maintain that Machiavelli's purpose was different, and was good: that he wrote satirically, to expose the tyrant, 'so that with the air of instructing

[1] Boccalini, *Advertisements from Parnassus* (tr. Cary), I, LXXXIX.

the prince he might instruct the people'.[1] But this view was given some prominence by being accepted by Rousseau in the *Contrat Social*, and some apparent validity by its adoption on the part of Alfieri, a more thorough reader of Machiavelli (on whom he based a large part of his own political doctrine) than Rousseau was. And since when Machiavelli came back into fuller view at the end of the eighteenth century it was as a patriotic writer that he came, Alberigo's defence of him was acceptable to the editors of the well-known Italia edition of 1813, as it had been to the poet Foscolo in the *Sepolcri* of 1806. Machiavelli was, in Alberigo's words, 'Democratiae laudator et adsertor acerrimus'; his purpose, that of making tyranny odious.[2] Such views are of historic interest only, in the form which they then took: but it is not uninstructive to see this feeling of conflicting elements, of something that needed, and was capable of receiving, explanation. It was left, at the time, for one of the most sympathetic of the French students of Machiavelli (and of Italy), who could be free from the necessity for patriotic interpretation, to point out that if the *Prince* had in reality been phoney, and meant to trap the prince who acted on it, it would have led its unfortunate author back to the Stinche and the strappado.[3] It was, in its way, a very conclusive observation.

Nevertheless, it was good that the patriotic impetus should have been available, for it carried Machiavelli through a number of editions at the end of the eighteenth and the beginning of the nineteenth century, some of which remain (in spite of accuracy of detail in the modern ones) the most readable presentation of his works. But when Machiavelli came to be assessed, in the second half of the nineteenth century, this view of him as writing to expose, not to advise, began to disappear, as was quite right since it is not founded. Unfortunately, in the process, what useful hints had been secreted here and there on the nature of Machiavelli himself, dating from the time when it seemed possible to have sympathy with him, disappeared also from view, and a picture was formed which owed more unconsciously to old misconceptions than to any new insight. Artaud, who had the merit of being first in the task of reviewing the fortune of Machiavelli through the centuries, might have afforded indications of some value. He had quoted Justus Lipsius, who in the matter of politics exempted from contempt Machiavelli alone, and found him 'vif, subtil, igné'.[4] They are adjectives to chew upon;

---

[1] Bayle, III, 1843.　　　　　　　　　[2] Preface, xxx to *Op.*, 1813.
[3] Artaud, *Machiavel son Génie et ses Erreurs*, 1833, II, 326.
[4] *ibid.*, II, 321, quoting Justus Lipsius, *Politicorum . . . libri sex*, I, 8.

and Artaud himself had seized their import when he asserted that
Machiavelli, in his statements on the need to ruin cities, was merely
carried away by his own arguments: 'L'auteur suit seulement avec
trop d'élan la force et la portée logique de son raisonnement.'[1]
Later critics, who have often used this matter as one for accusation
against Machiavelli, will find themselves owing to their view of the
man himself unable to add any such saving clause. Then Alfieri, in
the very passage which set forth the erroneous interpretation of the
Prince, had spoken firmer, surer words than had been uttered before:
'With regard to this author I must here note in passing a strange
oddity in the human mind. It is that from his *Prince* alone one could
here and there extract a few immoral and tyrannical maxims, and
these are put forward by their author (if one reflects well) much more
to reveal to the peoples the ambitious and wary cruelties of princes,
than to teach princes how to use them; since more or less they always
use them, have used, and will use them, according to their need and
ability. On the other hand, Machiavelli in his histories, and in the
discourses on Livy, at every word and thought breathes liberty,
justice, acumen, truth and high-mindedness, so that whoever reads
well, feels much, and enters into the author, can only become a fiery
enthusiast for liberty.'[2] *Igneus* was the word of Justus Lipsius for
Machiavelli; *focoso* that of Alfieri; and as an echo of these, before the
tide sets another way, I may add Laurent's remark in 1865 on 'le cri
d'un ardent patriote'.[3] If these epithets have any validity, may not
Artaud also be right in stating that Machiavelli was carried away by
the vigour of his own discourse at times?

Meanwhile, these almost casual remarks which had accompanied
this first modern turning to examine Machiavelli carry no weight in
the second half of the nineteenth century, which established Machiavelli's reputation on what seemed a basis of knowledge and historical
criticism. Villari had been the historian of Savonarola before he
turned to the latter's contemporary, and his sympathies went obviously
to the friar: so much so, that it is with him the antithesis between the
two originates: Savonarola all faith and spontaneous enthusiasm,
Machiavelli all analysis, doubt and searching.[4] It was an easy contrast
to seize hold of, flattering to religious sentiment on the one hand,
taking full advantage of distrust for Machiavelli on the other. Nor,
obviously, had its author given any credence to the adjectives of
Alfieri and Lipsius. Villari belonged to the school of historical criticism

[1] Artaud, I, 298.   [2] Alfieri, *Del Principe e delle Lettere* (in *Opere*, Italia, 1828, II), II, ix, 328.
[3] F. Laurent, *Etudes sur l'Histoire de l'Humanité*, X, 319.
[4] Villari, *La St. di G. Sav.*, I, 319–22.

(though he came too soon to have a historical view of Machiavelli) and was therefore in the opposite camp to De Sanctis, the champion of aesthetic, or impressionistic, criticism. Such adversaries should have different tales to tell. Yet, just as Carducci cursed De Sanctis openly, only to borrow quietly (as in the very case of Machiavelli and Savonarola) his judgments, so De Sanctis at times approximates, whether consciously or unconsciously we are not called on here to say, to his opposite number, Villari. The fact that De Sanctis was an impressionist in all his criticism, with a very limited capacity for understanding the Renascence, did not prevent him from saying some sound things about Machiavelli, though they were mixed with much that was unsound; and it is he, even more than the systematic historian Villari, who left the main directive. They came in an age of positivism, and between them they created the mirage of a positivist Machiavelli. The latter, for De Sanctis, is the founder of the science of history and politics for modern times, because he left out the supernatural from human affairs, abandoned syllogisms for the intelligent study of facts that could be seized as a series consisting of causes and effects.[1] That is, of course, not very different from what Bacon pointed to in a famous phrase, and no one after De Sanctis has challenged this part of the formula. But it is De Sanctis also who saw Machiavelli's thought as both a reaction, and an exaggeration: Machiavelli's conception of the State was for De Sanctis too much like the all-absorbing Divinity of the Middle Ages which it replaced. This is a hint which was not unnoticed afterwards: sanctioned by Croce as being accurate it was ready for use for various purposes.[2]

Nor did Tommasini, who intervened with his vast, and useful, volumes on Machiavelli, influence greatly the trend of opinion. Tommasini had sloughed many prejudices, but it was not a helpful formula that he chose: to quote everything apropos of one author baffles much more than it enlightens, and Tommasini's *magnum opus* is a monument to vast, and undiscriminating, scholarship. What does it matter that his viewpoint is often sober and always, of course, informed, if few can have the patience, or the leisure, to disentangle it from the two thousand five hundred grey pages in which he buried it? There was a *mot* of Professor Foligno that in Villari *C'è tutto, fuorché il Machiavelli*: one might say of Tommasini that here there is both everything and Machiavelli too. Do we want an instance? Let us look at the great chapter on Machiavelli and Religious Thought, which contains the most judicious exposition of the matter. Out of

---

[1] *St. d. lett. it.*, II, 61.   [2] Croce, *Teoria e st. d. storiogr.*, 212.

two hundred pages which trace the progress of religion from antiquity, sacred and profane, down to Christian Science and Shintoism, twenty pages here and there are directly relevant perhaps to the personal equation of Machiavelli. It is the bulk of Tommasini's investigations that has prevented his very moderate account of Machiavelli from being influential. If it had had a reasonable compass it might have cut short the run of books where Machiavelli figures still as the main villain in the world's sad farce. But as it is, it is still possible, is it not so much simpler? to write in the manner of Gentillet about Machiavelli: to cull the wicked maxims in a short and inaccurate excursus at the outset of a book, then trace to his immoral influence all that is rotten in the state of a nation. Does that seem too insouciant a formula still to work? It was the method of M. Cherel, considering Machiavelli in France in 1935, and it has not changed essentially since Gentillet. So little does one need, for this sort of criticism, to have read Machiavelli with one's own eyes, that M. Cherel was able to think his author preferred Alexander VI to Julius II because the latter was weak enough to neglect his opportunity of suppressing an enemy by a grandiose crime at Perugia![1] No one, at least, had formerly confused Julius, notable for his headstrong impetuosity, with Gianpaolo Baglioni. And after the first few carefree pages on the doctrine, then it is possible to pen the panegyric on one's own race, and to view all that is bad as an intrusion. 'Ce que Racine a glorifié ici, en l'opposant au machiavélisme, c'est l'esprit le plus authentique de la monarchie française.'[2] But was Racine thinking of Machiavelli in writing *Athalie*, about which this remark is made? No, he was, according to M. Cherel even, envisaging Louis XIV. Yes, but in so far as Louis XIV represents bad and absolutistic tendencies in monarchy he must be un-French. Therefore, he is the product of machiavellianism. It is an ironic commentary to this that much of what M. Cherel commends as being genuinely French, or genuinely medieval, or genuinely Christian, is in accord with views of Machiavelli of which he is unaware. The title of his book might better be *Not-Machiavel in France*, and the fundamental method is a familiar one with the propagandist: appeal to the idea of what a thing (let us say the French monarchy) ought to be—how admirable, how French, how realistic! Look at what it happens to be at a given moment (say in the time of Louis XIV), yes, of course, how unfortunate: but its state does not really affect the argument because it shouldn't be so, nor indeed would it be so if it weren't for

[1] Cherel, *La Pensée de Machiavel en France*, 15.   [2] *ibid.*, 196.

either Machiavelli or machiavellianism. Nor am I digressing from
my regrets at the bulk of Tommasini's volumes in expressing my distrust at this manner of procedure: for if Tommasini had been shorter
M. Cherel and his fellows might have found one of those sage
sentences, several of which are scattered in his two thousand pages:
'For a mind accustomed to dogmatic schemes history, when it does
not fit in with dogma, is as though it did not exist.'[1]

There has been room then, in our time as ever, for the books with a
thesis against Machiavelli, and without much of a basis in Machiavelli.
And even in the hands of criticism proper Machiavelli has not fared
too well. After Tommasini there came exponents such as Ercole,
whose views grew more Fascist as Mussolini seemed to him more
plainly the true Hero of the *Prince*. Obviously, Ercole accepted De
Sanctis's hint: was there not a Trucchi, in commenting the *Divine
Comedy*, who applauded Dante's conception of the State as Fascist?
Machiavelli, says Ercole, is neither immoral nor amoral; his categorical
imperative concerns the good of the State, to which all else is subordinated. That is the overriding morality of Machiavelli. If we
look back to De Sanctis's essay in the *Storia della Letteratura Italiana*,
we shall have no difficulty in seeing that he prepares the way very
plainly for a Fascist interpretation of Machiavelli. But there will be
few whose sympathies will be aroused now for Machiavelli by any
such twist as this to him.

The case of Machiavelli is a *cause célèbre*; but it is one in which the
evidence has not often been called or heeded, in which passion or
prejudice has commonly provided the verdict, and in which the
defence has frequently been as faulty as the prosecution. It is thus
that the simplest points with regard to Machiavelli have been mis-
stated. Let us pick up the contradiction latent between the indications
of Alfieri and of Villari. What sort of a man was he? 'Pour peindre
en un mot toute cette politique, c'est le génie appliqué à la scélératesse.'[2] Then he is bad and calculating? At least, that is how Villari
depicted him: 'Even if a brigand chief had had the daring and dexterity to upset a country and subject it to his rule, Machiavelli would
have admired his ability and courage without taking alarm at any
sanguinary and cruel action. . . . This all came from the nature of
his genius, the character of the times, and—it may be—the coldness of
his heart, which, though certainly not bad, was not easily inflamed
with any very ardent enthusiasm for goodness.'[3] We shall find before

[1] Tommasini, II, 601. [2] St. Hilaire, *Politique d'Aristote*, 1848.
[3] Villari, *N.M.*, I, 337.

long that modern criticism has not deviated in the main from that.
But we must notice first that what had been presented fugitively to us
as a fiery nature now seems cold; what was ardent is now *not easily
inflamed*. Yet even Villari could not quite leave the picture thus
without throwing in some contradictory elements. True, Machiavelli has his patriotism, and then, *aux bons moments*, 'the cynical smile
of the cold diplomatist disappears from his lips, and his physiognomy
suddenly assumes, to our eyes, a serious and severe solemnity, revealing to us the flame of genuine patriotism that is burning in his heart
and ennobling his existence'.[1] That has all the elements of surprise
about it: but it cannot make a wholly satisfactory picture, since the
two halves of it are incompatible. A cold heart, and yet it is inflamed
with patriotism! Even the petrarchists were more logical, since they
took care to keep the flames in their own bosom, while the ice was
in that of their mistress. But once more, as an interpretation of
Machiavelli's character it is not very far from that of De Sanctis.

Indeed, for the latter, the appropriate motto to suit Machiavelli is
nil admirari: 'Non si maraviglia e non si appassiona, perché com-
prende.' His is the *apathy* of the doctor: 'It is the apathy of the
superior mind, looking with compassion at the convulsive and
nervous movements of the passions.'[2] This was language dear to the
critics of the end of the nineteenth century, with their discovery of
the pathological, the clinical, viewpoint. So Pollock (I am indebted
to the erudition of Tommasini for the phrase) found in Machiavelli
'the pure passionless curiosity of the man of science'.[3] All this at a
time before a D'Annunzio had come to show that this sort of objec-
tivism could be (and usually was) as imaginative as romanticism,
though in a different way. In the meantime, De Sanctis was able to
make his usual (and prejudicial) point about the difference between
the age of Dante and that of the Renascence. The centre for Dante
was the heart; with Machiavelli, it is the brain. In the Italian Renascence the intellect is adult while the conscience has decayed. Hence
the equation: 'The God of Dante is love, a unifying force for intellect
ánd action—and the result was Wisdom. The God of Machiavelli
is the intellect, intelligence and regulation of the forces of the world:
the result is Science.'[4] And De Sanctis proceeds inevitably to the same
corollaries as Villari: *virtù* has changed its meaning, and Machiavelli
admires, when and wherever he finds it, the force and energy of the
mind that knows and dares. His Hero is the tamer of man and

---

[1] Villari, *N.M.*, I, 373.   [2] De Sanctis, II, XV, 66.
[3] Tommasini, II, 173, and see the rest of Pollock's remarks there or in *An Introduction to the
History of the Science of Politics*, 1893, 42.   [4] De Sanctis, II, 65.

nature, 'the one who understands and rules natural and human forces, and makes them his instruments'.[1] His *virtuous* man is Caesar Borgia, then.[2] And perhaps, if that stood alone, it would do duty. It was coherent and apprehensible. Does not such an attitude inspire most obviously the sublime nonsense which Tommasini's omnivorous appetite discovered in Mr. Draper's *History of the Intellectual Development of Europe*? 'His works thus offer the purest example we possess of physical statesmanship. They are altogether impassive. He views the management of a state precisely as he might do the construction of a machine, recommending that such a wheel or such a lever should be introduced, his only inquiry being whether it will accomplish his intention. As to any happiness or misery it may work he gives himself no concern, unless, indeed, they evidently ought to enter into the calculation.'[3] That is blood-curdling, Mr. Draper; but how would it affect the matter if the object of Machiavelli's calculation were, like that of Dante or Thomas Aquinas, if in a different way, the achievement of a good state of society? Must not happiness or misery evidently enter the calculation, since the first is what one aims to arrive at, the second what one desires to escape from? What sense can be left to the calculation if it has no such ends in view? It would be an addition sum without a total. Or at least, it would reduce Machiavelli to the simple recommendation which M. Cherel saw in him: 'Aux princes il dit: Soyez absolus, par tous les moyens.'[4] It might, of course, be true that Machiavelli makes it; but it is apparent, if he does, that he must have left his passionless curiosity and his objectivity, and start with a prejudice in favour of one method of government. So that we are led, from a desanctisian base, towards a contradiction.

It is because of this same question of the end in view, of the reasons for building this machine with all its levers, which can hardly exist without an intention, that there develops in De Sanctis himself the same blurring of the picture we have seen with Villari: as it unfolds, so it begins to be at war within itself. Machiavelli glorifies energy, even when at the service of the bad: that is the Italy of the Renascence. 'It was an adult intelligence, very alert but abstract, a formal logic with a complete indifference as to aim. It was knowledge for knowledge sake, as art for art. In the conscience there was no longer an aim nor a content.'[5] So we have the leer by which the Italian Renascence asserts its own intellectual superiority, and reveals its moral

---

[1] *ibid.*, 69. [2] *ibid.*, 66. [3] Tommasini, II, 21. [4] Cherel, 231.
[5] De Sanctis, II, 70.

decadence. We are still coherent. But then De Sanctis begins to
add the surprising touches: the true Muse of Machiavelli is irony,
and it is an irony which springs because his *poetic world* is too far from
reality. We had not suspected from the account of him as it so far
stood that he had, or wished to have, any poetic world. How can
De Sanctis arrive at so novel a discovery? It is his gloss to the last,
the embarrassing, chapter of the *Prince*, which De Sanctis sees as
something magnificent, written in poetic language unlike Machiavelli's wont, and testifying 'rather to the aspirations of a noble heart
than to the calm persuasion of a man of politics. They were illusions.'[1]
I quote the good De Sanctis a little baldly, because again the elements
of this portrait must make it enigmatic. We had seen established, or at
least asserted, that the centre was the head, and that the heart and
conscience were quite empty. Now it seems, on the contrary, that
the heart is good and *noble*, that it is full of illusions: a strange filling,
surely, for the heart of a pitiless realist! But De Sanctis did not pause
to ask himself where Machiavelli's apathy had gone: it was no wonder,
he continued, that Machiavelli had illusions, 'because there was much
that was poetical in his nature'. And by this sequence De Sanctis,
who had begun by making a formal antithesis of Dante and Machiavelli, now ventured to find much in the latter that he could call
dantesque.

A mind without a conscience, admiring force irrespective of the
use made of force, allied to a noble heart; illusions in a man who is
the impassive analyser of facts! The opposite of Dante, yet the
possessor of qualities which are Dante's! There is no sense that can
be made out of the picture of Machiavelli as De Sanctis and Villari
left it; unless, indeed, Machiavelli were some monster compound of
incompatibles. Nevertheless, they arrived quite simply at this picture,
and its origins explain its inconsistencies. Although De Sanctis had
proposed to put on one side *machiavellismo*, that something he claimed
as an incidental in Machiavelli himself, magnified to be an all by his
imitators, and the main obstacle between us and him, yet he has a
purely traditional base for his picture of Machiavelli. This observer
who adds nothing of his own in his analysis of facts, where have we
seen him? Is he not to be identified (when we have discounted the
scientific terminology of the nineteenth century) with the Machiavelli
who defended himself in Apollo's court of Parnassus in the words of
Boccalini? This Machiavelli who admires the wicked, as long as they
dare to do their worst, how far is he from that alias for Satan whom

Cardinal Reginald Pole denounced? But what, meanwhile, of the illusions, the poetic soul, the noble heart, the aspirations and the enthusiasm—all terms with which De Sanctis intersprinkled his account? They must have some connection with the identification of Machiavelli which we have seen established by the forgotten (and necessarily inadequate) criticism of the first half of the nineteenth century.

Now in the sequel Italian criticism, even where it has not been enmeshed in Fascist interpretations, has not often seemed able to realize clearly the untenability of these now well-established views. Modern labour has gone more often to the preparation of a definitive text (even when this, as in the Mazzoni and Casella edition, has been presented in a somewhat illegible form) than to the adjusting of the focus. Some writers, as Janni or Prezzolini, have merely heightened the colours of the traditional picture till it became caricatural. And we may say that this has been a habitual procedure outside Italy. Others, more sophisticated, as Luigi Russo, have restated it, not in the rather elementary style of De Sanctis, but in the stilted jargon which a nodding acquaintance with Croce and philosophy has too often bestowed on recent Italian literary criticism. It is this that has been made to supply the bridge which connects the two supposed sides of Machiavelli; and when Russo asks the old question of De Sanctis on why Machiavelli writes like a poet and a prophet in the last chapter of the *Prince* he has, in reality, no more valid answer than had his predecessor. It is a *revanche* for Machiavelli's opposite, Savonarola. The latter, indeed, 'is vindicated in the very mind of Machiavelli, who, by a curious but inevitable contradiction, after he has dissertated coldly on the arts of the lion and the fox, at the end of his treatise' turns prophet and speaks biblically.[1] If a thing is a curious contradiction it would not seem that it should also be inevitable; and I have a feeling that this convenient inevitability is merely an uncritical acceptance of the old equation. But elsewhere Russo covers up better the fact that he has no new views of his own. How is it, he inquires, that Machiavelli can at the same time write legislation for republics, as well as for 'the most anti-democratic monarchy'?[2] It is because he is endowed with an objectivity which is worn with something of a difference: it is not only 'nuda logica', it is as well 'questa poesia della tecnica pura', because it is the doing that matters to Machiavelli, not the value of the thing done. When this statement is filtered of its ambitious language it will be found not

---

[1] Russo, *Ritratti e Disegni Storici*, 1937, 15.　　　　[2] *ibid.*, 33.

to have advanced one scrap from De Sanctis and Villari; or if it has advanced, it has advanced to the position in which Machiavelli is recognized as being passionately dispassionate (or if we can tolerate it better, poetically unpoetical). And it is because Russo is still on their old ground that he can (and rightly, for that matter) throw in the assertion of the warmth of Machiavelli's nature alongside that of its coldness. The author who hated the middle course is by temperament an extremist. 'Meglio essere impetuoso che respettivo' he had written in the *Prince*, and Russo finds it fit the man himself. Does he not force events with his 'accesa immaginazione'? Use violence even on historic facts to draw them to demonstrations that are unexpected? This is poetic objectivity indeed.

Even so, in that it does not raise new contradictions, but only contents itself with refurbishing the old, it is to be preferred to the ingenious paradoxes of Toffanin. For the latter, what is valid in Machiavelli is the discovery of the need for absolutism, for the State (we are not really far from De Sanctis, or from Ercole); and because the *Discorsi* look more republican, and seem more a point of arrival than the *Prince*, the need arose to remove them from the argument. Toffanin did not content himself with the ready view of Perrens (and of others): that if Machiavelli wrote them both, then obviously he was indifferent to both.[1] He refutes the evidence of the *Discorsi* because, of course, Machiavelli was only playing to his gallery. He would have plumped for Tacitus, had not Buondelmonti and Rucellai (to whom he dedicated the work) been republicans! By this gentle sophistry Toffanin was able to dismiss the Livian Machiavelli of the *Discorsi* in order to come to the real one, 'il Machiavelli dei Tacitisti',[2] the Machiavelli of the *Prince*. It must be added, in fairness to Tacitus, that when Toffanin had got thus far he still had to find Machiavelli at the antipodes to Tacitus: a situation which, however, Toffanin (so great is human ingenuity) was able to claim as also an identity.[3] This, I think, is a perversity of criticism, not an avenue to understanding.

It was left for Chabod, in a brilliant and classic discussion of the dating of the *Prince*, to seize most firmly, and (since his polemic was quite a different one) without becoming involved in the old contradiction, the nature of Machiavelli. The latter's letters to Vettori between June and August, 1513, show him in the possession of a *furor politicus* that grows ever more fierce and heroic. There quivers in

---

[1] Perrens, *Histoire de Florence*, III, 384.　　[2] Toffanin, *Machiavelli e il Tacitismo*, 22–5.
[3] *ibid.*, 68.

these letters the same vehemence, the same urge to speak, as in the *Prince*. In both letters and treatise there is mingled sarcasm and indignation, grief and hope, and it is these sentiments which are transfigured in the closing chapter of the *Prince*. It is incandescent matter boiling in his mind. 'Chi ripensi la passionalità del Machiavelli, la natura sua cosí vivace e irruente . . .', such a one, reading the letters, will understand the genesis in the same period of time of the *Prince*.[1] This, without troubling to make the refutation, dismisses the *coldness* that Villari saw as a characteristic (so ready are men to find their own qualities in others), and the dispassionate *apathy* of De Sanctis. Irony belongs to the mind, but sarcasm springs from the feelings. We are back to the indications of Justus Lipsius and Artaud, and we may turn for confirmation from the muddle of the critics to one who should be as well informed as the next person on this matter of temperament: to Machiavelli himself.

Here indeed is a man whose main work is a commentary to an ancient historian, in whose unerring pages he finds all the recipes for the reformation of the present, or thinks he does; and his fate is that for centuries men hold him up as one who looked at facts in all their nakedness with never a glimmer of idealism. To escape from the political situation around him he turned back two thousand years towards the past; and critics write that we can understand why he was what he was because he was the product of his times. A Frenchman wrote a book on Machiavellianism before Machiavelli, and found the models for his theory in the Sforzas and their like. And long before Benoist waxed lyrical over the unscrupulousness that Machiavelli had found to inspire him Hume had remarked, in stating that Machiavel was certainly a 'great genius', that his reasonings on monarchy were defective since he had confined his study to the 'furious and tyrannical governments of ancient times, or to the disorderly principalities of Italy'. How could Machiavelli build his system (if he has one) on the realities of the Italian political scene, on the pattern of the Sforzas and the Borgias, when it is the inadequacy of these which brings him to the point of writing? His whole idea, often formulated, always operative, is to escape out of the present morass, to substitute for its corruption and failure something better. It hardly follows that the present corruption can at the same time provide him with his recipe; and indeed Machiavelli is quite explicit about this matter of recipes. 'Io non mi partirò mai con esempio di qualunque cosa da'miei Romani', he wrote, in the name of Fabrizio Colonna, at the

[1] F. Chabod, in *Archivum Rom.*, 1927, 376–7.

beginning of the *Arte della Guerra*; and Guicciardini was quick to see that such an infatuation was impractical, anachronistic. But Guicciardini could not have imagined that nobody would take his point for centuries, that all would see Machiavelli as a cold scientist, instead of as an idealist, with dreams of improvement.

It is the temperament of Machiavelli which conditions his writing, and is most clearly revealed by it. And if we look at his works we shall find the indications for it irrefutable, and irrefutably on the side of Chabod. *The coldness of his heart*, said Villari, *not easily inflamed*: and what did Machiavelli say about it? In the *Primo Decennale* he expressed his anxieties over the course of events, his fears for Florence, and he closes with the expression of the intensity of his feeling:

> Onde l'animo mio tutto s'infiamma
> Or di speranza, or di timor si carca,
> Tanto che si consuma a dramma a dramma.

It is a statement which confirms one at least of the contradictory impressions of De Sanctis. The latter, it will be well remembered by his readers, had a famous distinction between poets and artists, writers and men. Obviously, Machiavelli, tested at this touchstone, is no dilettante stylist: he is a *man* and not a *writer* only; and De Sanctis worked the equation out quite right. 'Qui l'uomo è tutto, e non ci è lo scrittore, o ci è solo in quanto uomo.' The result is that mere form is swept away: 'Quello che scrive è una produzione immediata del suo cervello, esce caldo caldo dal di dentro. . . .'[1] That is very true; but it would be quite impossible if Machiavelli was cold inside; if he was the frigid analyst, the clinical dissector of facts. The *Prince*, for instance, was written at white heat in a few months of 1513, it bursts into obvious flame in its close; yet, so much were its critics caught up with the often-stated views on Machiavelli, that until not long ago they were discussing how they could lop off the close as something extraneous, added as a sop, or as a cloak, at any rate quite different from the *coldness* of the rest of the book. The coldness is, of course, a figment; the close belongs to the book; one has only to start with an opposite idea of Machiavelli's temperament to find the *Prince* more explicable; and the indication of Machiavelli himself at the end of the *Primo Decennale* is amply confirmed throughout his other writings.

But if the temperament of Machiavelli is warm, it does not follow necessarily that it is also good. Perhaps he is hot and passionate? There is in the *Discorsi* a passage which adds admirably to the tercet

[1] De Sanctis, II, 64-5.

of the *Decennale*. Machiavelli has a chapter there in praise of those who found, not, as Villari must have imagined, of those who destroy, civil institutions; and he paraphrases Tacitus in a noble account of the contrast between the Roman world under good Emperors and bad ones. His conclusion is memorable. It is that the reader of his parallel will burn with the desire to imitate the good side rather than the bad. 'E sanza dubbio, se e'sarà nato d'uomo, si sbigottirà da ogni imitazione de'tempi cattivi, ed accenderassi d'uno immenso desiderio di seguire i buoni.'[1] The terms of that conclusion to Machiavelli's comparison can hardly be overstressed: not only does he burn himself with this immense desire to achieve a good state of society; but he asserts that nobody who is human will react in any other way on hearing it. All will burn as well with the same immense desire. Here is a coldness with a difference; or rather, something so plain and elementary that, had not the air been charged with prejudices since Machiavelli's time, none could have failed to recognize it. Yet, if we look at the modern interpretations of Machiavelli, we shall find that his plainest statements have gone unheeded. Mr. Eliot wished to use his Machiavelli as a stalking-horse for the Church. He picked up, then, from Lord Morley, the idea of Machiavelli only seeing half the truth (Lord Morley meant, he saw the bad about mankind, and not the good): 'What Machiavelli did not see about human nature is the myth of human goodness which for liberal thought replaces the belief in Divine Grace.'[2] The point is easy: read Machiavelli's account of the wickedness of man, and realize how sinful a creature he is left to himself, and in his natural state! But this piece of propaganda was a little irresponsible, resting on the legend of Machiavelli, more than on Machiavelli himself; and if the latter thinks of all men as likely to burn with a desire for good, when it is set in picture before them, he has some greater belief in human goodness than Eliot, or his predecessors in criticism, had realized.

⬤bviously, we are passing here from the temperament of Machiavelli to the kindred subject of his outlook. And here there has been sufficient unanimity for both Mr. Eliot and Benito Mussolini to speak the same language. He was, said the latter, a 'spregiatore degli uomini'.[3] He regards man as bad. And it is plain that we have only to add the theological part, which Machiavelli omitted, to arrive at a conformity with, shall we say, a Bossuet, who wrote of 'la tyrannie des passions, et la prodigieuse malignité du coeur humain toujours

---

[1] *D.* I, X, 47. [2] T. S. Eliot, *For Lancelot Andrewes*.
[3] B. Mussolini, *Scritti e Discorsi*, IV, 107.

porté à faire le mal'.[1] Or the conformity may be with Dante, in
M. Gilson's view of Dante's philosophy: 'mais la malice des hommes
est telle qu'ils ne vivront pas selon la vertu à moins qu'on ne les y con-
traigne'.[2] So that we might arrive, by the slightest adjustment, at
the conclusion that Dante's Emperor, Bossuet's absolute king, and
Machiavelli's Prince have all the same function, and the same
Christian sanction. Naturally, the demonstration that Machiavelli was
doing something different, though still doing something that was
intended to be good, does not arise here, and must await our consideration of the *Prince* itself. But we must note at this point that
this charge of pessimism, though it rests on notorious texts, yet
meets a plain check in the most explicit statements of Machiavelli.
Let us look once more at the remark I quoted: 'E sanza dubbio, se
e'sarà nato d'uomo, si sbigottirà da ogni imitazione de'tempi cattivi,
ed accenderassi d'uno immenso desiderio di seguire i buoni.' That is
neither the language of pessimism, nor of one who regards man as
naturally bad. But, strangely enough, it is not untypical of Machiavelli at the most crucial points of his writings. Why did he write his
Discorsi? He says in his Proem, after a little (which I had better
mention, for fear lest I should be accused of suppressing his pessimism)
on the envious nature of men, their being readier to blame than to
praise, that he is impelled to write by the natural desire which he has
always had to do those things he thought of common benefit to all:
'spinto da quel naturale desiderio che fu sempre in me di operare,
sanza alcuno respetto, quelle cose che io creda rechino comune
benefizio a ciascuno'.[3] A birthright which includes such natural
desires as this is clearly other than that of impotence to good as stated
in the *Discours sur l'Histoire Universelle*. Machiavelli is not speaking
the language of Bossuet, nor is he fettered in the fallen world where
Mr. Eliot meant to place him. He is speaking the language of the
humanists; and since this spirit of optimism, here the starting-point
for the whole of the *Discorsi*, conditions his writing it is useless to
counter it with the well-known texts in which Machiavelli, for
instance, talks of the necessity for a legislator to presuppose all men
as bad. Neo-classical precepts such as that may belie the temperament
of Machiavelli; they do not change it. And as well, the presupposition of the *Discorsi* is that the *ordini* of the world are wrong, through
lack of knowledge. It is not pessimism to see things as wrong, or bad,
if they are wrong and bad. That is only accuracy of vision. But the

---

[1] Bossuet, *Discours sur l'Histoire Universelle*, 1681, I, 8.
[2] E. Gilson, *Dante et la Philosophie*, 151.　　　[3] D.I., *Proemio*, 6.

Discorsi themselves are to give the right knowledge; and even if Machiavelli is not equal to his task, he hopes to bring it near enough to completion for a successor to finish it. That is pure optimism; and it does not need the cautious Guicciardini to remind us how rash it was as optimism. Few men burn immensely with the desire for the achievement of a common good; not all are capable of accepting knowledge, even when it is set forth. Is it not unexpected to find Machiavelli's enthusiasm overshooting our capacities? Even in him a pessimistic tinge creeps in among his later letters, at the end of his life when his hopes for Florence and Italy are further than ever from any fruition, when, instead, the dismal year 1527 is to bring him and Florence and Rome down to eclipse. But, again, that does not alter his nature, nor the tendency of his thought in his earlier, creative, period. And we can look to him with some hope that the praise which Alfieri gave to him (along with his wrong assessment of the actual scope of the *Prince* itself) may be justified when we have read him. In the meantime, we may feel assured that it is the coldness and pessimism of his nature which are myths carried forward from the long legend that has been woven round him.

II

THE BACKGROUND OF HIS TIME

THE theme of Machiavelli is inseparably bound to the history of his time. In its outlines this is probably well enough, if not over-well, known. Its significance, the reasons for its being what it was, that is more controversial. I have felt it necessary to include the briefest of introductions to this historical theme, setting out the table for the game that was being played, showing how the major pieces were disposed, and what the openings were. To add more would be to distract attention away from criticism of an individual writer, and to seem to move towards the writing of history. That I do not wish to do.

The nineteenth century had a thesis that it was the new culture of Italy which was responsible for its weakness politically and militarily. The history of the fifteenth century, with its despots and its mercenaries, with papal simony and iniquity, became an integral part of what is known as the Renascence; and the two sides, political and cultural, were treated together, as by Burckhardt or Monnier, and made to explain each other mutually. It was my purpose in an earlier volume[1] to establish some separation of levels; to detach the valid stream of ideas that constitutes the contribution of the Italian Renascence to modern civilization, and to show a cultural development at a level which was unable to affect political conditions (because it was, naturally, outside or beneath them); to claim finally that what has strength and point for us now could not have been a merely empty culture in its process of formation. It is my business here to examine the culture of the Renascence at the point where it becomes painfully aware of politics. This point is Machiavelli. For he does not represent (it is an assertion that I have made in my first chapter, but its proof will follow) the double degeneracy of both politics and culture. He represents instead the culture that is born of humanism becoming aware of political problems because they are at a crisis. It is because of this that he seeks to solve them from the elements with which humanism had endowed the western mind. But, for these reasons, we are obliged to examine the crisis which precipitates his writing.

[1] *Petrarch and the Renascence*, 1943.

It does not follow that because the princes of Renascence Italy were attracted by new art or learning to patronize them, so acquiring both as a veneer, that they had thereby changed the elements of the political situation which they inherited, or which they were in the process of creating. That is a confusion which arises in the wake of Burckhardt. If we went back beyond him, to the first examiners of the Renascence in modern criticism, we should find that this contamination had not germinated. Hallam saw the Italian fifteenth century as the 'golden morning of Italian wisdom'. But it was a morning only: the first studies of ancient wisdom were directed to Letters and to Arts, and this, joined with the movement of industry and commerce, inspired the first flowering of modern European civilization. And, Hallam continued, had not the fatal pressure of Spain perverted taste, altered the tendencies of the Italians, taking them away from the habits of industry which belonged to their fathers, only to substitute for these sloth and display, then the fruits of autumn might have followed so fair and promising a spring. It was the events of 1530 (Hallam might have said it was the battle of Pavia, in 1525), and not premature decrepitude, that brought subjugation to Italy.[1]

That is a very different thesis from the one of Jacob Burckhardt. It seeks a historical explanation for the rise and fall of culture, not a cultural cause for the events of history. It is one which has a theoretic confirmation where we need it most, in the explicit statement of Machiavelli himself. It has often been remarked that the latter seems insensitive to the art that was flourishing around him. He may have met Leonardo on his missions to Caesar Borgia; he lived in the same city as Michaelangelo, and there are even passages in letters to him which refer to suggested contact between the two—for the transmittance of a sum of money![2] But he himself speaks of neither, nor of their works. He breathes politics only. Yet in the eloquent close to the *Arte della Guerra* Machiavelli recognizes the merit of Italy in this resurrection of art and literature, so that he was not blind to its taking place: 'perché questa provincia pare nata per risuscitare le cose morte, come si è visto della poesia, della pittura e della scultura'.[3] He is almost willing to hope, in this context, that, since this is so, Italy will go one step further, and learn military science from the ancients. That tells us clearly enough, not that he regards the Renascence as something harmful or abortive, something that brings its

---

[1] Cf. Zambelli, xxii, for Hallam, *Europe in the Middle Ages*.
[2] *Lettere Familiari*, ed. Alvisi, 143 and 148.   [3] *A. d. G.*, VII, 423.

own punishment, but instead as something which needs extension, and is capable of receiving it. And in a famous text at the outset of his *Discourses on Livy*, where Machiavelli once again for a fleeting moment makes mention of works of art, it is to express a similar desire: 'Considering, then, what honour men attribute to antiquity, and how many times a fragment of an ancient statue has been bought at a great price, for a man to have it by him, and to honour his house with it, for him to be able to have it copied by those who take pleasure in this art' . . . to see all this honour given to one side of antiquity, and to see on the other hand all the noble deeds that histories relate of ancient kingdoms and republics, performed by kings, captains, citizens, legislators admired rather than copied, 'piú presto ammirate che copiate', that is to see both a gap and the hope of filling it. He hopes to draw men from this error (not the error of looking to antiquity, but that of not looking to enough of it), he hopes to use this culture also for the amendment of present faults.[1] Is not the text significant, and conclusive? It is not, in Machiavelli's opinion, the culture that is responsible for the faults of the fifteenth century: it is that its culture, its cult for antiquity, has not gone far enough: the history of the fifteenth century is its own, uninfluenced for the better by the backward glance of humanism. Now just occasionally one may find that statement still extant in modern writers. Thus Caggese, in his history of Florence, remarked that Humanism illumined with new thought and new ideals the human mind, but that the State remained stationary, immobile, fixed on old indivi-dualistic prejudices, an engine of oppression and no longer an instru-ment of progress. As it had emerged out of the communes into the *signoria* it was something that hampered: 'faced with the foreign States, set up on a more ample base . . . it no longer made any sense'.[2] That offers a very reasonable explanation, when we remember the long roots there are to the Italian situation. But it was a casual remark, lost in a tide which was flowing resolutely another way. It was, for various reasons, so much more attractive to say the culture caused decay. It saved distinctions, offered the master-key.

But, naturally, contemporary writers were not furnished with this modern theory; and it is as refreshing as it is necessary to turn back to them to see their comments on the situation which developed in Italy from 1494 onwards. The theorists, born at this moment, and born of the new culture of Italy, as of the political liberty of Florence —men like Machiavelli and Guicciardini—look for a reason for the

[1] *D. I, Proem*, 6–7.   [2] Caggese, II, 511.

downfall of Italy. They found it in disunity, for instance, a theme which both of them attach indissolubly to the agelong question of the papal temporal power. Guicciardini laments as well (how often!) the irreconcilable discord and the mad ambitions of the Italian princes. Both he and Machiavelli write of Lodovico Sforza as the prime causer of Italy's misfortunes. And if we look to the humbler fry we shall find that Lodovico's name occurred to them as deserving full opprobrium. Giovanni Cambi, that honest and attractive chronicler, rated his summons to the French as madness, and when he set down in his *Istorie* the capture of Lodovico in 1500 he added the pleasure that it gave in Florence: 'E chosí suciedevano e'fatti, e fu questo Moro chagione della distruzione d'Italia, e della nostra ciptà. Idio ne sia ringratiato, che cielà levato dinanzi.'[1] These were fairly general sentiments. Of course, if all Italy had been ready to unite against the coming of Charles VIII, which Lodovico provoked, then this initial action would have had no fatal consequences. It is here that we must bear in mind those statements on the role of the papacy as the main factor in the disunity of Italy—statements that have never been dismissed, and which are, I think, unexceptionable. And if we turn to Philippe de Commines we shall find an indication for the particular state of Lombardy itself which can throw light on the general state of Italy. For there was not only disunity as amongst the separate states of Italy: there was also disunity within the states themselves. 'Et ce que contient cette duché, je ne vis jamais plus belle pièce de terre, ni de plus grande valeur; car quand le seigneur se contenteroit de cinq cens mille ducats l'an, les subjets ne seroient que trop riches; et vivroit ledit seigneur en sûreté; mais il en lève six cens cinquante mille, ou sept cens mille, qui est grande tyrannie; et aussi le peuple ne demande que mutation de seigneur.'[2] That is a very understandable desire, (and we, who suffer in this same matter of taxation, may be ready to sympathize with it), even if it has no apparent connection with new learning. With the discontent of the old ruling faction under a new monarchy it explains the fact that there could be no cohesion within Lombardy.[3] Commines had heard of Francesco Sforza, and he noted that though he won Lombardy by conquest, yet he ruled it unlike a tyrant: 'Et la conquesta, et posséda, non point comme tyran, mais comme vray et bon prince; et estoit bien à estimer sa vertu et bonté aux plus nobles princes qui ayent regné de son temps.'[4] But hereditary rule tends to degenerate, and

---

[1] Cambi, *Istorie*, II, 147.   [2] Commines, VII, II, 192.
[3] Barbagallo, 236 ss.   [4] Commines, VII, IV, 195.

the passage down from Francesco to Lodovico is not one that needs explanation from contemporary movements in culture. Rather, it is something so ordinary that we may gloss it out of Villari, who remarked a general trend downwards in the princes of Italy during the fifteenth century, and explained it by the fact that it was their fathers who, through obstacles and dangers, had risen to power, while the sons, 'born in peace, and growing up among courtiers, had been bred to softness'.[1] As for the commentary of culture, as opposed to its influence, we shall find it sufficiently when we arrive at Machiavelli himself.

Since we are at present looking with Commines, who brings to this matter a fresh and authoritative mind, let us look a little further. He went as an admirer to Venice, and is perhaps the first who set down in lyrical language the strong impression that Venice in its wealth and beauty left on him, and he noted Venice's reaction to the coming of Charles VIII. Venice, no more than Lodovico Sforza, was thinking in terms of the establishment of the French in Italy. But she had lately passed from being a sea-power only, and a barrier for Christendom, to being one with mainland ambitions in Italy; and these had drawn upon her head distrust and execration from the rest of Italy. 'Pour toutes ces haynes sembloit auxdits Vénitiens que c'estoit leur profit que la guerre fust entre le roy et ladite maison d'Aragon, espérant qu'elle ne prendroit si prompte conclusion qu'elle prist, et qu'au pis venir, l'un party ou l'autre leur donneroit quelques villes en Pouille.'[2] One may divide in order to rule; or one may find division which obliges by making rule inevitable. And here it meant, as Commines observes a little later, that the one Power in Italy (since Lodovico Sforza was their sponsor, not a possible opponent) that might have stopped the progress of Charles VIII and the French was not inclined to trouble it: 'car voyant leurs forces, leur sens et leur conduite, ils le pouvoient aisément troubler, et nuls autres en Italie'.[3] So strong were the fears of Venice in her expansion that we shall find Florence (nor she alone) looking to the King of France as a protector against Venetian ambition.

But should not Naples itself, according to the anticipations of Venice and of Lodovico, have been able to make some resistance? The answer, for simple and familiar reasons, is in the negative. While the Peace of Lodi in 1454 had set up a rough balance of power between the major states of the peninsula, it had also eliminated any testing of their internal validity. Lorenzo, the 'needle of the balance', bent

[1] Villari, *G.Sav.*, I, 28.   [2] Commines, *ibid.*   [3] Commines, VII, XV, 214.

his efforts to securing an equilibrium; and in this he was following the policy of Cosimo, whose support for Francesco Sforza at the expense of the Venetians (to whom personally he was indebted, and who were traditional allies) prevented Venice from bringing all Italy under her sway. Henceforth, such episodes as were provoked by the ambitions of any member of the league of Italian states were brief and inconclusive, and had brought on the aggressor (or on the Power which seemed likely to advance) the charge of designing to destroy the liberty of Italy, and with that charge, the coalition of the rest. Since Italy before 1494 was held together, or at least was held apart, by age-long rivalries, that system could prevail. It is Commines who remarks that Pisa and Florence, for instance, had been enemies for three hundred years before Florence conquered Pisa in 1406; and those who came after him might have extended this observation further. Did not the Pisans (like the Sienese) desert their city when it was incorporated finally in the Duchy and Grand-Duchy of Tuscany, rather than live under the alien rule of Florence? Have not the streets of Pisa even still something of the silence that comes from that old feud, and from the losing in it? This rivalry, dating backwards long before Dante, is obviously no outcome of the Renascence. But we must remember it as a potential obstacle to the latter. And if the conscious policy of Lorenzo the Magnificent was dedicated to keeping things as they were, the act of Lodovico has thrust the lever within the fabric; and the rifts necessarily begin to appear. Naples had a cruel dynasty which up to now had been able to assert itself against the power of the feudal barons. Had not the latter been forcibly subjugated at the time of the famous conspiracy a dozen years before? But the monarchy could not command their loyalty, nor, with its oppressive taxation, could it command support from the people. In the words of a contemporary: 'Allora furono vedute balenare le menti, volubili e inconscie, dei nostri, e bramare nuova tirannide, e voler patire gli stranieri, e invocare quali padroni i Francesi.'[1] Naples, that is, is in the same unfortunate condition as Lodovico Sforza would be in were the first movement of the French directed against him.

What of Florence, author of this policy of balance? We may go back once more to Philippe de Commines. He saw the degeneracy of the Medici line (a thing, he said—lest we should think Piero rotten because he was the fruit of the Renascence—which happens in kingdoms and empires). The authority of his predecessors was harm-

[1] Cf. Barbagallo, 241.

ful to him. Cosimo's had been 'douce et amiable', suiting a city used
to liberty. Lorenzo had been moderate. But Piero had reached the
stage of arrogance: 'mais le fils cuidoit que cela lui fust dû par raison;
et se faisoit craindre . . . et faisoit des violences de nuict, et des bateries
lourdement, abusant de leurs deniers communs. Si avoit fair le père,
mais si sagement qu'ils en estoient presque contens.'[1] Italian testimony
to this descent is naturally abundant. The ingenuous Cambi writes
of Piero as 'chattivo di tutti e'vizj', hopes soon to be free of tyrants,
and sees him especially as wishing to turn into servants those whom
his father had left as his companions.[2] There is in the trial of Lamberto
dell'Antella, a creature of Piero who had grown disgusted with, and
fearful of, his master, a statement which cuts both ways at once: 'che
gli rimase el piú bello Stato, e'l meglio fondato di Italia, et in 31 mesi
lo perdé et rovinollo; e tutto per le sua bestialità, omicidii, tirannie et
usurperie che e'faceva'.[3] That is as much a testimony to the city we
think of as the centre of the Renascence, as it is a condemnation of
Piero, whose personal deficiencies did so much to ruin it. Critics
praise Cosimo, *Pater Patriae*; they debate on the enigma of Lorenzo;
but who has ever raised his voice for Piero? Rinuccini, one of a band
of Florentine chroniclers and diarists with a strong sense of liberty,
and a strong bias towards Savonarola, noted as early as 1466 how the
elder Piero (was not the name fatal in the line of Medici?) was
impatient with the 'vivere libero' of Florence, how in order to maintain his greatness he desired innovations there: he showed his temper
as being tyrannical, not civil. And Rinuccini added (what Machiavelli will restate in the *Discorsi*) that a republic which desires to live
in liberty must never let one citizen grow so far 'che egli possa piú
che le leggi': for the insatiable appetite of man, when it can more
than it ought, wishes and desires more than is licit.[4] We shall find
later that this is the language of Alberti and Castiglione, as well as of
Machiavelli. Nor is it surprising that this diarist, who put a heading
on the death of Lorenzo the Magnificent, that *malignant tyrant*, should
repeat his warning in 1494 at the time of the expulsion of the second
Piero.

But it was not only the ineptitude of Piero de'Medici, and the confusion following his going, that prevented Florence from offering a
barrier to Charles VIII. There was a factor which we may count as
an imponderable, as long as we are ready to attribute to that elastic

[1] Commines, VII, V, 198. [2] Cambi, II, 68.
[3] Document in Villari, *G.Sav.*, II, xxi.
[4] Rinuccini, ciii and cf. the repetition in similar words on cliii.

term both influence and weight. It was the preaching of Savonarola. Pasquale Villari, whose best work, perhaps, was his study of Savonarola, most diligently unearthed the facts round a personality for which he felt more attraction than he did for that of Machiavelli; but his judgments on Savonarola are often oddly inconclusive. Here at the end of the fifteenth century there arose a preacher in Florence whose following, incredible as it may seem, ran into five figures. Chroniclers speak of as many as fifteen thousand present every workday at his preaching.[1] It is a large number, and it might have seemed reasonable to explain it in terms of religious sentiment in Florence; in terms, for instance, of the two thousand couples of religious ('tra preti e frati e cherici') who walked in procession at the funeral of the Archbishop of Florence in 1513.[2] That was too simple an explanation; besides, it would have spoiled the obligatory picture. How could the fifteenth century be so corrupt, or, at least, so corrupt because it was so pagan, if that were true? Therefore Villari related the matter to the nature of the Renascence: this hectic following after prophecies, and rumours of prophecies, became the natural consequence of a century that had grown over-credulous, *by dint of having wanted to doubt about everything*.[3] It was because they had grown so sceptical that they were so ready to believe! Such an interpretation hardly seems as positivist, or as sober, as Villari's reputation would suggest. Yet this process of standing on his head to acquire a right perspective proved irresistible to him: he put it first in his preface, to show it was an underlying idea for him, then proved his reliance on the method by returning to it in the body of his work. With regard to the specifically apocalyptic preaching of Savonarola he observed that all were then the fonder of these supernatural visions *in proportion to their incredulity*.[4] Well, it was strangely credulous of them. Nor does it seem to me that Villari improved the matter by insisting on princes and their astrologers at the time of the Renascence; or when he worked it out as counterpoint, in which this exalted mysticism, in the midst of the corrupt and pagan society of Florence, produced an extraordinary effect.[5] The word extraordinary may, indeed, be the right one, for it is hard to accept it as the ordinary reaction of indifference or contempt. But it would be more reasonable to pay heed to the observation of Filippo de'Nerli in his *Commentaries* on Florentine popular credence to new prophets: 'e per insino a un certo Pieruccio pettinagnolo, e anche i tanti Romiti e fraticelli, che ci sono capitati, ed hanno predetto cose

---

[1] Landucci, 127.   [2] Masi, *Ricordanze*, 124.   [3] Villari, *G.Sav.*, I, xiii.
[4] *ibid.*, I, 352.   [5] *ibid.*, I, 141.

future, alle quali tanti nostri superstiziosi, benché anche onorati cittadini hanno creduto, o fatta vista di credere a qualche lor proposito, purché egli abbiano profetato o predetto futuri mali o rovine grandissime'.[1] After all, culture is not so widespread, or so deeply penetrating, as to have affected greatly the popular outlook in Florence. Instead, by this observation Savonarola can be attached to a long series, operating on a different level than that of Renascence culture. His own personal interest lies both in his individual equipment as a scholar as well as a prophet, and in the coincidence of Charles VIII's coming as an apparent fulfilment to his prophecy. Does not Commines, every time he remarks that Charles VIII's enterprise in its astonishing success was clearly conducted by the hand of God, pay tribute to the efficacy of Savonarola's doctrine? And here Villari seemed to see the point, while not attaching importance to it. *Ecce ego adducam aquas super terram*—and while these fervent prophecies were issuing from Savonarola's lips there came the news that a stream of foreign arms was descending from the Alps. Villari described the terror that the news inspired in Florence, and how rumour swelled the armies in number and made them seem invincible in battle.[2] How much, we may ask, was Savonarola responsible, not perhaps for Charles's coming, but for inability to muster any strength against it? No evaluation has ever been given to this, but we may feel that his influence is not to be rated low.

Since Florence is the birthplace of Machiavelli, the seat of his activities, and the object of his affections, we must define its position more sharply at this crucial moment, both in its backward and its forward view. It is made quite clear from contemporary observation, and we shall do well to note first a remark of the same Filippo de'Nerli, once more (lest we should still be tempted to attach the phenomena of the fifteenth century to some new cause) relating her situation back to ancient custom. Indeed, the observation will take us back beyond the time of Dante himself to that origin of faction in the twelfth century. It is one that Nerli himself consciously extends to cover the whole sequence of Florentine history, 'come chiaramente si può vedere in tutto il corpo delle Fiorentine Storie', nor shall we find it unrelated to what happened elsewhere in Italy. It was, that following the habit of faction and civil strife the reformation of the State of Florence had always been for the benefit and

---

[1] F. de'Nerli, *Commentarj*, I, 125; and cf. the episode of the friar who said God had told him Savonarola's doctrine was true, and that whoever resisted it would have his tongue torn out and given to the dogs (Landucci, 157).

[2] *G.Sav.*, I, 203.

convenience of the dominating faction, and never for the benefit of all, so that never therefore could there emerge a quiet republic or a durable state.[1] Guicciardini stated the matter in identical terms: 'Questo è il fine delle divisioni e discordie civili: lo sterminio di una parte; il capo dell'altra diventa signore della città; i fautori e aderenti sua, di compagni quasi sudditi, il popolo e lo universale ne rimane schiavo: vanne lo stato per eredità; e spesse volte di uno savio viene in uno pazzo, che poi dà l'ultimo tuffo alla città.'[2] Was not this last the office of Piero de'Medici? so that the same passage lights both the theme of faction and that of degeneracy in hereditary rule. And in the matter of faction, what obtained in Dante's youth, and at the time of Dante's exile, is still true in 1434 and 1494. The Medici replaced an oligarchy (they did not, of course, obliterate a democracy); and they left unsatisfied the powerful families that had been accustomed to share in government. It was a State, its supporter in Guicciardini's important dialogue on the *Reggimento di Firenze* is bound to confess, usurped by means of force and faction. And though in that same work Bernardo del Nero rebuts his interlocutor's charge that the Medici—as always when power is concentrated—disarmed the Florentines to hold them, thus making them degenerate from the warlike virtues of their ancestors, he only does so by rejoining that this was a process which had begun long before them: the work of former rulers, or of the very richness of Florence, given over more to merchandise and profit, until for a youth to take to the profession of war became *almost infamous*.[3] That, according to the angle we are looking from, may seem desirable or to be reproved. We might think of it in terms of Horace Walpole, who praised the nobles of Florence in his own time because they were too civilized to fight in any circumstances; or we might think of it from the viewpoint of Machiavelli, who found that such an attitude boded no good for the meeting of external danger.

At any rate, we can accept it as supporting the statement of the interlocutor Soderini at another point that Florence reached her present state (the dialogue is ideally dated 1494) 'parte suffocata dalla sua ricchezza, parte dalla forza de'suoi cagnotti e partigiani'.[4] If we looked to Cambi we should find that while he traces moral corruption in Florence to the high dowries demanded (so that three thousand marriageable girls between the ages of eighteen and thirty found neither their virtues, nor their honesty, nor their beauty, nor even

[1] F. de'Nerli, I, 105–6.   [2] Guicciardini, *Storia d'Italia*, IV.
[3] Guicciardini, *Reggimento*, 25 and 90–1.   [4] *ibid.*, 95.

their being noble, sufficient to secure a husband), he did not think of linking it with a new trend of ideas.[1] And in his very honest way he writes with indignation against it. Guicciardini, in the same dialogue, connected vice in Florence with its size and riches.[2] Did not the Romans also turn their excellent virtues into vice, not because of discord, but because of wealth, 'dalle ricchezze, dalle grandezze degli imperi e dalle sicurtà'.[3] It is a text which may turn us, since before long we must look towards Livy in his association with Machiavelli, to Livy's own conclusion on the Romans: 'Prona semper civitas in luxuriam, non ingeniorum modo vitio, sed affluenti copia voluptatium, et illecebris omnis amoenitatis maritimae terrestrisque; tum vero ita obsequio principum et licentia plebei lascivire, ut nec libidini nec sumptibus modus esset.'[4] We do not, perhaps, need to pursue the parallel, or to do more than seize its general implications. But it is important to grasp the fact that Florence after the flight of Piero is not capable of organizing itself easily and reasonably: it was not used to popular rule, having never seen liberty, and in the ensuing confusion the minds of its citizens, so freshly freed from Medici rule, were full of suspicions.[5] We must bear these facts in mind in answering the question why Florence made no opposition to Charles VIII.

Such was the Florentine situation in its process of formation: was it to be any better, or any more stable, by virtue of the reforms associated with the name of Savonarola, which seemed to the honest *popolano* Landucci to be, for all those who wished to live well and without partisanship, 'el piú degno governo ch'abbia avuto mai Firenze'?[6] That it may have been; but as it did not satisfy the ambitions of the families humiliated by Medicean rule, nor of those either who had profited by the Medici, its popular basis, resting with people who had been below the constitution before, and who therefore had no political experience, had its inherent weaknesses. The fear that the major citizens were hankering after a Medicean restoration was endemic; and Piero de'Medici represents only one of two danger-points, the other being Pisa. The latter town was obstinately intent, after Charles had granted what was not really his to give, its liberty, on maintaining its independence from Florence. And Italian conditions were such that the Pisans would never lack supporters ('che è impossibile che manchi loro spalle', as Guicciardini wrote picturesquely): for all who wish to exert pressure on Florence will see to it that the

[1] Cambi, *Ist.*, II, 253. [2] *Reggi.*, 145. [3] *ibid.*, 157.
[4] Livy, XXIII, 4. [5] *Reggi.*, 141. [6] Landucci, 107.

wound of Pisa is kept open.[1] Add this to the other difficulty, that of
an inability to place reliance on the more able, or more prominent,
citizens because of the fear that they are looking for external difficulties in order to stifle liberty, or at least in order to find employment
which in time of peace is not available for them (that is, when they
are not actively leaguing with Piero for the return of the Medici),
and it will be seen that it is hard for Florence to pursue any clear
policy. In this testing-time she has her most experienced and com-
petent citizens standing aloof, under suspicion. It will have fatal
consequences for her position.

Of the five major states of Italy I have made no mention so far
of the Church. There is in one of the collected articles of Ojetti an
anecdote which we may not think irrelevant in this context. It was
on the occasion of Ojetti's introduction by Anatole France to the
young Marcel Proust, then in his full admiration for France. The
latter had mentioned Venice, and Proust inquired, affably but somewhat distantly, if Ojetti was a Venetian. 'Non, je ne suis pas vénitien.
— Mais, d'où êtes-vous?' with a hint of impatience in his voice.
Ojetti answered modestly, 'Je suis romain.' To which Proust replied,
'Oh, c'est trop grand!' And Ojetti added the reflection that Proust
was right in this, for there has never been a Roman writer in Italian
literature. A trivial anecdote, perhaps, lent value by the names of
its protagonists? But yet it is significant that Rome should have
contributed so little to art and to literature. Raphael and Michaelangelo come to Rome; they did not come from it. The writers, from
Dante down to Ariosto (to keep near our period), come from elsewhere. Is there not something of the desolation which the Baron
Bonstetten, or Lady Morgan, or the Président de Brosses were later to
record so movingly in the Roman Campagna, about the spiritual
landscape of Rome? The papacy was an institution which had
known absolute corruption centuries before it fell into it again with
the advent of Paul II in 1464. Even Villari, while maintaining that
the age was most corrupt, yet saw a general discomfort in Italy at the
state of the Church.[2] He might have looked a little further, and
remembered that Lorenzo the Magnificent, when he spoke of his
son Giovanni's cardinalate as the biggest achievement of his house,
appended the warning that Rome was a sewer of corruption, 'che è
sentina di tutti i mali'.[3] Must it not mean something that this judgment coincides with those of Savonarola, of Machiavelli, of Guicciardini, or of Giovanni Cambi? Note how these Florentines speak with

---

[1] *Reggi.*, 70 and cf. 164.   [2] *G.Sav.*, I, 25–7 and cf. 83–4.   [3] Caggese, II, 449–51.

unanimity. 'La vera religione è spenta', says Savonarola, in one of those fierce denunciations of Rome.[1] 'Chostui fu pessimo Ponteficie al mondo, in modo che lui spense quasi la fede di Christo pe'sua mali esempli,' wrote Cambi on the death of Alexander VI.[2] And Machiavelli, who is not always out of tune with Savonarola, uses the same language: 'Abbiamo, adunque, con la Chiesa e con i preti noi Italiani questo primo obligo, di essere sanza religione e cattivi.'[3] As for Guicciardini, his condemnation of the priestly government which it was his function as an official to serve is nothing less than notorious. I omit the other diarists, because the case is so straightforward. Florence, from Lorenzo the Magnificent to Machiavelli, expresses itself as at an opposite pole to Rome; and we must pay all the greater heed to this unanimity of opinion about Rome when we remember that the Renascence is the creation largely of Florence, and something which is imported only into Rome.

> Oh! se'tu Roma, o d'ogni vizio il seggio?[4]

Nearly three hundred and fifty years after the sonnets of Petrarch against Rome, Alfieri in the same verse-form utters the same accusation. It is not easy to attach this theme to that of the Renascence; though it would be quite easy to apply M. Cherel's method, to appeal to the principle of what the temporal power should have been, and find out from that what in effect it must have been. Even, perhaps, we might find a more expeditious way than that, and follow the last historian of the Roman question in his discussion of the principle of Temporal Power: 'Assuming that the civil principate was a necessary adjunct to the Pope's spiritual mission, the fact that he administered it badly or incompetently would not affect the issue.'[5] Would not affect the issue, Professor Binchy? Then, if God means the Pope to be a king, it is a matter of indifference, to God and to us, whether he is a good, or a bad, king? I take it that it may be easier, and honester, for us to assume, with Dante, that God meant no such thing; and that the intrusion of the papacy into temporal matters where it had no competence, which Dante saw as vitiating so long a period in the Middle Ages, was not the least unfortunate episode in its history. For we must not forget that, though I quoted Alfieri and Petrarch in this matter, for the excellent reason that they both wrote it in sonnets, it is Dante himself who opens the prosecution. It is a case, then, which lasts both before, during, and after, the

---

¹ Villari, *G.Sav.*, I, 428–9.   ² Cambi, *Ist.*, II, 195.   ³ *D.* I, XII, 54.
⁴ Alfieri, *Opere*, IV, *Son.* XVI.   ⁵ D. A. Binchy, *Church and State in Fascist Italy*, 1941, 7.

Renascence: to which the Renascence itself is incidental; not which is incidental to the Renascence.

It may be also that we should bear in mind the mad words of Julius II. Somewhere (it was a useful observation of Toffanin) in the passage from the Middle Ages the universal claims of the papacy had shrunk, and its stature had diminished until it was reduced to the level of a Signoria without any having the courage to recognize the transition openly.[1] Perhaps it was only that the claims of the medieval papacy were expressed *in vacuo*, or with only one idea, that of the Empire, to compete with them. They had therefore the room to expand to their theoretic limit, while later, with the growth of other political entities, they received a nearer check. At any rate, the disproportion is obvious when Julius II, bent only on completing the work of his immediate predecessor Alexander VI in creating a temporal state, claims the encroachments of Venice in Romagna as an offence against him, and, therefore, against God. In so doing he is, M. Gilson would remind us, speaking the language of St. Thomas Aquinas, not that of Dante;[2] but the contrast may only serve to show us that, on this matter of separation or hierarchization of temporal and spiritual orders, Dante spoke a different and a more reasonable language than did Aquinas. And Julius II? 'In this purpose of recovering our territory we have been from the beginning tenacious, still are, and always will be. . . . We must neither dissemble nor neglect so great an offence made against God, and such a challenge to our dignity. . . . No intimidation, no compact, no condition can turn us from the firm purpose to recover these towns and fortresses. It is demanded by God and by our Saviour Jesus Christ, who entrusted us with the government of the Church; it is demanded by our pastoral office.'[3] So Julius fulminated; and the policy which he pursued to implement such words is common property. We shall see arising in the fifteenth century the idea that power corrupts: is it not plain that the theoretically limitless power of the Popes was always a potential source of corruption, and was most often an actual one? That source of danger is no invention of the Renascence; but like other corruptions it may well have been fomented by the material prosperity of the fifteenth century.

There is a footnote to be appended on the state of the Church temporal. It also is one of those that carries us back to immemorial times: Rome as well was torn with faction. Commines, when he

[1] Toffanin, *Mach. e il Tacitismo*, 72.
[2] Gilson, 183, giving the striking parallel texts from *De Monarchia* and *De regimine principum*.
[3] Barbagallo, 223.

came there, found Orsini ranged against Colonna as they had always been, 'et est toute la terre de l'église troublée par cette partialité. . . . Et quand ne seroit ce différend, la terre de l'église seroit la plus heureuse habitation, pour les subjets, qui soit en tout le monde. . . .'[1] Well, of course, the hypothesis may be correct, but it never could be tested. 'E a dí 20 d'aprile 1482, è nato scandolo a Roma tra gli Orsini e'Colonnesi; e mandorono sottosopra la città ccme si suole fare sempre. Per le quistioni de questi grandi ne patisce tutto el popolo.'[2] These barons were, said Jovius, gyves for the Popes, 'ceppi dei pontefici'. And there were others to see that the temporal power could never be quiet until these turbulent barons had been hushed. Was not Julius II (often taken too readily as the restorer of the temporal patrimony) in a stronger position than the earlier Popes had been precisely because Alexander's policy had depressed the Orsini as well as bringing Romagna to unity? Even Julius, little as he can be suspected of partiality towards his predecessor, spoke of Alexander as having deservedly deprived the papal vicars in Romagna of their turbulent possessions.[3]

'Et de tous costés le peuple d'Italie commença à prendre coeur, désirant nouvelletés. . . .'[4] It is a very usual thing for the mind of man to desire, and before we have finished we shall find it as an observation in classical, and neo-classical, guise that men, whatever their condition, are liable to wish to change it for another. Once they are invoked there is no revocation of these novelties. Is it not plain that in an age when there is no embracing concept of nationality to appeal to, there is no means of resisting the intrusion of the foreigner (not felt as a *foreigner*, but as a *barbarian*, which is slightly different), once it has been made? The begetter of the enterprise of Charles VIII, the unlucky Lodovico il Moro, did not wish to think of it as a permanency; Venice connived at it because it only seemed to modify the Italian situation somewhat in her favour, not with the realization that it would create a new Italian situation; Naples had discontented factions, and no compensating adherence to the dynasty, while it had also a traditional Angevin connection; Florence and Rome were unarmed, and the former at least in a fit frame of mind to acquiesce in Charles's coming rather than to oppose it. Was it so much a miracle that the expedition was accomplished with such celerity, and without opposition? The house divided fell open; and as for the smaller states of Italy, in a pretty phrase which we shall

[1] Commines, VII, X, 205. [2] Landucci, 40–1.
[3] Barbagallo, 222. [4] Commines, VII, VI, 200.

find again, they went with the flood, once the flood was running. It is wise to add, though it will be readily conceded, that all this did not assure any future contentment with the results of the French coming. Already in his *Dialogue* Guicciardini counted the prospects, and found them unattractive: others would follow Lodovico's lead if it succeeded for him, further their own ambition, or else insure against their fear, if they had no other way of doing so, by calling in the foreigner. 'You see that now people have begun to talk of Germans and Spaniards to drive out the French; therefore not only do I see no assurance that the French will not stay or return to Italy, but I fear as well lest the way be opened for some other people. And this would be the final ruin, for while they remain in concord, they will eat up Italy; if they come to a rupture, they will rend it; and if perchance one foreigner drives out the other, then Italy will remain in utter slavery.'[1] That was not quite a prophecy, or rather, it was a dantesque prophecy, since the dialogue was written about the time of the battle of Pavia, when it seemed as if France had been written off as a major Power, although its ideal date is 1494; but it had only gained in accuracy through the knowledge of those thirty intervening years.

Finally, we must, I think, reverse the direction of our vision for a moment. We have, from the French side, contemporary accounts of the impression Italy made on its invaders; and we have, from French critics contemporary with ourselves, estimates of the importance of that impression. It was an 'éblouissement'; it was a discovery comparable to the one made by Christopher Columbus. Charles VIII himself exclaimed: 'Vous ne pourriez croire les beaux jardins que j'ay veus. . . . Car, sur ma foy, il semble qu'il n'y faille que Adam et Eve pour en faire un paradis terrestre.'[2] The contrast was so strong with northern barbarism that the conquerors were 'almost intimidated' by the novelty of the objects which they found. They were not, however, so intimidated as to refrain from laying hands upon them. The desire to emulate was aroused, and was to become operative; but the immediate question was to remove. From Italy the French took back pictures, statues, clothes, jewels, works of art of all kinds, without counting books and manuscripts.[3] When Charles VIII returned there was a transport fee of 1593 *livres tournois* for the carriage of 'plusieurs tapisseries, librairies, painctures, pierres de marbre et de porfyre et autres . . . lesdites choses pesant en tout

---

[1] *Reggi.*, 72.   [2] M. Lemonnier, in Lavisse, *Hist. de France*, V (1), 150.
[3] *ibid.*, 160.

87.000 livres ou environ.'[1]   M. Chamard, in an interesting book on
the importance *inter alia* of the Italian influence on the French sixteenth century, added a footnote on this process, which, in its concern with one side only of the equation between France and Italy,
is particularly revealing: We must bear in mind, he said, that these
Italian wars lasted no less than sixty-five years, from 1494 to 1559,
that each new descent of the French into the peninsula brought new
contacts with this marvellous civilization, and then we shall understand better *how much these repeated contacts must have been fertile.*[2]
It is I who have added the italics to that naïve statement; and, indeed,
we may well understand how fertile those contacts were. But, for
which party to them?   M. Chamard at least had no tremor in his
voice: the effect on Italy was foreign to his thesis, and far from his
thoughts.   Nor is he alone in his ingratitude for a transfusion which
was carried out at the expense of so large a blood-letting.   It is an
attitude given a quasi-official status by Lanson in his *History of French
Literature*: a page or so to echo Michelet's original statement of the
wonder, of the French captivated 'par tous les sens et par tout l'esprit,'
the natural consequence that they transported home all that had
ravished them in Italy, the logical conclusion: when they went
back to France, the whole Renascence went back with them,
somewhat confusedly, in their brains as on their wagons.[3]   It is so
convenient a heritage, and Lanson takes it so coolly as something
granted, that he also makes no mention further of the donor's
state.

Indeed, if French criticism has added anything further, it is as
likely as not the insult added to the injury.   So did Texte, in a rather
dated essay, observe that we (I mean, the French) of course took from
antiquity its right side, making it a school for writing well, whereas
the Italians were enmeshed in a 'dilettantisme épicurien'.[4]   That
observation ignores a great deal, very prudently.   France had to
slough the tasteless confusion of the sixteenth century before there
could emerge the classic expression of the seventeenth.   She had the
leisure, and the independence, to do so.   But if there are misdirections,
and unwanted elements, in the Italian fifteenth century (and I should
be the last to deny it) the sixty-five years of Italian wars foreclosed
upon the Italian scene before there was time for the clarification
that took a century and a half in France.   The sixteenth century in
Italy can only partially fulfil the hopes aroused by the fifteenth before

1 M. Lemonnier, in Lavisse, *Hist. de France*, V (1), 161.
2 H. Chamard, *Origines de la Poésie fr. de la Ren.*, 223.
3 Lanson, 225.   4 Texte, *Etudes de Litt. Europ.*, 25–50. Cf. esp. 48–50.

we come to the spiritual frustration which is the corollary of physical frustration.

Nor can I omit, in this context, that other charge made often by French critics, and which we touched on in Chapter I, in the person of M. Cherel. The ideas of Machiavelli, said Charbonnel, represent a systematization of the methods of usurpation and of rule that flourished with too many princes of Italy; but they have only rarely seduced French minds. 'Nos compatriotes ont, d'une manière générale, éprouvé une instinctive répugnance à l'égard des maximes et des exemples proposés par le Secrétaire florentin.'[1] It is very reassuring to know that one's own hands, and those of all one's nation, are and have been clean. That does not prevent the fact that M. Cherel, in listing the French kings who had learnt ruses and faithlessness, even before the publication of the *Prince*, but because of their Italian campaigns, took care to omit Louis XI. He had, of course, good reason to, for Louis XI was most averse to the idea of Italian adventures. But in spite of this, it was he who said of his son Charles VIII: 'If he knows these five Latin words, *Qui nescit dissimulare nescit regnare*, it will suffice.'[2] And perhaps that one reminder will suffice; though if it is insufficient we shall find enough to buttress it.

That short account may seem an excursion of a type that I have not hitherto allowed myself to make. But it is, I hope, a necessary one. We cannot understand the interplay of emotions, or the reactions of Machiavelli, unless we have in mind the two sides to the same picture. It was indeed all summed up anticipatorily by that honest, and valuable, fellow-townsman of Machiavelli, Luca Landucci, when he noted in his diary the first occupation of Florence by the advancing army of Charles VIII in 1494. 'And note that they were not in hundreds, but in thousands, so that the whole city was occupied throughout; that those who were not billeted, when the horse and infantry arrived, occupied at once all the suburbs and the streets within the city, saying: *Open here*; and they did not mind whether the house was rich or poor. They gave it to be understood that they wished to pay; there were few who paid. And if they did pay something, they paid for the horns and ate the ox. *E se pure pagava qualche cosa, pagava le corna e mangiavasi el bue.*'[3] It is not only Machiavelli

[1] Charbonnel, *La Pensée Italienne au XVIe Siècle et le Courant Libertin*, 434.
[2] A. H. Johnson, *Europe in the Sixteenth Century*, 5.
[3] Landucci, 72.

who had a talent for the vivid phrase; and, indeed, we shall find that the Florentines were well enough informed on matters of payment for their native wit to be stimulated. It is when we have savoured the full bitterness of the situation, as seen from the Florentine side, that we shall be ready to approach the problem of the *Prince*.

III

HIS EXPERIENCE

WHAT I have established in outline in the last chapter is the position of Italy in face of its invaders, and of its invaders in the face of Italy, at the moment of crisis as the fifteenth century draws to its close. What we must look to now is Machiavelli's view of events as they unfold upon that basis, and it is in the *Legations* which he wrote that we shall find it. In reading these nothing strikes one more than the recurrent marginal statements of the modest position, and the modest character, of Machiavelli himself. He is the Florentine envoy without the title or the authority: even his pay is scaled below that of a fellow-envoy such as Francesco della Casa. It is only when one turns to a person of different status that one seizes the background to this. Guicciardini, in his youthful *Storia Fiorentina* (a work as able, and more charming than the big history of Italy), sees the Florentine scene from a very different angle. Machiavelli is the intelligent employee who brings his energy, his abilities, and his faith to the service of his city: that is a position which is inevitably a little un-critical, quite irrespective of those abilities. On the other hand, Guicciardini is the *grand seigneur* born on the level at which the affairs of Florence are conducted, predisposed to see the interplay of forces as a whole; and obliged, by the force of events, to see them from an angle of detachment. While Machiavelli is giving proof of his devotion to Florence, Guicciardini is noting down its weakness internally. 'In che s'ha a intendere, che e'sarebbe difficile immagi-narsi una città tanto conquassata e male regolata quanto era la nostra.' The short periods of office, the forbidden degrees of relationship, meant weakness and inexperience: the suspicion of leading citizens as favouring the return of the Medici meant the alienation of 'cittadini savii ed esperti'. While the long deliberations went on, the latter stood aside; they put themselves *a specchio*, as debtors to the State and so ineligible for office.[1] Hence the need for humble envoys, 'perché non volendo andare gli uomini savii e di riputazione, bisog-nava ricorrere a quegli che andavano volentieri'.[2] Among the names that Guicciardini adds at this point, to exemplify these humble

---

[1] Guicciardini, *Storia Fiorentina*, XXV, 272–82.   [2] *ibid.*, 274.

emissaries, Machiavelli's does not occur, only perhaps because it is
swallowed up in a comprehensive 'and other such that I need not
mention'; but this establishment of distinctions is accurate, and
must not be forgotten. Machiavelli will arrive gradually at a position
from which he can criticize, not Florence only, but all Italy; but he
begins from underneath, and his energies are absorbed in service.
He works for Florence, while Guicciardini's eye runs easily over all
the flaws in her structure.

It is this status of Machiavelli which accounts for the contrast
between the *Legations* and the *Scritti Inediti* as collected by Canestrini.
No volume is more disappointing than this latter, which contains
the outgoing letters written by Machiavelli in the performance of
his secretarial duties. His hand held the pen, but his employers
provided the words. Besides the fact of his devotedness one learns
very little about the mind or personality of Machiavelli from the
Scritti Inediti. On the contrary, in the *Legations* lie the elements of
Machiavelli's experience, and they have the attractive qualities of
his style. If Machiavelli is a seer of facts, of things as they are, not as
they ought to be, then, quite obviously, it is with the *Legations*
that any consideration of him must begin, for this is what he saw.
The critic of Machiavelli who does not trouble to complete his
apprenticeship with them will find himself without a valid line of
approach towards the *Prince*. Machiavelli, as we shall see him here,
cannot criticize Florence, and only gradually will he arrive at a
picture of the affairs of Italy: his intelligence is reflected in his statement of what comes under his eye, and it is obvious throughout that
he is one of those who serve, not one of those who rule, the city which
calls him in its Instructions to him 'nostro carissimo cittadino'. This
situation accounts for a certain limitation of focus in the *Legations*;
but for this very reason the points which must have borne themselves
in permanently on Machiavelli's mind stand out all the more clearly;
and it is for these we must look, even more than for the general
pattern of events. And whereas, in my last chapter, I quoted from
others than Machiavelli, here I shall quote from him mainly; and
with him, from the Florentines who stood near him, so that we may
be sure of a synoptic vision.

The series begins with minor journeys in which the burden of his
business varies little. It is the negotiation of *condotte* with the minor
rulers of Italy who served Florence with mercenary troops. Though
there was no trade union of *condottieri* each looked to his salary. The
pay of others has been raised?—then why not mine? The Lord of

Piombino does not feel himself inferior in any way to Conte Rinuccio. Then should not his pay go up with the latter's? Naturally, that is his view of the matter, and not Florence's. They have looked up the books and seen their promise to him: so Machiavelli is sent to answer fair and general words, 'con termini larghi e molto generali, i quali non ci obblighino a cosa alcuna'. So it is on the visit to Caterina Sforza too. She and her son had let the time-limit elapse, and Machiavelli is to tell them this, but he is to add immediately that in spite of this Florence desires to satisfy her; and if she alleges the increase in other *condottieri's* pay, he is to use what best words he can. If she complains that the instalments are late he is to say that the deal with her is made for no necessity of Florence's, and, burdened as the city is with expenses, payments may at times be slow. Offer excuses she can understand! 'E in questi effetti ti distenderai con efficacia di parole, e con quelli migliori termini che ti occorreranno.' But Caterina bargained hard: Milan was a competitor for her services, and to put her down while others went up in pay seemed shameful to her. She had kind words for Florence, and Machiavelli answered suitably, but, he added in his report, if you made some allowance for her past services, or widened the terms of this *condotta*, it would be more efficacious. I omit the details; but one thing I must not omit, for it adds another side to the picture. On his way to Forlí Machiavelli wrote from Castrocaro, on the confines of Florentine territory. The people of this district were in fear of armed incursions from over the border; and Dionigio Naldi, who terrorized them, had the aid of Caterina, though she was on good terms with Florence. Only a day before there had been one of many incidents ('e cosí fanno ciascun dí simili insulti'), so that the people of the district came to Machiavelli weeping, complaining that Florence had abandoned them. Yet Machiavelli was bound for Forlí to guarantee its lord 10,000 ducats a year. It is a situation like that which provoked Landucci to write in 1480, about payments to the Duke of Calabria: 'Ogniuno che viene a'danni nostri, quando egli à disfatto el contado e rubato, e Fiorentini ànno per un savio uso di dare danari per pagamento di quel danno ci ànno fatto. E non è solo una volta stato, ma sarà ancora per l'avenire. Chi vuol danari da'Fiorentini, ci venga a fare male.'[1] On the one side, the process of buying soldiery at as good a price as possible; on the other, the sight of their lawlessness at the expense of Florence. Machiavelli's mission was inconclusive, Catherine's mind having been made up before his arrival; but he

---

[1] Landucci, 35.

could see the strong position of militia-producing states, and the constant blackmail to draw more money out of Florence. Nor can the proceedings with regard to Paolo Vitelli in September, 1499, have done other than strengthen the lesson with regard to *condottieri*: win with them, you are at their mercy; lose, and you lose in the ordinary way, as he was later to express it.

So far the scene is limited to the petty courts of Italy; but Machiavelli is soon favoured with a wider view. This time we know the irony of the situation from the witness of the *Scritti Inediti*.[1] In September, 1499, Louis XII had received with affection Florentine congratulations on his success in Italy. He had even shown this *ab effectu*: he had renewed Florentine commercial privileges in France; and, indeed, Louis seemed ready to redeem those brittle promises of Charles VIII in 1494 on the return of Pisa and the fortresses. He sent Beaumont and an expeditionary force to take Pisa. The outcome was far from Florence's bright hopes. The expenses had been calculated at 24,000 ducats a month, to be paid all by Florence, who hoped that the fear of the French name would limit the need to two months' service. But first there came two thousand more Swiss troops than stipulated for, 'a quali fu forza dare dua paghe'.[2] Then, there were other tasks on hand. The Lombard towns had had to pay ransom to the victorious French,[3] and the Cardinal of Rouen was anxious to squeeze it from the Bentivogli also, under the plea that they had favoured Lodovico Sforza. So the expeditionary force took their road via Bologna, and one month's pay 'ne andò in fummo senza profitto alcuno'. Their first arrival on the scene of action was heralded by violence against a confederate of Florence, the Marchese di Massa; and their indiscipline and ineffectiveness is common knowledge.[4] As also is the abortive end of the expeditions for the same reasons.

At this juncture Florence was advised to justify herself. In this dishonour to French arms it was to be expected that Louis's captains would try to turn the blame on Florence. It was an accurate expectation. And Francesco della Casa was sent with Niccolò Machiavelli to France to put the Florentine case, which was retrospective only, for Florence had no wish to renew the enterprise. The facts seemed clear: Florence had borne all the expense, had supplied even in double quantity for a force which refused to use even an ounce of

---

[1] ed. Canestrini, 1857.   [2] Buonaccorsi, 30–1.
[3] *ibid.*, Milan, 300,000 ducats, Pavia, 100,000, Parma, 60,000, etc. Bologna got off with 40,000.
[4] Cf. Machiavelli, Buonaccorsi, Guicciardini, etc.

their own goods.[1] And the military failure was due to the disorders of the troops themselves. Even so, the envoys were to beware of openly accusing Beaumont of cowardice and corruption either to the king, or especially to the Cardinal, of whom he was a protégé. And when they got to the French court, they found their task hard. King and Cardinal were ready with accusations that failure was due to Florence as well, and when the envoys offered details, they cut off the argument. As Trivulzio, an exile at the court, told them: 'E vorrebbono pure sotto il dire che da ogni parte s'è fatto errore, la colpa che è tutta loro accomunarla con altri.' Meanwhile, their reception from Rouen depended on the reports to him of Beaumont and the other captains, so that they were reduced to urging Florence to billet them on Florentine territory to their satisfaction. Then they would write back more charitably! When the two Florentines complained of the Swiss troops' behaviour, the answer was that such was their nature; and again the discussion was cut short. The French would hear nothing against the Lucchese (who favoured the Pisans and purchased good opinions in Louis's entourage), and it was left for della Casa and Machiavelli to lament that 'i Lucchesi, con qualche loro mezzo ed amico a loro proposito, potessino più che la verità'.[2] It is here that the graphic phrases of Machiavelli (is one wrong in discounting della Casa before his illness left the whole legation in Machiavelli's hands?) begin, and in a context as far removed from the legend of Machiavellianism as could be possible. The Lucchese have made friends with the Mammon of unrighteousness ('e tutto nasce dal sapersi acquistare *amicos de mammona iniquitatis*') and the rulers of Florence think fondly that *reason* will help.[3] The point at issue is that of money: the French brush aside the Florentine refusal to pay the Swiss because they hadn't served (and even had refused to) and were all dissolute. But if you don't, we've got to!—and that would never do. The Florentines would have had Pisa if only they had spent ten thousand ducats on the captains . . . 'e in simili cose si vuole avere il sacco aperto, perché facendo così si spende un tratto, e facendo altrimenti si spende sei'. This matter of payment becomes the focus of the whole legation. It is, for Machiavelli, the occasion for summing up French policy, Louis's nature with regard to spending, and his conduct in Italy up to this time, *di volerne trarre e non mettervi*: to take out, and never to put in.[4]

That being so, what of French views of Florence? The French,

---

[1] VI, 51. Cf. *Op.*, P.M., III, 41–5, which seems to settle the contradictory passages in Guicciardini, *St. Fior.*, 227 and 229.
[2] VI, 77.   [3] VI, 94.   [4] VI, 97.

reports Machiavelli, are blinded by their power and their present profit: they esteem only those who are armed or those who are ready to pay, and it seems that Florence fails on both scores, 'la prima dell'armi per l'ordinario, e la seconda dell'utile non sperano piú'— has not Florence been burdened with the Pisan War since 1494? And here jumps out the brilliant writing of Machiavelli: 'E reputanvi ser Nichilo, battezzando l'impossibilità vostra, disunione; e la disonestà dell'esercito loro, cattivo governo vostro.'[1] And then again a little later: Louis's discontent is founded on two heads: because of you he has suffered dishonour in Italy, and he cannot recover his honour with your cash ('né potere . . . ricuperare l'onore suo co' danari vostri'), and secondly, having to pay out 38,000 francs of his own money to the Swiss.[2] In this last lies 'l'importanza del tutto,' in it consists 'la somma di ogni cosa'.[3] At least, if Florence was not prepared to pay, Pisa was; and there were reports that the Pisans were offering 100,000 francs, and yearly tribute also, to win the grant of independence.[4] Even, Pisa would go further; they suggested a puppet to be set up by Louis over a state centred round Pisa. Then Florence would have a rope round her neck, and the Florentines would give *carte blanche* to Louis. Machiavelli adds: 'Sono queste cose ascoltate . . .'[5]

I abbreviate, of course, the details, because they are so accessible in the pages of Machiavelli's *Legations*. It is the essence of the situation that is important. On the side of Florence, a belief in honesty of policy, good faith and fair words. It is in this very year that Landucci notes the League against France, with a place left open for the entry of Florence, and adds, 'E non volemo mai lasciare el Re, che doverrebbe conoscere la grande fedeltà de'Fiorentini, che siamo diventati nimici di tutta la Italia e con grandissimi pericoli.'[6] Such sentiments recur generally among the Florentines of this period; and Florence remained faithful to the French alliance till it dragged her down in 1512. But, on the other side, there is a jockeying for position to be able to lay Florence the better under contribution: there are the petty *condottieri* with their constant jealousies and their claims for financial betterment, to be placated as well as possible; then, behind these, the power of France, whose broken promise of the return of Pisa had involved Florence in war and expense since 1494, and whose failure in arms and discipline during Beaumont's expedition could so easily be glossed over by Louis and Rouen at Florentine expense.

[1] VI, 99.	[2] VI, 103.	[3] VI, 112.
[4] VI, 107.	[5] VI, 124.	[6] Landucci, 208.

Di volere trarre e non mettervi: that is the intention of the world outside the Florence Machiavelli serves.

It is at this point in his career that two things, both of which we may consider as of great importance, take place. In 1502 Vitellozzo, whether independently of his chief Caesar Borgia, or under the latter's orders (for whatever one's estimate of Caesar Borgia is, one must remember that Florence lay across the line of Caesar's advancement), gave assistance to the rebellion of Arezzo and the Valdichiana. It is not so much Machiavelli's letters on this event which are valuable: it is his brief discourse on the way of treating rebel cities, which shows for the first time (since it is the first of his theoretic writings) the gap between events and his opinion on dealing with them. In reality Florence did what the diarist Masi noted down:[1] she relied on an appeal to Louis XII, with payments to conserve his benevolence and to act as a check on his favours to Valentino, whose power had already cost the city a *condotta* in 1501 (without the obligation of personal service, the condition being to supply three hundred men-at-arms at need). Even at this sacrificial cost Florence had not been able to avoid pillage of outlying territory by Valentino's army, waiting for better terms. And she had paid twenty thousand ducats to Louis to keep him considerate towards Florence. And now, instead of transferring troops from the Pisan front to meet the danger at Arezzo, there were consultations: the small-minded were suspicious still of the intentions of the bigger citizens, they questioned the reality of the danger, and procrastinated. Florence lost Arezzo (it is Guicciardini who points it out[2]) through the defects of her constitutional position: she recovered it through the services of the French.

But Machiavelli, when he comes to deal with the matter, does not propose to start at home, and alter Florence's constitution; or offer practical remedies for avoiding the humiliating dependency on Louis XII. He quotes Livy, *ad verbum*, as he puts it himself, for a page and a half.[3] It is true, we do not know anything of Machiavelli's upbringing; but at least as early as 1503 he has jumped out of the present into the past. Lucius Furius Camillus, whom he quotes at length, speaks with the right of one who has made his own contribution in terms of military victory. There is a sharpness and a strength in his putting of alternatives which does not suit with the conditions of Florence in 1502: 'Dii immortales ita vos potentes huius consilii fecerunt, ut, sit Latium deinde, an non sit, in vestra manu posuerint.'

---

[1] Masi, *Ricordanze*, 50-1.   [2] *St. Fior.*, XXIV, 257; and cf. Nerli, I, V, 145.
[3] *Del Modo di Trattare, etc.*, II, 385. Cf. Livy, VIII, 13-14.

The speech makes wonderfully firm and fortifying reading. It is the classical Machiavellian *aut-aut*. But Florence was not in the shoes of Lucius Furius: the military victory was that of France, not of Florence, and Florentine policy had French brakes on it, besides having very different internal conditions than obtained in Rome. Machiavelli appealed in this discourse to a humanist conception of history,[1] but he has established a gap between the *verità effettuale*, to which he is often considered to be glued, and his opinions.

The second factor which may have equally sharpened Machiavelli's views is his contact with Caesar Borgia. So far, he has seen in Italy minor rulers with no policy save trimming, and no aim, save cash. In the *Legazione al Duca Valentino* he approaches someone of more substance. Machiavelli is not, of course, deceived by Caesar Borgia's position. It is due to the favour of the King of France and the Pope, in combination, 'le quali due cose gli fecero tanto fuoco sotto, che bisognava altra acqua che coloro a spegnerlo'—as Caesar Borgia said to Machiavelli about his captains in their first important conversation.[2] But as well: 'Ha tanta artiglieria e bene in ordine, quanto tutto il resto quasi d'Italia.'[3] For his part, Caesar Borgia, at this moment of danger to his plans, gives fair offers to Florence. Machiavelli listens to them with pleasure, and with diffidence. My office, he says, to write his words, and yours to judge them and to think 'che sia bene che lo dica, ma che sia meglio non avere a fare prova'.[4] It is difficult to assess precisely the situation, because the pattern of possibilities is intricate. France protected Florence; but there is an advantage to a protector in the protégé being weak and unfortunate. It makes him more pliable, unlooses the purse-strings.[5] On the other hand, it is often taken too much for granted that Caesar Borgia was responsible for the actions of the captains under him. The fact that he had taken into his pay the majority of available *condottieri* does not mean necessarily that he had them at his control; and the break of La Magione gives validity to that point. As well, there is a sort of unanimity amongst the Florentine writers in speaking of the Orsini and Vitellozzo, rather than Caesar Borgia himself, as being the fomenters of trouble, the backers of the Medici. We may take two plain statements of Cambi as typical, and as supporting what Machiavelli will say in this legation.[6] But if it seems that Caesar

---

[1] Whitfield, *Petr. and the Ren.*, 101. [2] VI, 191. Cf. also, e.g., 231, 235, 258.
[3] VI, 199. [4] VI, 317.
[5] Buonaccorsi, 60: 'Aggiugnendo che quello havevono fatto Vitegli, e Orsini lo facevono con consenso del Re per sbattere la città, e farla piú facile alle domande sue.'
[6] Cambi, II, 161 and 185.

Borgia was not responsible for Vitellozzo's actions against Florence
(they came when he was occupied elsewhere; they threatened to
make him lose the favour of Louis XII), he may not have regretted
them. But after the Diet of La Magione the aims of both Caesar
Borgia and Florence are clear: the immediate enemies of Florence are
Vitellozzo and the Orsini. They are those of Caesar Borgia also.[1]
That is why Machiavelli finds his words so reasonable: 'le parole
sono state sempre, e sono, tanto buone, quanto io ho scritte, e dette,
e parlate con ragione'.[2] That is why he begins with the intention of
preventing, in so far as he can, any agreement between Caesar and
his captains. I did not fail, he writes, to do my office of fostering the
opinion in him 'che non si possa e non si debba mai piú fidare di loro,
facendogli toccar con mano molte cose seguite per il passato, quando
si mostravano amici, che tutti loro macchinavano e ordivano contro
Sua Eccellenza, e tanto egli fu capace'.[3] We have no clue to help in
identifying any of these many things; but that deficiency does not
excuse us from giving its value to so clear a passage when we estimate
the attitude of Machiavelli and Florence, or the personality of Caesar
Borgia. It is for these reasons that Machiavelli notes with assurance
the mutual suspicions of the *dieta di falliti* (the phrase is Caesar Borgia's
own), as well as the latter's resentment of their treachery. And
Machiavelli, from the beginning, judges that Caesar Borgia will be
the victor, not only because of the support of Louis XII ('il maestro
della bottega'—in Caesar Borgia's own phrase), but because he
stands by himself against disunity; and holds his counsel admirably,
and his course.[4]

Now Machiavelli notes throughout with satisfaction that Caesar
Borgia does not desire agreement with his late captains any more
than Machiavelli himself desires it. And we may bear in mind his
assessment of their like in a text from his next big legation (to the
court of Rome): there he calls them, in their constant feuds, 'piuttosto latroncoli, che soldati. Ed essendo obbligati alle proprie passioni loro, non possono servire bene un terzo. E queste loro paci
che fanno, durano quanto pena a venire occasione l'uno all'altro
offendersi. E chi è qui ne vede ogni giorno l'esperienza, e chi gli
conosce, pensa di temporeggiarli, tanto che possa dare loro i termini.'[5]
To temporize till one can give them terms: it is Caesar Borgia's
attitude as Machiavelli sees it in the legation to Imola; and we must
not forget the nature of the captains with whom he was dealing. But

[1] VI, 349. [2] VI, 347. Cf. Dell'Oro, 124. [3] VI, 220.
[4] VI, 220 and VI, 278. [5] VI, 372.

what of the climax at Sinigaglia? Was it mere treachery on the part
of Caesar Borgia, or was it diamond cut diamond?

It is known that Machiavelli wrote two accounts of these events:
one which is easily to be found in most editions of his works, the
Descrizione del Modo tenuto, etc.; the other which was not published
at all until the Passerini-Milanesi edition. It has been hard to find,
and so has been proportionately easy to reject. The difference
between them is that in the set *Descrizione* Machiavelli writes as
though Caesar Borgia was the only one who thought in terms of a
trap at Sinigaglia. In the other, which is the autograph fragment of a
letter to replace the one missing for December 31, 1502, from Sinigaglia itself, Machiavelli states explicitly that distrust (as throughout)
was mutual, and that the captains had their plan to trap Caesar
Borgia, which failed because he came in force. This is a *locus classicus*
for the plastic nature of evidence in the face of conviction. Because
the letter is explicit Tommasini felt the need to diminish, or abolish,
its testimony, by inventing the circumstances in which it was written.
It cannot be the copy of the missing letter, because, of course,
Machiavelli didn't keep them; he must have written it after January 13
when Salviati was coming as the new ambassador and Niccolò had
not yet left Valentino. And because he didn't know into whose
hands it might fall, so he is ambiguous in his terms: thus he can 'put
as true the tales which Valentino had handed out,' all out of prudence.[1]
This is ingenious, but it is conjectural; and it might invalidate the
whole series of Machiavelli's letters up to this one. For Tommasini's
attribution of special circumstances is gratuitous, supported by no
evidence, but arising from the desire to explain the letter away. On
the other hand, the *Descrizione*, as Dell'Oro pointed out,[2] has its
Achilles' heel: it mentions Monsignor d'Euna 'che fu poi cardinale'.
Such a phrase gives considerable recession to the event of his becoming
cardinal; and as this was not till May 31 of 1503 it would seem to put
the *Descrizione* considerably later than the summer which saw the
death of Alexander VI. The point is a delicate one, but the letter is
not dismissed until concrete proof is brought to show that Machiavelli, against his wont, had falsified his information. And in the
meantime it may be taken that the later account reflects a literary
tendency (as in the *Vita di Castruccio*): Caesar Borgia has acquired
something of the sharpness Machiavelli found in Lucius Furius
Camillus.

But even if we leave that point properly in suspense, we must

[1] Tommasini, I, 258-9.   [2] Dell'Oro, 131.

see Sinigaglia in some perspective. For those who have begun with Caesar Borgia as the hero, and Machiavelli as the hero-worshipper, it has been possible to embroider richly round this theme. What account could be more lyrical than Benoist's one of the 'bellissimo inganno'?[1] If one starts from that side, naturally Caesar's captains are a set of men with whom one should have full sympathy; if that is excessive, and beyond human ingenuity, one solves the matter by leaving them unscrutinized, a set of dummies, but foully betrayed. It is not quite right to do so. Mazzoni and Casella (who accept an early date for the *Descrizione*, and distrust the letter) point out that Vitellozzo and Oliverotto da Fermo had deserved their end.[2] It was the conclusion of Julius II. If we, as heirs to the humanitarian reforms in justice that begin in Europe with the eighteenth century, are unduly hurt by the method of execution, yet we must remember to put that in perspective too.[3] It will have been noticed that I used the word *justice*: what, M. Benoist would ask quickly, has justice to do with Sinigaglia? Well, it is the unanimous reaction of such good Florentines as Cambi and Landucci to think of it in terms of justice, and even (still unanimously) of divine justice. 'E non volendo la divina giustizia sopportagli piú gliaffatti rimanere presi nel laccio giustamente.' That is Giovanni Cambi; and Landucci says the same on the abasement of the house of Orsini: 'Guarda come la divina giustizia paga alle volte el Sabato.'[4] While for Nerli, too, the enemies of Florence who have so often troubled her, who entertained the Medici's hopes, and instigated the ambitions of Caesar himself in the direction of Tuscany, have disappeared by this stroke.[5] We have seen already that Machiavelli has reasons for taking up the standpoint of his fellow-citizens; and it is only if we insist absolutely on a Machiavelli who admires wickedness when it is operative that we can ignore so much evidence, or make the legendary appeal to Sinigaglia.

My task was to look at Machiavelli's *Legations* only as a means to determining the formation of his ideas; but since the crux arose here in what he said himself, it was necessary to consider its resolution. Nor has that taken us far afield. Instead of the irresolute Florence, under contribution to her captains, and dependent on France, here is a man who metes out to the treachery of his captains the stern treatment of L. F. Camillus; who looks beyond the temporary favour of Louis XII to a permanent structure of his own. Caesar

---

[1] Cf. Benoist, *Le Machiavélisme*, I.
[2] *Op.*, M.C., xli–xlii. Cf. Dell'Oro, 133–6, and Whitfield, *New Views on the Borgias*, 77–89.
[3] For contemporary justice, see, e.g., Landucci, 219.
[4] Cambi, II, 185; Landucci, 252.   [5] F. de'Nerli, I, V, 152; and cf. 140.

Borgia (as his *friend* told Machiavelli) knew the Pope might die at any time, and that he needed another foundation. 'Il primo fondamento che fa, è sul re di Francia; il secondo sulle armi proprie.' The friend added that these two might not prove enough, and that therefore he wished to make friends with his neighbours, with Florence, Bologna, Mantua, and Ferrara.[1] And if the Florentine envoy is a little apprehensive at the rise of Caesar Borgia's power, mistrusting its implications for Florence, there is yet something here that he can grasp. It is, once more, partly his subordinate position: Guicciardini would have been more Florentine. But Machiavelli has mixed in his apprenticeship to affairs (working his way, not so much up, as underneath) a vent-hole through Livy. It is this that makes him write back to Florence 'che si ha a fare qui con un principe, che si governa da sé';[2] and to put down the pregnant phrase that one must not measure Caesar Borgia by the other rulers of Italy, 'ma ragionare di lui, come di un nuovo Potentato in Italia'.[3] One must not suppose, even for one moment, that any admiration Machiavelli may have felt for Caesar meant a weaning from the viewpoint of Florence only. His sense of a resolute strength in the one is expressed instead in terms of exasperation with the weakness of the other. Contrast his statement of the *new ruler* with the bitter reflections which arise out of extraordinary expenditure on Caesar Borgia's part, but which overflow on to the nature of Florentine policy. 'This I have written willingly, he reports to the Signoria, so that you may see how when a ruler is in disorder he spends no less than you do, nor is better served by his soldiers than you are; and on the other hand, he who is armed well, and with his own arms, produces the same effect whichever way he turns.'[4] They are melancholy reflections, which we may transfer at our will.

Machiavelli has not, then, transferred allegiance, even if he has found one who is potentially a model. Nor is there, of course, in this legation, a boundless admiration for Caesar Borgia. Just as before he has spoken of Alexander VI as insatiable in his ambitions, so here he gives warning against specific misdeeds of Caesar: his army, in its passage back to Rome, will be likely to follow its old ways and live at the expense of what towns in the states of the Church lie in its path.[5] Let Florence look to any of her merchants' goods in Ancona, lest there be a sack there. Nor, to be fair to the tenour of the letters, does Machiavelli ever doubt that Caesar would find a way out of,

---

[1] VI, 258.   [2] VI, 267.   [3] VI, 261.
[4] VI, 288.   [5] VI, 292.

or break openly, any agreement with his disaffected captains (that does not prejudice the point as to their intentions, or as to what actually happened). Machiavelli is so far receiving impressions, and there are wide gaps, of many sorts, between the minor Florentine Secretary, and Caesar Borgia; just as there is a gap between his reading of Livy and the realities of Florence. Thus the germ for the *Prince* is obviously prepared in the pages of this legation, without Machiavelli being ready to do more than think in terms of Florentine interests; and without any prejudice to his moral judgments on certain aspects of Caesar Borgia; as without him being carried off his feet. The essential, and the self-evident, fact is that this is the central point of Machiavelli's experience in the negotiation of Florentine embassies, in spite of its slightly previous date. He does not lose the viewpoint of Florence only (so touchingly asserted in 1504 in the *Primo Decennale*), he applies to the benefit of Florence the ideas on the value of being, in the current phrase, 'in su l'armi'; but the succeeding legations centre, as had the earlier ones, round the question of blackmail levied upon Florence. His city clung, with pathetic good faith, to the French alliance, and the reward of that was the catastrophe of 1512. But before that, and preparatory to it, there are new factors and new blackmail levied on Florence.

The first legation to the court of Rome has drawn men's eyes more than the others because in it is recounted day by day the collapse of Caesar Borgia's hopes, down to a last and brilliant, if contemptuous, phrase, 'e cosí pare che questo duca a poco a poco sdruccioli nello avello'.[1] Think no more of him as a problem for Florence, he is slipping down into his grave! Much has been made of this treatment by Machiavelli of his *hero*. It has been commonly connected with his cynicism: he admires success, at any cost, despises failure. Such criticism is partisan: it rests on an idle supposition, that Machiavelli had expressed some boundless admiration for Caesar Borgia. But if he does any such thing (and we shall hardly find that matters are quite thus), it is in a famous chapter of the *Prince*, which is very safely posthumous to the career of Valentino. It posits also that Machiavelli is blind to anything but somebody else's success, when there is no possibility of such a theoretic detachment on his part. He is thinking of the interests of Florence, as he was during the legation to Imola. His judgments on the Borgias in the *Decennale*, a year later, are admirably stern; and there is here a passage on the capture of one of Caesar's captains which is significant. This latter

[1] VI, 472.

event pleased Julius II immensely, since it seemed to give the opportunity to discover much of the cruelties, robberies, homicides and all
the rest 'che da undici anni in qua si sono fatti a Roma contro Dio,
e gli uomini'.[1] Those *eleven* years cover the period 1492 to 1503;
they coincide with Alexander's pontificate. And even in the degeneracy of the papacy from 1464 it is right that we should pay attention to this contemporary roping of them off; for the seekers after
sensationalism have been so prone to view the Renascence in terms
of the Borgias. 'They do sum up the political and moral ideas
prevalent in Italy of those days,' as a recent English writer chose to
put it.[2] It would be better to refer to the *Decennale*, and to the indignation of the Florentine diarists, to establish a separation, rather than
to spread these generalizations. Nor must we forget the nature of
the Roman nobles, characterized in this legation, which gave colour
to Caesar Borgia's aim, expressed to Machiavelli in the preceding
mission, to free all the patrimony of the Church from tyrants, judging
thereby that a new Pope would be grateful to him when he found
himself no longer enslaved to the Orsini and Colonna, 'come sono
sempre suti i Papi per lo addreto'.[3] But if, as I have said elsewhere,
the assessment of the Borgias is an intricate matter there is nothing
to be explained, or explained away, in Machiavelli's attitude to them.
He is an observer in the interests of Florence, and of the general
welfare: as he says himself, 'staremo a vedere che seguirà, e preghe-
remo Iddio che dia vittoria a chi rechi salute e pace alla Cristianità, e
alla città vostra'.[4] And he had said much the same thing, as this
which is written when awaiting news of the armies on the Garigliano,
on the election of Julius II.[5] Nor must it be thought that these are
idle or hypocritical words: the Machiavelli who notes so accurately
the temperament of Julius II ('e non lo avendo per uom doppio,
ma piú tosto rotto e impetuoso'[6]) is himself quite innocent of being
doppio.[7] That is why the *Legations* are such a necessary preliminary
to Machiavelli's works: they encourage no misconceptions as to the
honesty of his character.

What are the forces that Machiavelli sees at play? First, in the
minds of all observers, the power and ambition of Venice, object of
universal hatred. Her hands stretch out as those of Caesar Borgia
relax their grasp, and the latter's ambiguous position is due to Julius II's

[1] VI, 465.   [2] D. Erskine Muir, *Machiavelli and his Times*, 52.   [3] VI, 339.
[4] VI, 450. Cf. identical formulas in the ingenuous Florentine diarists, e.g. Paolo Paoli,
clxxix.
[5] VI, 380: 'Che Iddio lo faccia utile Pastore per la Cristianità.'
[6] VI, 428 and 451.   [7] Cf. IV, 178, *Istruzione a un ambasciatore*.

possible need of him as a counterweight to Venice in Romagna. Is there not here the best proof that Machiavelli is not thinking either in terms of success, or of a national State, in 1503? Caesar Borgia has fallen; but Venice might dominate all Italy. It is true; but Machiavelli thinks *against* Venice and *for* Florence. We must not think of him as one who had an anachronistic sense of patriotism. He notes in Rome the current judgment that the Venetian enterprise against Faenza will be the gateway to open all Italy for them, or will be their ruin.[1] We are only five years from the League of Cambrai. It is this enmity, as much as his promises, that causes Julius to hesitate in his attitude to Caesar Borgia. Elected partly with the aid of the Spanish cardinals he had promised largely to Caesar, as to others; but he would not be sorry for a pretext not to keep his word. Thus he encouraged Florence in hesitating to give safe conduct to Caesar Borgia's men, and Machiavelli deduced aright that, while the Pope left it to Florence's judgment, 'arà piú caro se gli dia la pinta'.[2] Yet, when Venice prepared to lay her hands on Caesar Borgia's state of Romagna, Julius bethought himself that it might be better for the latter to have it than them. Nor does Julius escape Machiavelli's censure for his treatment of Caesar Borgia. When there are rumours of his having been thrown in the Tiber, and Machiavelli realizes that they embody a fact, or something soon to be one, he adds: 'e vedesi che questo Papa comincia a pagare i debiti suoi assai onorevolmente, e li cancella con la bambagia del calamajo'.[3] It is one of those typically Machiavellian phrases of the *Legations*, sharp with the language of every day used to express something of importance. When Machiavelli writes ironically (which, *pace* De Sanctis, is somewhat rarely) it is the full irony of indignation, scornful, not sneering. And this is the prelude to a famous condemnation of Julius II which we shall find later.

And Florence? The Venetians look beyond Romagna towards Florentine territory: have they not already been a major obstacle to the recovery of Pisa? Where must Florence look for help against them? Julius is new elected; he has neither troops, nor money. The French are freshly engaged in their struggle with the Spanish for the Kingdom of Naples, and for more than that. You cannot hope, he writes to his superiors, that the French or the Pope should employ men or money for you; you have then 'a fare fondamento sopra ogni altra cosa, che sopra i danari, o gente d'altri'.[4] *Fare fondamento*: it is the idea Machiavelli had learnt at the court of Caesar

[1] VI, 444.   [2] VI, 431.   [3] VI, 448–9.   [4] VI, 436.

Borgia being put to the service of Florence; it is the overture to his
service for the Florentine militia.¹ And Machiavelli rubs the lesson
in a little later. Blame if you like, he says, the wickedness of the times
'e la cattiva sorte degli impotenti'.² It is perhaps to be meditated on
that in this legation there first appears in connection with Machiavelli
the idea of the end and the means; and that in this world which has
such pitfalls for states like Florence the phrase originates in somebody
quite different from Machiavelli himself. It is part of his experience,
not of his nature. He had a letter of excuses to present to a cardinal;
and it is the latter who made the generalization which has often been
imagined as the sum of Machiavelli's doctrine: 'Lui disse che di tutte
le cose gli uomini guardavano piú al fine, che ai mezzi.'³ Men look
to the end, not to the means. Machiavelli did not forget the lesson;
though it will be evident later that his views bear little relation to
the vulgar version of the end justifying the means. But in the present
is it not one more reinforcement to the warnings to Florence in her
impotence? For there is another danger that appears on the horizon
in this legation: the rumours of the Emperor's desire to join the party
being held upon Italian soil. 'L'Imperatore voleva passare *infallanter*,
e presto, e che lo animo suo era circa le cose di Pisa volere dua cose;
la prima darne la possessione a chi piú danari gli ne dava; l'altra di
volerne in ogni modo un censo ogni anno come di terra sua, e dato
in feudo ad altri.'⁴ This was no time for those who had no foundations except in reason.

Indeed, the legation to Rome can be thought of as a breathing-
space for Florence; but it is scarcely over before the dangers to the
impotent mature. First, we must note two marginal certificates: the
first, to Machiavelli himself, in the letter from Cardinal Soderini
which followed his return. Hold the said Niccolò dear, he writes to
the rulers of Florence, 'perché di fede et diligenzia, et prudenzia non
se ne ha a desiderare multo in lui'.⁵ Faith, diligence, and prudence:
they are good qualities. But, after all, are they in good employ?
for the value of faith depends on its principal. The answer, perhaps,
lies in the second certificate. All the Instructions to Machiavelli in
his settings-out are interesting, some specially revealing. The one
on his hurried departure for the French Court again, to urge the need
of Florence after the victory of Consalvo on the Garigliano had added
a new danger to the other ordinary ones of Italy, is no exception.
The necessity is, to seek the salvation of Florence where it can be

---

¹ For the phrase, e.g. VI, 258.   ² VI, 442.   ³ VI, 373.
                    ⁴ VI, 456.   ⁵ VI, 494.

found; and here again a prophetic phrase slips in, not Machiavelli's yet, but to be Machiavelli's, even to be ironically one of the corner-stones on which rests the idea that he preached the supremacy of the State: 'perché noi non dobbiamo preporre alla conservazione nostra alcun altro rispetto'.[1] Yet, even so (and this is the second testimony of which I spoke), Florence does not hasten to desert the setting star of France. It is still her desire and her intention to arrange things so that 'noi possiamo stare in fede, e mantenere gli obblighi'.[2] Such is the role of the Florence to which Machiavelli's devotion is given. And there is a sidelight in the same Instruction. Florence had always tried to impress upon the French the advantage they would gain from a strong Tuscan State in central Italy. The French had not listened, for reasons we have seen quite clearly already. But now they may, when Consalvo threatens to overturn all their influence in Italy: it is their own interest to preserve us; point this out to the Governor of Milan, that he may pass it on to Louis, 'perché la sperienza ha mostro che pochi ricordi gli muovono piú (move, that is, *kings*) che quelli di loro medesimi'.[3] Florence thinks in terms of obligations to others; kings think in terms of themselves. And Niccolò Valori, the Floren-tine ambassador proper at the French court, in whose name (and in whose style, duller than that of Machiavelli) most of the letters of this legation are written, supplies a further commentary: 'se si ha ad aver fede a parole di re'.[4] It is interesting, is it not, that one of the pronouncements which the hunters after machiavellianism found most machiavellian is that of a pamphleteer in 1741, who wrote: 'En fait de politique et d'intérêts, il n'y a ni reconnaissance ni traités qui tiennent'?[5] Perhaps it may have been possible for him to have someone else than the Florentine Machiavelli as his informant on this matter.

Although there is still a second volume of the *Legations*, there is not so much to detain us. My purpose is not to paint the background of contemporary history—that has been often done;[6] but to show the traits that presented themselves most insistently to Machiavelli. And what comes after is a reinforcement to what has come before. Thus, the short legation to G. P. Baglioni goes back again to the conditions of the first missions. In 1505 Baglioni refused his services, against the terms of his *condotta*, and this, as Buonaccorsi says, was a major concern to Florence.[7] Machiavelli's commission was the usual humiliating one: to find out whether he would serve, or not; and if

---

[1] VI, 496.   [2] VI, 499.   [3] VI, 500.   [4] VI, 550.
[5] Cherel, 207.   [6] Cf. Barbagallo, for a recent survey.   [7] Buonaccorsi, 100.

not, why: whether it was to better the terms of his *condotta* at Florentine expense, or had some deeper cause; and finally, 'che non si
rompessi seco . . .'¹ Fair words, then, as to the Lord of Piombino or
to Caterina Sforza. Similarly, the legation to Siena in 1505, due to the
fear of Bartolomeo d'Alviano, then in the process of losing his *condotta* with Consalvo, and therefore in that of looking for territory,
arises from a situation resembling the Florentine fear of Vitellozzo
and Caesar Borgia. Perhaps, one remark urged by Machiavelli on
Pandolfo Petrucci needs glossing: Bartolomeo, he says, is the type
to be feared by all rulers, 'essendo lui armato, e senza stato, ed essendo
di natura fiero, e senza rispetti, e l'Italia trovandosi piena di ladri, e usi
a vivere di quel d'altri'.² It is a statement to be illuminated by juxta-
position with Guicciardini's account of the change in conditions after
Consalvo's victory on the Garigliano. Up till then, soldiers had been
licentious, but yet they had lived largely on their pay, their licence
had not been intolerable. But the Spaniards first in Italy began to
live totally on the substance of the people because they were badly
paid by the Spanish king. Guicciardini adds Petrarch's reflection on
the imitation of good falling short of its exemplar, while the imitation
of evil always exceeds it: and from this start (1504-5) they all began,
whether Spaniards or Italians, whether paid or not, to do the same,
till friends and enemies came equally to be feared.³ This important
passage, which must be read in conjunction with another of the same
historian on the deterioration of conditions for Italy at the time of the
League of Cambrai throws essential light on the downfall of Italy.

Sufficient prominence has been given, in the various accounts of
Machiavelli's life, to his exertions on behalf of the Florentine militia,
to meet the threats of the situation: and in so far as this represents a
working out of his opinions in practice, not the formation of them,
the writings with regard to the militia (though the whole matter
testifies to his earnestness, and to his devotion) are uninteresting to us.
The legation to Julius II, arising out of the Pope's request for Florentine help in his expedition against Perugia and Bologna, is also not
very much to our purpose. Its highlight, to which I shall return, is
in the *dappocaggine* of G. P. Baglioni, who neglected his opportunity
of taking advantage of his rash adversary.⁴ But also, and we must
link the idea with those statements of Guicciardini on military
conditions in Italy at the time, there is in Machiavelli's mind a feeling
that Julius II may accomplish something: if he succeeds at Bologna,

¹ VII, 4.   ² VII, 21.
³ *St. d'Italia*, VII, 232, and cf. also VIII, 136.   ⁴ VII, 95.

all believe that he will lose no time in trying bigger things, 'e giudicasi che o questa volta Italia si assicurerà da chi ha disegnato inghiottirsela, o non mai piú'.[1] Have not the critics failed to see that for a brief moment Machiavelli attaches to the person of Julius hopes which he had not attached to Caesar Borgia? His sphere of vision is enlarging, and this is the first time that he ventures to think of a general solution.

One detail, too, is added here to remind us of these swallowers-up of Italy: Julius builds (a *fondamento* once again) much of his hopes upon Swiss mercenaries. He has remitted to Milan some 30,000 ducats on their account, equivalent to three months' pay in advance, which they demand before they will stir, 'come sanno benissimo le Signorie Vostre'.[2] Indeed, Florence knew well enough the price of things. The next legation to the Emperor will emphasize that again; but before it there is a curious prelude, in the legation to Siena in 1507. The rumour is of Maximilian's coming, and Machiavelli's business is to learn the reaction of Siena, a town that might be thought to favour traditionally the Imperial cause. Yet Machiavelli finds Pandolfo displeased at the news, 'come colui che sta bene, e non vede piú guadagno ne'travagli'. *Nondimanco*, and it is already the disturbing Machiavellian word, he is preparing for Maximilian's coming; firstly, to make it thought in Siena that he is on good terms with the Emperor, to prevent favours for those discontented with his rule; and secondly, in order really to be on good terms with Maximilian.[3] It is in miniature the picture of Italy as it must have appeared to Machiavelli.

It is after this that he proceeds to join Francesco Vettori in the attempt to buy off, or to determine if it is necessary to buy off, the Emperor Maximilian. To pay blackmail, or to omit it on the principle that blackmail, like blockade, is only legal when it is effective? It needed a shrewd observer to determine the conditions. Therefore, the instructions are elastic: Machiavelli could offer up to 50,000 ducats, but he was to start the bidding at 30,000, and to offer a series of instalments which might allow for an escape out of the contract. What was he to ask for in return? The restitution of Pisa, and the conservation of the dominion of Florence as it was.[4] But the Signoria built no rash hopes: if it was too much to ask for restitution, then he should leave that out.[5] The bidding began inauspiciously: the answer to Machiavelli was that they offered something less than in 1502, and

[1] VII, 137.   [2] VII, 122.   [3] VII, 153.   [4] VII, 164.
[5] *ibid.*, 'Quando la restituzione non si potessi avere, si lasciassi addreto.'

asked for something more. There must be no talk of restitution!
And as well, Maximilian, with his thirst for ready money, would
prefer an immediate cash loan; against which he was prepared to
deposit with the Fuggers a letter decorated with the Imperial seals,
guaranteeing the integrity of Florence—to be handed over to Florence
when ulterior agreement had been reached.[1] Lang, the Imperial
Minister, dilated on the honesty of this arrangement, observing
that if Florence desired the Emperor's esteem she ought to give him
this pledge of her affection. To which Vettori, for most often the
letters are in his name, though the style smacks more of Machiavelli,
replied that it did not sound very acceptable to Florence, 'vedendo il
pagamento dei danari certo, e la sicurtà incerta';[2] but that it was his
business to report it back to Florence for consideration. And so the
haggling went on, while the Florentine envoys noted the balance of
gains and losses in the Imperial plans: the summer coming, but the
period for which the Diet had granted pay to the Imperial soldiery
rapidly going. In blackmail of this sort there are two dangers: to
pay too soon, and so contribute to the weakness of one's own
position; or to pay too late, when the price is harder. Small wonder
that the Florentine envoys complained that the thread was spun so fine
that it could not be woven. I skip the details of the bargaining,
because it is the situation that concerns us, and that is plain enough;
partly, as well, there is the scruple that the signature is Vettori's
almost throughout. But naturally, Machiavelli looked over his
shoulder; and we have found out before that he has ears enough to
listen to other people's observations. Here also there is one, on the
nature of the Emperor, which may lie at the base of a notorious
passage in the *Prince*. Maximilian is a man of talents and experience,
one whose reputation as emperor stands higher than his predecessors
for a century back. But he is so kind and humane, that he is too easy-
going and credulous; and though he holds his troops together by
money, yet he is too liberal to make money last. For sure, liberality
is a virtue in a prince—*nondimeno*, it is no use satisfying a mere
thousand when you need twenty thousand, 'e la liberalità non giova,
dove la non aggiugne'.[3] Things that seem virtues, and lead to one's
undoing: we shall meet them again in the theory of Machiavelli.

Once more, we can pass over much: the activities of Machiavelli
in the death-throes of Pisa do not concern us, especially as we see
nothing here of the play of blackmail between France and Spain,
anxious both that Florence should not emerge from this interesting

1 VII, 169.   2 VII, 170.   3 VII, 186.

situation which kept her under permanent contribution. For that, one must look to Buonaccorsi.[1] Or we could find the theory of it in Guicciardini's *Reggimento*. Then in the legation to Mantua in 1509 Machiavelli merely goes to pay the ransom-money which the failure of Maximilian's earlier venture had only postponed. True, he manages to learn something which he did not forget: the Venetians, their territory terribly handled in the brutal hounding of them begun with the League of Cambrai, put up, upon the places they recaptured, a St. Mark who bore a sword and not a book; so that they seemed to have learnt at their own expense 'che a tenere gli stati non bastano gli studî e i libri'.[2] But the period of the legations is drawing to its close. In the play of powerful forces in Italy it is becoming hard for Florence to cling to the French alliance; and the projected council of Pisa in 1510 makes the dilemma painful. With Florentine territory embraced by that of the Church, and with Julius on the papal throne, how can Florence give hospitality to councils meeting to depose the Pope? Just a sentence, significant for Machiavelli's conclusions, and we can pass on from the legations: Florence must decide, 'senza aspettare che i tempi venghino loro addosso, e che la necessità gli stringa'.[3] It was, alas, what Florence was in no position to do: she could only temporize, as she had done in that first legation to Maximilian; and the policy led downhill. With the disappearance of the French prop after the battle of Ravenna in 1512 Florence is open, militia or no militia, to the opposing forces. The Spanish army carries out the singularly cruel sack of Prato, and the reimposition of the Medici is inevitable.

I must not leave the period of the legations without pointing a moral that will already have occurred to the observant reader. There is a striking unanimity in the group of Florentine onlookers with their insistence on Florence's keeping faith. The frequent assertions of this in Landucci's *Diary* are clearly spontaneous, and they are echoed by Cambi, Nerli, Paolo Paoli, Guicciardini.[4] I may make two references to Buonaccorsi, Machiavelli's friend and colleague, who also has the usual Florentine pride in the good faith of his city, 'sendo stata la città sempre osservantissima della fede'.[5] And we must bear that pride in mind to contrast it with his remarks on Ferdinand of Aragon ('ce bon et parjure roy Ferdinand', as Brantôme dubbed him). Frederick of Naples chose to flee to his enemy, Louis, rather than to

---

[1] Buonaccorsi, 134–9.   [2] VII, 312..   [3] VII, 355.
[4] E.g. Cambi, II, 265–6; Nerli, 142; Paolo Paoli, clxxi; Guicciardini, *St. F.*, XXIII, 248; with Landucci, 80, 127, 208.
[5] Buonaccorsi, 43.

his relative Ferdinand, to whom he had appealed for help, and who had come to betray him 'senza rispetto alcuno di parentado, o di fede, che cosí era solito in tutte le cose sua, come nel processo si vedrà, ove si harà a fare mentione di sua Maestà'.[1] And the Emperor? In 1512 Florence sent Soderini to Mantua to honour him, and the Emperor took the opportunity of asking for 100,000 ducats. Florence refused, pointing out his guarantee not to offend, or allow to be offended, the city of Florence; they would pay, since he was always in need of money, when he was in strength in Italy, since they could do no other, and since he took no account of his obligations, or his word, 'da che non teneva conto alcuno degl'oblighi, né della fede'.[2] As there was no immediate cash forthcoming, the Bishop of Gurk, the Imperial Minister, turned to the Medici, who had promised much more for their return to power; and the Republic of Florence fell in consequence, because it had ventured to remind a monarch of his word. For the King of France the testimony is more abundant: was not he the recipient of Florentine faith during this period? But the promises which he swore on the altar of Santa Maria del Fiore in 1494, 'innanzi a Cristo Giesú, come parola di re,'[3] were never to be kept. We can find easily enough the stern words that chroniclers like Rinuccini or Landucci used against Charles VIII.[4] Or we may seek the pendant to this 'word of a king' in the statement of Guicciardini, also on the King of France: 'Sendo lui bisognoso di denari, e non piú osservatore della fede che gli altri barbari.'[5] Nor must we forget alongside this the change in the management of war on which the same Guicciardini wrote an important passage in his *Storia Fiorentina*.[6] If it was Spanish soldiery who carried out the cruel sack of Prato in 1512, at the end of this period we have been concerned with, it was the French who had introduced bloody warfare into Italy at its beginning. It was Jovius who remarked on the sack that opened their career on Italian soil that the fame of this cruel act went out, causing great terror, but inspiring 'uno incredibile odio alla nation Francese, la quale molti pensauano che non fosse differente in tutto da'costumi nostri'.[7] What would Cherel and Charbonnel have thought of this piece of impertinence, if they had had the misfortune to read it? I do not really know; but I do not think they could suitably appeal here to any moral superiority upon their side, or maintain with any equity that Charles and his fellows must have been imbued so much

¹ Buonaccorsi, 48.   ² *ibid.*, 180.   ³ Landucci, 86.
⁴ E.g. Rinuccini, cliii–cliv and clviii; Landucci, 264–5.
⁵ *St. F.*, XXX, 345.   ⁶ *ibid.*, XI, 105.
⁷ Paolo Giovio, *Istorie del suo Tempo*, tr. Domenichi, I, II, 48.

with machiavellianism as to have outstripped their teachers before they had made contact with them. And Machiavelli, who uses the adjective *bestial* for the French soldiery, observed on the departure of the Cardinal Georges d'Amboise from the Roman Court that he was liked by all, since he had been found more easy and more human than had been expected in one who was 'gran signore, e Franzese'.[1] Is it not clear now why no one can afford to ignore the experience of the years lived through during these legations before looking to the *Prince*?

[1] VI, 481.

IV

THE *PRINCE*

THERE is, in one of the startling chapters of the *Prince*, an opening sentence which has seemed to many the confirmation of Machiavelli's cynicism. It is on the subject of faith in princes. The first half pays lip-service to the virtue of keeping one's word, and then his terrible *nevertheless* steps in to point to the reality: 'Nondimanco si vede, per esperienzia ne'nostri tempi, quelli principi avere fatto gran cose, che della fede hanno tenuto poco conto, e che hanno saputo con l'astuzia aggirare e'cervelli degli uomini; e alla fine hanno superato quelli che si sono fondati in sulla lealtà.'[1] This is, indeed, one of those texts on which it is customary to base the attack not only on Machiavelli, but on the Italian Renascence as well: so pagan, and ergo, so wicked, how could it reckon in terms of keeping faith? Machiavelli is, said Oriani, the artist who depicts faithfully the faithless picture of his own time: *artista, non uomo*, if I may add a rhetorical counter to De Sanctis's classic *uomo, non artista*.[2] And those whose business it is to blacken the Renascence have been quick to follow up the issue.[3] So neat, so symmetrical a position: the Italians were corrupt (it was Machiavelli's own word for them) because they had abandoned the Age of Faith, so that their punishment came at the hands of the incorrupt; at the hands of those who, presumably, still lived in the Age of Faith, and of faith. Does not Alexander VI come later in the chapter as a concrete example of faithlessness? All that is most convenient for those who like the ready-made in pictures, or who have the cause of medievalism at heart. But it is precisely because of this that the background of the *Legations* is essential to any comprehension of the ideas current in Machiavelli's mind at the time he wrote the *Prince*. When we know that background is it not clear that it is Florence who built on loyalty, and that it is Florence who has gone down before the faithlessness of Charles VIII, Louis XII, Ferdinand of Aragon, and Maximilian, to keep the list short? This chapter which has given so much offence to the moralists north of the Alps has an opposite function to the one always lent to it. It is not Machiavelli

---

[1] P. XVIII, 34.   [2] A. Oriani, *Fino a Dogali.*
[3] Cf. Whitfield, *Petr. and the Ren.*, 14, etc.

codifying Italian corruption for the use of would-be despots. Once more, there would be little use his codifying formulas that had led to defeat as a recipe for securing success. Nor, if we read this chapter with any attention at all, can we accept the idea of Janni, for instance, that a cardinal principle with Machiavelli is this one of not keeping faith.[1] On the contrary, the Machiavelli whose letter to Vettori of December 10, 1513, the birth-certificate of the *Prince*, contains four times in four of its closing lines the statement of his own faithfulness (*fede . . . fede . . . fedele e buono . . . la fede e bontà mia*),[2] is not insensitive to the matter. The praise that he gives to the virtue of keeping faith is quite sincere; but the bitterness arises from the fact that the policy of keeping faith has proved inadequate.

Vis mea lex, wrote Roger North in 1564 in the margin of his copy of Jovius's *Istorie* at the point where Charles VIII confronted Alexander VI, the one armed, the other disarmed.[3] The balance between Italian states was possible in the fifteenth century, though it was precarious and needed the personal ability of a Lorenzo to preserve it. But once the short-sightedness of Lodovico Sforza had introduced the bigger fish into the pool it is nature that asserts itself, not abstract ideas of supernatural penalties; and it is, from Machiavelli's point of view, the good and weak (that is, Florence) who suffer at the hands of the unscrupulous, the bad and strong.[4] Of course, there are cross-hatchings in the map of Italy: that is why I said that Pandolfo Petrucci's dilemma of 1507 represented the Italian scene in miniature. Thus, for instance, the liberties of Ferrara are threatened by the Venetians, with their ambition to found a mainland power; then later by Julius II, with his desire to extend the temporal dominion of the papacy; and later still by Leo X, in his desire to found a new state for his nephews of the House of Medici. In all these contingencies it might be natural for the Estes to regard the French King or the Emperor as a possible guardian: an important point to bear in mind in assessing, let us say, Ariosto's so-called indifference to the fate of Italy ('he built imaginary palaces, while his country crashed around him'). And Jovius's remark (*we thought them like ourselves*) has to be read in a wide context; in the context, for instance, of that universal hatred towards the Venetians, the general dread of their designs. Then we can see how, in a picturesque phrase common to Vettori and Machiavelli, the

[1] Janni, 241. [2] *P.*, ed. Lisio, 6–7.
[3] Giovio, *Ist.*, 75. My copy, from the Wroxton Abbey library, was bought by Roger North at Rome in 1564, and inscribed by him with the motto *Durum pati*, which might have done for Italy.
[4] Cf. esp. *D.* III, XLIII, 438–9.

smaller states of Italy go with the flood, once it is running. They lack cohesion, just like the disaffected captains of Caesar Borgia. What can they do, ultimately, but pay blackmail like Florence? *Trarne e non mettervi*: it is not only Louis XII who might take this as a motto; and with the deterioration in the behaviour of soldiery that we have seen associated by Guicciardini with Consalvo's victory of 1504 and the League of Cambrai in 1508 it is a situation that brings despair. It is the context, that is, of Machiavelli's *Prince*.

Italy, Machiavelli repeated three or four times in various of his writings, and in various guises, was all exposed to rebellion and muta-tion, it had weak arms, and out of this there came miraculous gains and miraculous losses.[1] The years 1494 to 1512, in short, seem unreal as a nightmare. But Machiavelli may be, as they say, pitiless in his analysis of what is: he is nevertheless untiringly optimistic with regard to what might be. When Florence falls, and his life-work might seem wasted, the real life-work of Machiavelli begins. He turns back to two parts of his experience: to what was different from con-temporary reality—that is, to Livy; and to what had seemed a formula of opposition, to Caesar Borgia. Now, if we are scrupulous with Machiavelli it must give us pause that his author is Livy, not Suetonius. It is not only the reflection of the enthusiasm of the humanists, though it is that without a doubt; it is also the proof that he is looking for a remedy.

> Nous pouvons conclure de là
> Qu'il faut faire aux méchants guerre continuelle.
> La paix est fort bonne de soi;
> J'en conviens: mais de quoi sert-elle
> Avec des ennemis sans foi?[2]

Is not Machiavelli as realistic, and less cynical, than the good La Fontaine? But Caesar Borgia? To take as a *hero* a man to whose name some opprobrium must cling, both from his own actions, and those of his father, and to propose him as a model? Yet, in reality, this is the easiest point to take; and it involves no particular wickedness on Machiavelli's part; and not a shred of that presumed Renascence magnification of the individual. Here is Italy *stiava e vituperata* in 1513;[3] who in it has the means to stand against the intruders? The Este, with their cannon-founding duke? the Marquis of Mantua? the battered Venetians? subject Naples or Lombardy? some stateless *condottiere*? Merely to ask those questions is to supply the answer: the states of Italy are under a flood with which they cannot compete,

---

[1] E.g. *D.* III, 292; *P.* XII, 26, etc.   [2] La Fontaine, III, XIII.   [3] *P.* XII, 27.

and against which they are unable to combine. There is no single ruler with power sufficient to challenge the King of Spain or the Emperor, or even the King of France, now in eclipse. But there had been one, whose aim, said Buonaccorsi, was to be a monarch in Italy,[1] and who had come near to founding his own power. Fortune had played him false when his father died, and he fell ill, together. Now we must not make the mistake that even cautious supporters of Machiavelli have fallen into, and imagine that because he turns to Caesar Borgia in 1513 as a model he also must have done so in 1502.[2] He regarded him then as a potential enemy of Florence. But the elements that made for his success were valid ones: he had behind him the favour of the Pope, and because the King of France desired the amity of the Pope, he had the favour of the King of France as well. And because he knew that favour was a substance that might melt away he tried to capitalize it while it lasted, and to transfer it wholly to his own account. 'He had more artillery than all the rest of Italy.' Why did Machiavelli condemn Caesar Borgia in 1503 in his reports from Rome? or in 1504, in the scornful lines of the *Primo Decennale*? In the first, because his concern was for Florence; in the second, because of moral considerations. Why does he praise him in 1513? Not because he has forgotten the latter, but because Caesar Borgia is dead, and yet, and yet, the bases on which he might have built to greatness lie self-evident before Machiavelli, and are still available.

Indeed, it is so crystal clear that it is hard to see how critics have wrangled and juggled with the *Prince*. Did he want a tyrant? What a question to ask a drowning man! Did he really mean the last chapter of the *Prince*, or did he gum it on afterwards, to bamboozle the Medici and mystify the public for four centuries? And in especial, did he really believe that these second-rate scions of the House of Medici were worth making an appeal to? It is with this last point that we can most conveniently begin: we know the Lorenzo and Giuliano who sit over *Michaelangelo's* tombs with features other than their own. Their sculptor said, Who will care what their features were in a century's time? We know instinctively, that is, that the genius of this branch was exhausted with Leo X, perhaps even with Lorenzo the Magnificent. This pair are nonentities. So we take it for granted that Machiavelli passed that judgment anticipatorily in 1513, and wrote his Dedication from some base, unworthy motive which we may interpret at our leisure. But it did not happen like that. Machiavelli

[1] Buonaccorsi, 134.   [2] Cf. Zambelli, lviii.

had no personal knowledge of either—what contact had there been between them and him? between the exiles and the functionary? And far from having discounted their achieving something, Machiavelli shared the hopes and expectations of Florence that they would recall in their own actions the genius of Lorenzo the Magnificent. The texts are abundant, and they are explicit.[1] We cannot, then, take the Dedication of the *Prince* as a piece of servility towards the winning side. Machiavelli was far from knowing that this pair would do nothing with their opportunities. But he did know that they had an opportunity which no other had in Italy. They reproduced exactly, potentially, that is, the formula of Caesar Borgia: they had behind them the favour of a Pope; and by his favour they had also that of a monarch, not the King of France this time, but the stronger power of Spain and the Empire. Giovanni de'Medici was elected Pope on March 11, 1513; and Machiavelli, who in his new enforced idleness had turned to Livy, and to those commentaries he was to call the *Discorsi*, raised his eyes from the past to the present, saw in a flash the possibilities of the situation, turned aside from his commentary, or twisted part of it to his new purpose; and wrote, at fever-heat, with all the marks of enthusiasm and inspiration, *Il Principe*. That was from July to December of that same year, 1513. Prato had been sacked at the end of August, 1512; the Medici returned to Florence in the first days of September immediately following that. And Machiavelli began the *Discorsi* because he had no key to the problems of the present from the present. But when the significance of Leo X's election broke in upon his mind he wrote the *Prince*. Let no one say that he was slow, in taking three months to appraise the situation, and assemble his discourse: after all, it has taken the rest of the world four centuries of reading the *Prince* before it has occurred to anyone to point out the obvious nature of its genesis. Instead, authoritative writers like Villari and Tommasini, or Lisio, have linked it lower, with designs of Leo X on specific cities, whether Parma, Piacenza, or Urbino, as dowries for his nephews. But Machiavelli reverts three times in his last chapter to the idea of a *redeemer* and of *redemption*—something that is as theologically sharp as Dante's association of beatitude with Beatrice in the *Vita Nuova*—and it is hardly consonant with that for the scope of the book to be determined by Leo's acquisitiveness.

Nor is it the slightest use considering his personal feelings with

[1] *Lettere Fam.*, ed. Alvisi, CXXXV, 298–9; Masi, 195; Paoli, clxxix; Nerli, I, 179; and Tommasini, II, 103–4, for the letter of Alfonsina.

regard to Medicean rule in Florence from 1434 to 1494. He had said in 1504, in his *Primo Decennale*, quite clearly, about the loss of Pisa, that this had stopped Florence from rejoicing as it should have done at escaping from the yoke that for sixty years had weighed the city down.[1] But what has that to do with the situation of 1513? when he has seen all Italy under a grievous yoke; and when a *Florentine* may alter everything? Nor, and even more essentially, is it the slightest use approaching the *Prince* as though it is a piece of disinterested theory, written from the angle of Machiavelli's considered views on the problem of the State. What a moment it would be, when the one State he loved was broken, and there were no dykes in Italy to stave off disaster, to write the theory of something one did not know! Yet this is what Tommasini took to be its purpose.[2] Or, if it is urged that this is what Machiavelli was going to do in the *Discorsi*, to do it in a hurry! And those who have chosen to see a doctrinaire origin to Machiavelli's thought have done better still. Charbonnel quotes Nourrisson to the purpose that Paduan rationalism, Alexandrianism, and Averroism bring necessarily in their train 'une politique destituée de toute notion du juste et de l'injuste, faite, par conséquent, d'égoïsme, d'astuce et de violence, — à la lettre, la politique du *Prince*'.[3] There is a fine frenzy of indignation about that. The point that M. Charbonnel missed, since he began with a non-existent theoretical attachment instead of from a consideration of the historical environment, is that by the *Prince* Machiavelli is endeavouring to find a way out of exactly this policy which Charbonnel has described, and which is, *à la lettre*, the policy of Charles, Louis, Ferdinand, and Maximilian. That makes a little difference to the matter, I presume; and unless the *Prince* is read as the specific remedy to an otherwise insoluble problem it is divorced from its context and its sense. It becomes the *ghiribizzo* which Machiavelli himself baptized it when he realized, perhaps, that his expectations of the younger Medici were misplaced.

'E della fede mia non si doverrebbe dubitare, perché, avendo sempre osservato la fede, io non debbo imparare ora a romperla; e chi è stato fedele e buono quarantatré anni, che io ho, non debbe potere mutare natura; e della fede e bontà mia ne è testimonio la povertà mia.'[4] Thus does Machiavelli end his famous letter to Francesco Vettori of December 10, 1513, one of the most eloquent, as one of the most likeable, of human documents. To whom, according to the same letter, is the *Prince* to be of use? It is to a

---

[1] *Primo Decennale*, 25–7.   [2] Tommasini, II, 101.
[3] Charbonnel, 431.   [4] L.F., M.C., 886, 1.

new prince, 'a un principe, e massime a un principe nuovo'.[1] And
so, he adds, I dedicate it to Giuliano de'Medici. And two details
in the book confirm this concentration on the present problem.
The first sentence of his second chapter leaves consideration of
republics to the *Discorsi*; the opening sentence of his last chapter
looks round to the conditions of Italy to see if they are such as to
warrant a *new prince*, and it comes to the conclusion that no other
time is more fitted for one than this, 'che io non so qual mai tempo
fussi piú atto a questo'.[2] And he proceeds to the picture of the woes
of Italy which has seemed to some so extraneous to the matter of his
book: more enslaved than the Hebrews or the Persians, more
scattered than the Athenians, there has been up to now only a glimmer
of possible redemption. Italy awaits someone to heal her wounds,
to put an end to sack in Lombardy, ransom in Tuscany and Naples.[3]
And his language rises to a prophetic fervour, which might aptly
be compared with that of Savonarola, against whom he is usually
contrasted as the cold and cynical scoffer.[4] Only, Machiavelli's
prophecy was a dream of the salvation of his Italy, while Savonarola's
imagination dwelt on swords coming to strike her down. *Gladius
Domini super terram Cito et Velociter*. It is here, faced with this fervour,
with its biblical language, that we should examine, and reject, such
statements as that of Gautier Vignal, that Machiavelli never shows
in all his work 'un sentiment de tristesse ou de pitié à l'égard de
l'humanité misérable et souffrante,' and that we must therefore accept
Voltaire's judgment that in all his works there is never a word to make
virtue lovable, 'pas un mot qui parte du coeur'.[5] Did they not read
the last chapter of the *Prince*, the summary of Machiavelli's experience from 1498 to 1512? It burns because it has been packed into
so small a compass. Its urgency makes other things irrelevant; and
that is why those two initial sentences, of the second (I had almost
said, the first, so brief is that) and the last chapter, are the sheet
anchors of the *Prince*.

> La paix est fort bonne de soi;
> J'en conviens: mais de quoi sert-elle
> Avec des ennemis sans foi?

Now is the moment to cast a smile on the difficulties of Lord Morley,
wrestling with Baumgarten's theory of the incompatibility of the

[1] L.F., M.C., 885, 2. [2] P. II, 5, and P. XXVI, 49. [3] P. XXVI, 49–50, q.v.
[4] Cf., e.g., D. E. Muir, 28: 'To these sermons Machiavelli came as a scoffer, and as a scoffer
he went away.'
[5] Gautier Vignal, 218.

last chapter of the *Prince* with all the rest,[1] as on his quotation a little earlier from the pseudo-elevated language of Symonds: 'Italian society admired the bravo almost as much as Imperial Rome admired the gladiator: it assumed that genius combined with force of character released men from the shackles of ordinary morality.'[2] That is very childish, though it will always remain attractive to the ordinary reader, satisfied to be assured that others are no better than they should be; but it is transferred into more solemn form by more ambitious thinkers. 'C'est sur cette admiration esthétique de la force qu'est fondée, chez Machiavel, la nouvelle estimation des valeurs morales.'[3] As if the *Prince* was written with some nice dilettante detachment! Such is the penalty awaiting those who regard the *Prince sub specie aeternitatis* before they look at it from the point of view of its context, or even of its statement. Far from the *Prince* representing the apotheosis of the Renascence admiration for the individual untrammeled by scruples, it is a remedy prescribed when the civilization of the Renascence is abased.

What is the key-word of the *Prince*? Is it not *necessity*, which, as noun, participle, or adjective, occurs seventy-six times in this short treatise of only twenty-six chapters? Nor, even if we take it that a few of those occurrences are discrepant, is it unaccompanied by other words, more or less energetic, more or less synonymous, that would swell the count. Even the variations in its frequency may be spied out with profit: is it merely an accident that *necessity* crowds nine times into the two or three short pages that constitute the famous Chapter XVIII on the keeping of faith in princes? It is the external necessity of Machiavelli's times pressing on him that makes him write it. Divide the matter of the *Prince* into what concerns external affairs and what concerns internal ones, and it will be seen that what has seemed most blameful belongs all to the first part. That does not mean that Machiavelli put it forward (in his *necessity*) with any evil thoughts. Take the *Prince*, as we must do, if we are to put it back in its real meaning, as the call to a native prince to master at least some part of Italy to save it: that is no wicked enterprise. Rather, justice and necessity go here together, and it is no accident that Livy springs naturally and forcefully to Machiavelli's lips: 'Qui è iustizia grande: "iustum enim est bellum quibus necessarium, et pia arma ubi nulla nisi in armis spes est".'[4] Does not the second passage which I quoted as an anchor to the *Prince* continue that in looking round there was matter for a prudent and virtuous man (and it

---

[1] Morley, 30.   [2] *ibid.*, 18.   [3] Charbonnel, 410.   [4] P. XXVI, 50.

matters little here which sense we give to *virtuoso*—if we take the *virtue* out in favour of *force*, *prudent* and *honour* will put it back again) to give shape to something that should do honour to himself and good to all?[1] Read a little further in this last chapter of the *Prince*, and it is still the note of *honour* that is offered: 'for nothing honours a man so much as do new laws and constitutions he has founded'.[2] Turn back a couple of chapters, to this part which was so lightly taken to have no connection with the final chapter (and for that matter, look at the close of Chapter XII, and see how already it foretells the close of all the book), and we shall find the statement that lies in between the internal and the external fields of vision, linking them both together: 'E cosí arà duplicata gloria, di avere dato principio a uno principato nuovo; e ornatolo e corroboratolo di buone legge, di buone arme e di buoni esempli; come quello ha duplicata vergogna, che, nato principe, lo ha per sua poca prudenzia perduto.'[3] There is no irony in this repeated tender of *honour* and *glory*, nor has this anything to do with the usual characterizations of Machiavelli's *Prince*. *Se maintenir à tout prix* is the common view,[4] but it is clearly inaccurate: its authors have forgotten the first necessity, which is *s'établir*. The problem of maintenance is quite another, and when we come to it we shall find that Machiavelli's formula for it is such as to exclude any idea of hypocrisy from this trilogy of good laws, good arms, and good examples. But we must not anticipate, and before we come to maintenance we must consider the necessity to be met.

The ethics of self-defence is very largely a matter of common sense. We frowned on flame-throwers in the war of 1914–18; we recognized their necessity against a foe who used any methods in 1939. Doubtless, the world is nicer without such toys, and we shall one day be able to insist upon their abolition. But the point is that at the present time we have not the choice. We English love the rules of the game: but there is little sense in playing cricket when the other side plays it with machine-guns. This, of course, and not initial wickedness on Machiavelli's part, is the point of the notorious opening to Chapter XV. *Saepe enim tempore fit, ut quod plerumque turpe haberi soleat inveniatur non esse turpe.*[5] Or, if we wish to keep to Machiavelli, there are two texts in which he says specifically that the defence of one's country is no matter for niceties. 'Niuno uomo buono riprenderà mai alcuno che cerchi di difendere la patria sua, in qualunque modo se la difenda.'[6] That is the first, in which the significant

[1] P. XXVI, 49, 2.   [2] *ibid.*   [3] P. XXIV, 47, 1.
[4] Charbonnel, 402.   [5] Cicero, *De Off.*, IV, II, 332.   [6] L.F., M.C., 417, 2.

word is *buono*. The second has received more notice, and on it has
been built the proto-Fascist and Fascist distortion of Machiavelli's
thought. It is in the *Discorsi*, and it is something to be observed,
Machiavelli says, by every citizen: 'perché, dove si dilibera al tutto
della salute della patria, non vi debbe cadere alcuna considerazione
né di giusto né d'ingiusto, né di piatoso né di crudele, né di laudabile
né d'ignominioso; anzi, posposto ogni altro rispetto, seguire al tutto
quel partito che le salvi la vita, e mantenghile la libertà'.[1] And here
the vital words are the *al tutto*. It is a statement identical with that
of Livy in Book XXIII.[2] And we must relate it to the whole picture
of Italy that we have seen underlying Machiavelli's political writings.
If we omit these considerations, and the *al tutto*, then we sail straight
forward with Francesco Ercole to the supremacy of the State which
Machiavelli did not know, and to the amorality of politics; to what
Ercole chose to call the categorical imperative of the Machiavellian
ethic, formulating it as the absolute, unconditional, total surrender of
private interest to that of the collectivity.[3] We have seen that there
is a history to this interpretation before it reaches a Fascist exponent:
Charbonnel, or the very respectable authors of the handbook *Italy,
Medieval and Modern*,[4] speak similar language, and have no other text
to adduce for this supposed glorification of the State. But I call it
Fascist because once we accept it we are inevitably on the path to the
apotheosis of Mussolini (or of Hitler). Indeed, how can the individual
be subordinated totally to the collectivity (to speak this jargon)
unless the collectivity speaks with a single and authoritative voice
which is other than that of the individual, or of the individuals?
It follows, then, inevitably that the collectivity must be personified
in an individual for it to acquire the requisite detachment and
authority. So we come to what was put most lyrically, perhaps, by a
follower of Ercole in a book which he called, significantly, *Machiavelli, Lo Stato*, and I mention it to show, as it were, the bomb explod-
ing, Caesar Borgia pushing his sharp chin out and assuming the
portliness of the expanding bull-frog of La Fontaine's fable. I cannot
quote it all, it is too long, this page in which the hero of the *Prince*
assumes identity with the Founder of the Empire, but its conclusion
I must quote: 'E del successo si fa un imperativo inevadibile, la legge
della sua esistenza insonne, dura e aspra. . . . E, vincitore, egli non

---

[1] *D.* III, XLI, 435.
[2] Livy, XXIII, 14: 'Ad ultimum prope desperatae reipublicae auxilium, quum honesta
utilibus cedunt.'
[3] Ercole, *Pensatori e Uomini d'Azione*, 198.
[4] 232, on this same passage: 'Nowhere have the paramount claims of the State been more
emphatically urged'—which is true, except for the fact that they are not urged here.

trionfa. Egli non è neppure il vincitore. È l'eroe. . . . Egli è lo Stato, la Patria, Tutto.'[1] So one could write in Italy in 1939; but the echoes answering *Duce*, *Duce* are fainter now, and we can recover breath to measure the gap from Machiavelli's text, and context, the more easily. We shall do better to put back the crucial *al tutto*, and prevent the descant at its starting-point. One is hardly at the right point for writing in terms of success, success, success, when it is failure all around. And besides, one other marginal word shows us that we must pause: it is the use of *cittadino* on the edge of the last text quoted from the *Discorsi*. Machiavelli often uses the word *patria*, and he means Florence; or if not Florence, some other city-state, whether Rome or something more recent. When he comes to write of a country he is, without being aware of it, at a loss for a word: so he calls it constantly a *provincia*. So innocent is Machiavelli of any glimmering of the great Moloch which the later theorists were to call the State.[2]

It is time, then, that we went back to the text of self-defence, and to the idea of Cicero which I intruded. Cicero's example was the crime of killing a fellow-man; but who finds fault with the killing of a Hitler? Is such a thing a crime? It did not seem so to the Roman people, who thought it most acceptable. *Vicit igitur utilitas honestatem, imo vero honestas utilitatem secuta est.*[3] All those who note that social-democracy (or pacifism) is not sufficient to stand in the face of Hitlerism must concur with Cicero's conclusion; and it does not affect the issue that Cicero was in reality distorting contemporary opinion on the killing of Caesar for his own purposes. But Machiavelli has been blamed for coming to the same conclusion, with the same regret at doing so. In the eighth chapter of the *Prince* he introduces a question to which he will return at the beginning of the seventeenth: he does so with the remark on cruelties well or ill used.[4] And although he adds immediately, and I would add, sincerely, a by-your-leave (*se del male è licito dire bene*), and makes his point—which is identical with that of Cicero—quite clear, yet it has been held great wickedness in him to have done so. That is because it has been taken for granted that this idea of clemency and cruelty is to be attached to some sinister doctrine of the *ragion di stato*. Hence it is something which can pass almost unperceived in another writer than Machiavelli. Let Mentor say it to Idoménée in Fénelon's prose, or Ercilla hide it among the stanzas of the *Araucana*, and none will

[1] Collotti, 57–8.
[2] Even *v.* Zambelli, xv, for the question of whether Machiavelli thought of a unified Italy.
[3] *loc. cit.*   [4] P. VIII, 20, 1.

blench.[1] Yet Fénelon's words might be a translation of that definition in Chapter VIII, or derived from the example with which
Machiavelli illustrates the theme in Chapter XVII: where Caesar
Borgia is pronounced less cruel than Florence on the basis of the
effects of their actions respectively in Romagna and Pistoia. Nor, if
it was the place to digress here, would it be hard to multiply the
parallels between ideas of Machiavelli and ideas of Fénelon.

But it is evident that, if we must accept the historical accuracy of
Machiavelli's judgment on Florence and Caesar Borgia at this point
(and responsible criticism has accepted the validity of his improve-
ments in Romagna), it does raise behind it a further issue. The judgment of Chapter XVII on the Florentines and Caesar Borgia damns
the former in spite of their intentions; and praises the latter in spite of
his initial actions. 'Era tenuto Cesare Borgia crudele; nondimanco
quella sua crudeltà aveva racconcia la Romagna, unitola, ridottola in
pace e in fede. Il che se si considerrà bene, si vedrà quello essere stato
molto piú pietoso che il populo fiorentino, il quale, per fuggire
el nome del crudele, lasció destruggere Pistoia.'[2] We are still, that is,
concerned with the insufficiency of social-democracy, but we must
examine it also from the angle of the end and the means. Now it is
very easy to twist this to an odious light. That is why it is useful to
point out that we have not moved away from the text of the *De
Officiis*. Cicero went on, a few pages later, 'Addunt etiam, quemad-
modum nos dicamus, videri quaedam utilia quae non sint, sic se
dicere videri quaedam honesta, quae non sint.'[3] And Machiavelli,
who keeps his eye on the *De Officiis*,[4] paraphrased this as a conclusion to a very short and very famous chapter of the *Prince*: 'perché,
se si considerrà bene tutto, si troverrà qualche cosa che parrà virtú, e,
seguendola, sarebbe la ruina sua; e qualcuna altra che parrà vizio,
e, seguendola, ne riesce la securtà e il bene essere suo'.[5] If we had only
to translate either of these statements into the language of common
sense, or of tradition, doubtless the matter would be easy enough:
The proof of the pudding is in the eating. Or, The road to hell is
paved with good intentions. Or, By their fruits ye shall know them.
But it is not quite so simple as that, or at least we cannot stop at the
translation, for in clinging to Cicero (and to what he called in the
same chapter the *verità effettuale*) Machiavelli has overturned a citadel.

---

[1] Cf. *Télémaque*, XII, 500; *Araucana*, IV, 1–2.
[2] P. XVII, 32, 2.   [3] *De Off.*, IV, III, 342.
[4] Cf. Burd, 285–7, analysing the ideas on liberty in the next chapter; though Burd has missed this point.
[5] P. XV, 31, 1.

Perhaps it is put most sharply in a remark that Machiavelli had had in his head since the Cardinal of St. George made it to him in 1503, and which comes out again as his own (how often are the *Legations* rich with the raw materials of Machiavelli's works!) in the *Ghiribizzi scritti in Raugia*: 'Donde io credo, non con lo specchio vostro, dove non si vede se non prudenza, ma per quello de'piú, che si abbia nelle cose a vedere il fine come le sono fatte e non il mezzo come le si fanno.'[1] That is something more important than the statement of political expediency, to which it has often been reduced. It is not that if one gets the right answer to the sum the working may be fantastically out: because, quite obviously, if the working is all out the sum will not come right. It does not therefore begin by sanctioning any means in order to arrive at any end. In fact, it does not shift the valuation from the *intention* to the *result*; but, and this is quite different, from the *intention* to the *intention plus the result*.

At this point we may turn back to Dante for the orthodox position:

> L'altro che segue, con le leggi e meco,
> sotto buona intenzion che fe'mal frutto,
> per cedere al pastor si fece greco:
> ora conosce come il mal dedutto
> dal suo bene operar non li è nocivo,
> *avvegna che sia'l mondo indi destrutto.*[2]

So Constantine can take his place in Paradise; and Dante, as often, rests his interpretation of merits directly on St. Thomas Aquinas, who had laid down that the outcome afterwards could not make an action that was good bad, nor one that was bad good.[3] For Machiavelli to mean well is insufficient to the task of doing good; he establishes a different, but an equally logical, and an equally moral, criterion. If the intention is inadequate to its scope, then it has elements of badness. One cannot destroy the world and take no blame for it.

It is at this point, though, that a further problem confronts us; and brings us back at once to the question of intentions. Horace Walpole once wrote to the Countess of Ossory: 'I told her it was a settled maxim of mine "that no great country was ever saved by good men," because good men will not go the lengths that may be necessary.'[4] The good man, that is, may object to the flame-throwers, and the clement cruelties; he may prefer to be a sacrifice. On the other hand, the man who can be cruel, may be bad. This is a dilemma

---

[1] *Op.*, M.C., 879, 1.   [2] *Paradiso*, XX, 55–60.
[3] 'Eventus sequens non facit actum malum qui erat bonus, nec bonum qui erat malus.'
[4] *Letters to the Countess of Ossory*, III, CCCXLIV, 214.

which Machiavelli does not state in the *Prince* (when, as we have seen, he is too preoccupied with immediate needs, and immediate possibilities, for it to occur to him: an omission which has done much to discredit him). But he does state it plainly in the *Discorsi*: in the important Chapter XVIII of the first Book, which is not far from being a Machiavellian commentary to the text of Fénelon to which I referred. 'E perché il riordinare una città al vivere politico presuppone uno uomo buono, e il diventare per violenza principe di una republica presuppone uno uomo cattivo; per questo si troverrà che radissime volte accaggia che uno buono, per vie cattive, ancora che il fine suo fusse buono, voglia diventare principe; e che uno reo, divenuto principe, voglia operare bene, e che gli caggia mai nello animo usare quella autorità bene, che gli ha male acquistata.'[1] That is a painful dilemma, furnished by life, not put forward by any cynicism in Machiavelli; in fact, it is clear that it is a scruple of honesty which expresses it. How, if at all, does Machiavelli resolve it? He does not do so by any acceptance of, still less by any admiration for, the wicked one who performs his wickedness so long as he does so strenuously. He does so in terms of both intentions and results, in a chapter of the *Discorsi* which has been held up against him rather because people have disliked his example (of Romulus killing Remus) than because of any other defect. But it is plain that if it is attached to any other form of necessary cruelty it still holds valid, as we may find when I return to the discussion of this chapter later. 'To be violent in order to spoil something, that is to be rebuked; to be violent in order to mend it, that is to be excused.'[2] The proposition thus becomes quite clear: Bad intentions produce bad results. Good intentions may produce bad results. Good intentions may produce good results; but they may be confronted with a situation in which they cannot begin by good actions. They cannot, however, at this point, renounce either the goal which is good, or the beginning towards it which is bad. *Vicit igitur utilitas honestatem, imo vero honestas utilitatem secuta est.* We are back where we started from; and we have the context to the statements of the *Prince* that have aroused so much hostile commentary. We may crystallize Machiavelli's deductions from the proposition in the half sentence from Chapter XVIII of the *Prince* (*Quomodo fides a principibus sit servanda*): 'non partirsi dal bene, potendo, ma sapere intrare nel male, necessitato'; or in the warning at the beginning of Chapter XV: 'perché uno uomo che voglia fare in tutte le parte professione di buono, conviene rovini infra tanti che non

---

[1] *D.* I, XVIII, 74. [2] *D.* I, IX, 42.

sono buoni'. Machiavelli may have had in mind the words (though
uttered in a different context) of the gilded youths who regretted
Tarquin, That it was dangerous, amongst so many human errors,
to live by innocence alone.[1] But he did not need to think any further
than Florence, for this is only the epitome of what he had seen.
Therefore, neither of these statements can be taken as presupposing
an abandonment of good intentions: the essential word is still *necessity*,
and the matter one of the choice of necessary means. Once more (and
I would add, not accidentally) Machiavelli quotes Cicero in a relevant
context. The choice is not always between a simple black and a simple
white; it is more usually through grey towards a white; and by a
constant Machiavellian warning, one snag suppressed is always the
begetter of another. What is prudence then? It consists in assessing
the value of the snags and in 'pigliare el men tristo per buono'.[2]
'Non solum ex malis eligere minima oportere, sed etiam excerpere
ex his ipsis, si quid inesset boni.'[3]

In this consideration of the meaning of certain statements of the
Prince I have referred to the *Discorsi*. Is this legitimate? and how is
the procedure affected by the opposition that critics have often
asserted as existing between the two works? The first, said Taine, is
the theory of monarchy; the second, that of republican government.
And many have been quick to see in this some cynical, or clinical,
detachment on Machiavelli's part. It is the occasion for such remarks
as that of a recent Italian commentator: Machiavelli assumes the
impassivity of the doctor, he does not feel, he understands (it is the
formula of De Sanctis—*intelligere*, not *sentire*) what is, after all, merely
another 'elegant problem to be resolved'.[4] Such talk is, of course,
loose and careless: one does not expect the doctor who is diagnosing
one's malady, or removing one's appendix, to be at the same time
falling on one's neck, or waving his arms in excitement; but one
imagines on his part a reasonable desire for the good of the patient.
No good doctor puts his passions into his analysis of a case. He is
not responsible for its elements, and his task is first to comprehend
them. But he may put his passion into the righting of them, which is
most strictly his business *qua* doctor. If Machiavelli is indifferent to
that, he is no doctor. If as well he is incoherent, writing now one
thing, now its opposite, then naturally our confidence at any one
point is shaken thereby. That is why the problem of the reconcilia-
tion of the *Prince* with the *Discorsi* is the prime problem in the examina-

[1] Livy, II, 3.   [2] *P.* XXI, 45, 1.
[3] Cicero, *De Off.*, III, I. For repetitions of the idea throughout Machiavelli, *v.* Burd, 344–5.
[4] Ruiz, *Pagine Scelte*, xxviii.

tion of Machiavelli. That being so, it is a matter which arises principally in the consideration of the *Discorsi*, when their statement begins to lie alongside that of the *Prince*, rather than here, where the *Prince* stands by itself. But something may be said here anticipatorily. If the *Prince* represents the comprehension of a particular remedy, existing ready to be seized at a particular moment, we do not really need the evidence of that brilliant little poem, the *Capitolo dell'Occasione*, to assure us that when the opportunity has passed one will gain nothing by restating it. The *Discorsi*, in other words, must inevitably be other than the *Prince*, not because Machiavelli has changed, or is indifferent in either, but simply because he is forced to look at something else. There is no need, then, to imagine a different outlook for Machiavelli, nor shall we find this really to exist. Still less can we throw the bridge over from the one work to the other in the manner of Burd—so diligent as a commentator always, so blind often as an interpreter! He assured us that we should find the methods suggested in the *Discorsi* quite as unscrupulous and quite as little determined by moral considerations as those of the *Prince*; and he proceeded to enumerate a score of pages from the *Discorsi* that seemed to him immoral.[1] I should prefer to make the opposite remark: that the healthy observations of the *Discorsi* find their counterpart in the *Prince*. But they are not usually noticed there for the very sufficient reason that people read this treatise in search of other attractions.

Where were we in our examination of the *Prince*? It was at the necessity of establishing a new prince, with the possibility of the same. Yes, but does he not go on to fasten his absolute power over the people's unhappy heads? 'Soyez absolus par tous les moyens!' Or, if we prefer it in Hanoverian English, George, be a king! Fortunately for Machiavelli, there is no theory, even no hint of a theory, of absolutism in the *Prince*. It is a prejudice that has been carried over from the matter of *s'établir* to that of *se maintenir* because no one has ever sufficiently recognized the existence of the former problem. I do not put this forward as a rash assertion: it is susceptible of immediate proof. Let us look for the word *absolute* in the *Prince*. We shall find it in a significant sentence of the chapter on Civil Principates: 'Sogliono questi principati periclitare quando sono per salire dallo ordine civile allo assoluto.'[2] They come to grief (for this is the obvious sense of the word *periclitare*[3]) when they abandon the

---

[1] Burd, 42 n.   [2] *P.* IX, 21,2.
[3] As shown by the clear use in *P.* XVI, 31, 2, in spite of Lisio's note to *P.* VI, 42, 18.

constitutional for the absolute form of rule. I am not certain that I
have adduced the only example of the word *absolute* in the *Prince*;
but for very good reasons there is nothing that can diminish the witness of this particular one. Machiavelli, it has already been recognized,[1] is preoccupied in all his works, from the *Prince* to the *Istorie*,
with the permanence, the stability of institutions: *mantenere, durare*,
and their like are recurrent key-words no less in the *Prince* than in the
Discorsi. We also have seen already that trilogy which Machiavelli
offered to his new prince as foundations to his State—good laws,
good arms, and good examples. Let us, however, put the question
open once again, suppose for a moment that what he says in his last
chapter might prove dissonant from what he says in the body of the
book. What recipes for permanence does Machiavelli recommend?
A ruler must build on sound foundations (did we not see him when
he was a-learning of the word?), or he will come to ruin. The main
foundations of any State, new, or old, or mixed, are good laws and
good arms.[2] His critics have often insisted on the latter, but they
have usually failed to add the former. It is necessary for a prince to
have his people friendly: otherwise he has no remedy in his adver-
sities.[3] There are two humours: that of the nobles, who are anxious
to oppress; that of the people, anxious not to be oppressed. Of the
two, it is the second which is honester, and to which the prince
must give assent: the nobles are few, they owe their reputation to the
favour of the prince; but the people are many. 'È necessitato (note
the recurrence of this sovereign word) ancora el principe vivere
sempre con quello medesimo populo; ma può ben fare sanza quelli
medesimi grandi, potendo farne e, disfarne ogni dí . . .'[4] That is
why the foundations of Caesar Borgia's power were good in
Romagna, since he had there 'guadagnatosi tutti quelli populi, per
avere cominciato a gustare el bene esser loro'.[5] And the historians
have accepted that as a just account of Caesar Borgia's administration there. It is considerations such as these that make untenable the
glib views of those who come to Machiavelli looking for sensationalism. Thus, on cruelties well or ill used: 'It is the plea brought forward
in every case of a *coup d'état*, or of the use of violence when it is
meant to teach a salutary lesson.'[6] It may indeed be; and without
Machiavelli having any responsibility for that. In fact, he gives the
plainest warning at the end of the very chapter in which he first
introduces the idea of cruelty well used: 'E debbe sopr'a tutto uno

[1] Collotti, 25.   [2] P. XII, 24, 2.   [3] P. IX, 21, 2.
[4] P. IX, 21, 1.   [5] P. VII, 16, 1.   [6] Muir, 140.

principe vivere con li sua sudditi in modo, che veruno accidente o di male o di bene lo abbia a far variare.'[1] If he does not do so, it will be too late to try and win their favour in any adversity: for men have no gratitude for favours wrung by force of circumstances.

Found on the people, and you found on mud. That is the popular proverb, and already in the *Prince* Machiavelli alleges it only to riddle it: if it is a private individual who builds his hopes on the people, then it may pass; but if it is a prince who plays his own part, then he will never be deceived by the people, and he will find that his foundations are well laid.[2] What are the means to hold the favour of one's subjects, other than seeing that they are not oppressed by a nobility? For those who think in terms of *coups d'état* and rule by violence it must be disappointing to find Machiavelli arguing against the building of fortresses. Your castle is a great encourager of oppression: you will trust in it, and not mind being hated by the people.[3] But even if you have fortresses they will not save you, if the people hate you.[4] Even in the necessary compression of the *Prince* Machiavelli finds room for a discussion which is a prelude to the important tenth chapter of *Discorsi* I. The prince must love virtues (in their ordinary sense); he must honour those who are excellent in their professions. He must encourage ('animare') his citizens in the quiet exercise of their occupations, in trade and agriculture and all other activities of men; so that one does not fear to adorn his possessions lest they be taken from him, nor the other refrain from opening a business through fear of levies on it.[5] In an age when we earn money only to pay it in taxation, and are prohibited from building handsomely because it would be ruinous in rates, we may find this Utopian. And Machiavelli elsewhere has his counsel on taxation: his prince is not to fear being rated parsimonious. If by his parsimony his revenues are sufficient for his needs without grievous burdens falling on his subjects they will find that he is liberal to all those from whom he does not take, and these are infinite, and miserly only to those to whom he does not give, and these are few.[6] Nor, to return to Chapter XXI, when Machiavelli has insisted on the ruler's duty to reward these categories, and all who add to the greatness of the city, need we suspect anything sinister in his addition that it is the ruler's duty to occupy the people at suitable seasons in the year with festivals and spectacles.[7] For this innocent advice derives from the Renascence concept of 'magnifi-

---

[1] *P.* VIII, 20, 1.   [2] *P.* IX, 21, 2.   [3] *P.* XX, 43, 1.   [4] *ibid.*
[5] *P.* XXI, 45, 1.   [6] *P.* XVI, 31, 2.   [7] *P.* XXI, 45, 1.

cence' rather than from any dark doctrine of political soporifics; if it does not derive from Livy. This picture, as I said, is close to the one of the Roman world under a good Emperor in the *Discorsi*; and the permanence of this theme throughout the *Prince* is proof enough that it is essential to Machiavelli's thought. If the foundations of the State are good arms and good laws, the first of these, and all who know anything of Machiavelli know this, must be one's own; and the second must give the constituents of one's forces the desire to fight for one, and not against one. Nor is Machiavelli unaware, in rejecting mercenaries in favour of citizen-soldiers, that the people love quiet, and so love a modest prince, while it is the professional soldiery who desire a prince to be insolent, cruel, and rapacious.[1] But the prince, who has two causes of fear, one internal, from his subjects, and one external, from other rulers,[2] since he can only rely on the first of these elements as a safeguard against the second, is bound to build upon their favour. That is why the warnings to the prince to avoid the hate, and to secure the benevolence, of his subjects punctuate the *Prince*.[3] If anyone had told its author that men would read his book without lighting on them he would have been surprised, and shocked.

It has been said so often that the *Prince* is (sincerely or satirically) a manual for tyrants, that it is worth inquiring what is left to tyrannize over when the prince has accepted Machiavelli's advice to him. For instance, a ruler can avoid being either feared or hated, and will always do so if he abstains from the property of his citizens and subjects, and from their womenfolk.[4] Add this to the parsimony in taxation, and the rest of what we have seen, and we shall have an odd formula for tyranny! We see, then, that it is possible to begin consideration of the *Prince* from one angle, and to find it innocent. That is because we have looked at it from the viewpoint of Machiavelli's *intentions*, which, without the slightest shadow of doubt, are blameless. And this, surely, is the place to point out that, if Machiavelli would exclude Constantine from his place in Paradise, Dante and Aquinas would have had no right to exclude Machiavelli. Constantine was the one

> sotto buona intenzion che fe'mal frutto.

He has his place

> avvegna che sia'l mondo indi destrutto.

[1] *P*. XIX, 37, 2.   [2] *P*. XIX, 36, 1.
[3] For instance, cf. *P*. VII, VIII, IX, X, XII, XIX, XX, XXI, XXIV. Cicero, *De Off.*, II, VII, is wholly consonant.
[4] *P*. XVII, 33, 1.

We cannot claim one criterion for the judgment of Constantine, and another for Machiavelli. Either intentions are valid passports, or they are not. I mean, to Paradise; or as a test of goodness, to put it untheologically. Thus Machiavelli is not at all removed from the idealism Cian noted in a very similar passage of the *Cortegiano*: rather this is one of the significant identities. 'E perché la laude del ben far consiste precipuamente in due cose, delle quai l'una è lo eleggersi un fine dove tenda la intenzion nostra, che sia veramente bono, l'altra il saper ritrovar mezzi opportuni ed atti per condursi a questo bon fine designato.'[1] That is, at the same time, both Ciceronian and Machiavellian.

It is clear also that some of Machiavelli's so-called cynicism dissolves in this light. There is (on that matter of goods and womenfolk) one of the most brilliant of the aphorisms in the *Prince*: *that a man will sooner forget the death of his father than the loss of his patrimony*.[2] Lisio found it true, alas! but terribly malignant: which does not seem to make much sense. Tommasini saw the light better when he remarked on Machiavelli's obvious faith, as expressed in the dedications of the *Discorsi* and the *Arte della Guerra*, that he was carrying out the office of a good man, and his obvious hope in the efficacy of education on human nature, that it was such as to remove from his nature even the slightest trace of pessimism. An educator is not a pessimist.[3] Nor, one should add, is he a cynic. Cynicism is not the quality of looking at truths: it is that of sneering because things are worse than they might be, and because one is glad to find them so. But it is because people have come to Machiavelli with a wrong line of approach that one must insist on the identities with a writer as blameless as Castiglione. The latter is only concerned partly with political matters in the *Cortegiano*, and he speaks often frankly with an idealistic, or shall we say a theoretic, tone. Yet Machiavelli would have been willing to put his own name to one or two of the finest passages of the *Cortegiano*, where Castiglione rises to a Machiavellian level of intensity in expression. Two of these I quote, because the separation of the idea of admiration for the tyrant or the conqueror from Renascence Italy needs witness. In the first, Castiglione is considering matters akin to Chapter XXIII of the *Prince*; he observes, as Machiavelli does elsewhere, that one error leads to infinite others, and that the ignorance of the prince, accompanied by a false idea of infallibility and the notion that his power proceeds from wisdom, will lead him on to the use of every means, just or unjust, to occupy

[1] *Cortegiano*, IV, 412.   [2] *P.* XVII, 33, 1–2.   [3] Tommasini, II, 144.

boldly others' territory, *if only he can do so*.[1] In the second passage
he notes of States not organized for the enjoyment of peace that they
will be led on to perpetual rapine: 'E lo star sempre in guerra, senza
cercar di pervenire al fine della pace, non è licito: benché estimano
alcuni principi, il loro intento dover essere principalmente il dominare
ai suoi vicini, e però nutriscono i populi in una bellicosa ferità di
rapine, d'omicidii e tai cose, e lor danno premii per provocarla, e la
chiamano virtú.'[2] There is a fine ring of scorn in that, not lessened
because the basis for the passage is in Aristotle's *Politics*. Nor does it
put Castiglione apart from Machiavelli. If the range of Machiavelli's warnings to the prince throughout this treatise is not sufficient
to show already what he had in mind, we have still other, and major,
statements of his to come to.

There is, however, one further safeguard in the *Prince* itself against
our taking too literally a remark such as the one that has stuck in
people's throats, 'Facci dunque uno principe di vincere e mantenere
lo stato: e'mezzi saranno sempre iudicati onorevoli e da ciascuno
laudati; perché il vulgo ne va sempre preso con quello che pare, e con
lo evento della cosa; e nel mondo non è se non vulgo.'[3] Or, at least,
against us giving this a general application. For instance, Burd quotes
at this point, along with Cicero and Ovid on judgments *ex eventu*,
Sallust on any methods of retaining power.[4] Sallust is one of Machiavelli's favourite historians: does the authority of the Roman world
carry him on into this doctrine of sticking at nothing? But if it did,
where would go all the understructure of the prince's rule? If he is
led on to a violent tyranny he has to incur, sooner or later, the hatred
of his people; and there is no remedy to this. So that what was put
forward as a means of retaining power would be at the same time
the sure means of losing it. We are brought back to the bitterness of
the world of 1513, and the threats from outside. Yes, but the safeguard? Well, Machiavelli did not only write the maxim quoted
at the beginning of the paragraph, which would be cynical enough
if we could give it unlimited scope. He also wrote the eighth chapter
of the *Prince*. He noted that Agathocles obtained, and retained,
power; and he condemned him. 'Non si può ancora chiamare virtú
ammazzare li sua cittadini, tradire li amici, essere sanza fede, sanza
pietà, sanza relligione; li quali modi possono fare acquistare imperio,

---

[1] *Cortegiano*, IV, 415: 'E da uno errore incorrono in infiniti; perché la ignoranzia loro accom-
pagnata da quella falsa opinion di non poter errare, e che la potenzia che hanno proceda dal
lor sapere, induce lor per ogni via, giusta o ingiusta, ad occupar stati audacemente, pur che
possano'.
[2] *ibid.*, 438.   [3] *P.* XVIII, 35, 2.   [4] Burd, 306–7, n.

ma non gloria.'[1] That is *Ciceronian* still: 'Si gloriae causa imperium expetenda est, scelus absit, in quo non potest esse gloria.'[2] But why should there be any need to trouble about glory, if it is enough to rule? We are brought back to the circle of considerations with which we have been concerned so far. We are brought back to the specific tender of a task involving honour and glory in Chapters XXIV and XXVI. The maxim from which we started here belongs obstinately to its context in Chapter XVIII. Once we have satisfied ourselves as to this, we are ready to look forward from the *Prince*.

Before we do so, though, there is one other point which has prejudiced (and will still prejudice) many against Machiavelli. We saw a long time back that he turned from the present to the Roman past, where he felt he saw more whole remedies, not inadequate half measures. We saw his admiration for Lucius Furius Camillus, and for the resolution of problems to a sharp *either-or*, of the sort which, when he comes to theorize, he says does not exist in life. Does not one *inconveniente* lead to another? and is there not an *inconveniente* lurking for us in every line of conduct? That is very Machiavellian. Yet, on the other hand, he likes the wholesale treatment: to finish with a problem by a gesture of a one hundred per cent solution of it. And this, which springs from his idealism, from his optimism, leads to expressions which seem, or often are, in themselves, outrageous. Moreover, the trick of thinking in what we may call Livian terms leads him to rearrange past events so that they fit this pattern which works out by such treatment. We can take as a typical example in the *Prince* the case of Remirro de Orco, Caesar Borgia's minister in Romagna. Nothing sounds more sinister than Machiavelli's account of his end: put, it seems, in charge because he was cruel, to create an example, and with a view to his latter end, also to serve as an example.[3] But, of course, it is not true that it happened like that: Machiavelli's procedure is to take a synopsis of what occurred, strike a line through it, and then go back to the beginning *as if the actors were now to plan it as it had fallen out*. In the case of Remirro, alias Ramirez de Lorqua, the facts were suggested already by Alvisi: that his erring in the administration of Romagna was not Caesar Borgia's doing, but his own fault; that his trial was juridical (in the words of the diarist Bernardi); and that in the severity of his punishment we must look to Caesar Borgia's firm intention for Romagna 'che siate per l'avvenire con iustizia et con integrità recti et governati'.[4] It is the anxiety

---

[1] *P.* VIII, 18, 2.
[3] *P.* VII, 16, 1–2.
[2] *De Off.*, III, 340.
[4] *v.* Dell'Oro, 82–6, for documents.

to secure the lesson out of a sequence that generates the uncompromising and disturbing note in Machiavelli. Thus it will seem in the *Discorsi* as though he recommends us to kill our brother, if we have one, before venturing to found a State; or to put our children to death before we reform one to liberty.[1] There has been a lot of indignation over those children of Brutus: would it seem so warranted if we followed Machiavelli's practice, and glossed ancient precepts in the light of our own times, to assert that there could be no new state of liberty in Germany if the S.S. were left with their lives? But it is time as well that someone pointed out that to take Machiavelli literally on such matters as Romulus and Remus is not necessary. He is carried away by his enthusiasm for the lesson. It fits so neatly that Romulus happened to kill Remus, and was then left alone as legislator, as of course theory demands. Did not Tommasini discover that he marches here, rather than with any revolting writer, with a father of the Church?[2] What is excusable in St. Jerome cannot really be blameworthy in Machiavelli: both have a theory of unity, the latter in legislation, the former in rule, and both are pleased to find the case that falls pat to prove it. But it is in these places, the excrescences of Machiavelli's thought, that men have found the wickedness they wished to associate with him. Start from the presumption that Machiavelli's doctrine is damnable, and your eyes will be riveted upon them. That is the path by which one reaches the rapture of Frederick the Great (or is it Voltaire?): 'L'intérêt, ce seul Dieu qu'il adore, est compté pour tout; il préfère la cruauté à la clémence. . . . Le Docteur du crime . . . de la scélératesse.'[3] It is only when one starts with the essential problems that faced Machiavelli, with his main attitude, and with his temperament, that they assume their right proportions, and their right place.

---

[1] Cf. *D.* I, IX, for Romulus and *D.* I, XVI, for the 'figliuoli di Bruto'.
[2] Tommasini, II, 590.   [3] *L'Antimachiavel*, 182, 198, and 69, e.g.

V

MACHIAVELLI AND SAVONAROLA

WE have just seen, and it may have been an occasion for surprise, Machiavelli coinciding with St. Jerome. Perhaps it is the moment, while we are at a transitional stage, to examine his relationship with another Hieronymus of his own time. I am not sure that I can do more than make tentative suggestions for the examination of this problem, and I approach it with no intention of speaking finally upon it. Machiavelli and Savonarola were, we remember, established by nineteenth-century criticism as opposites. Before that there had only been a casual coupling of them together as equally pernicious, the one a false prophet, the other a preceptor for heretics.[1] It is, then, the nineteenth-century judgment on them that holds the field without a rival. Yet, as we have progressed, we have seen hints that it was not a final judgment. Was there not some embarrassment over the biblical fervour of the ending to the *Prince*? And if we are to revise our estimate of Machiavelli to include some dose of goodness, are we not bound to consider again the question of this relationship?

It was a matter on which the nineteenth-century critics did not allow themselves the luxury of many doubts. There was not only Villari with his dictum of their conflicting temperaments (the one all faith and spontaneous enthusiasm—that is Savonarola; the other all analysis, doubt, and searching). He by himself might not be authoritative for us: if the estimate for Machiavelli's character is wrong, where does the contrast stand? But there was as well De Sanctis, who thought of Savonarola picturesquely as the last ray of a past day setting on the horizon, while Machiavelli was the rising dawn of modern times. 'The one was the last exemplar of the old medieval man; the other, the first exemplar of modern man.'[2] And as Russo observed, Carducci turned this idea into images in a well-known passage: the Renascence was shining all around in marble with its pagan face when Savonarola preached. He did not realize that the purely religious reform was to be for others who were more sincerely Christian than Italy; and amongst the circles of his *piagnoni*, poor monk, he failed to see in some corner of the piazza *a pitying smile on the pale face of Niccolò Machiavelli.*[3] And Russo, who, in spite

[1] Tommasini, I, 19.   [2] *Scritti varii*, etc., I, 15.   [3] *Svolg. d.l.n.*, IV, *ad finem*.

of his unoriginality, was anxious to add his mite, and get the picture
accurate in its detail, only objected to the pair being put as representa-
tives of different ages: they are antithetical tendencies of the human
mind, each unreceptive to the other. 'Savonarola is pure religion,
and Machiavelli pure science, technique, politics.'[1] Russo even put
them further apart than Villari, whom he disliked. The latter had
claimed a change of attitude for Machiavelli, and based it on the
remarks of a chapter in the *Discorsi*: Machiavelli, according to this
view, began by distrusting Savonarola, when he was, as Villari
thought, inclined to be of the Arrabbiati; later he was more ready
to do justice to him.[2] But Russo, as Toffanin, dismisses the idea of
revision: Machiavelli was sarcastic in the praise he seemed to give,
he was thinking of his audience in the Orti Oricellari.[3] After which,
perhaps there is only to add that Toffanin, apropos of this same
passage, sees in the malicious eyes of Machiavelli his 'immutable
contempt for the republican monk';[4] that Janni saw Machiavelli
meditating on Savonarola, 'but the result of his meditation was a
sneer'; and Janni added as a corollary that, since the law of politics is
exquisitely anti-christian (do unto others what you would not have
them do unto you), Machiavelli's grudge against Savonarola arose in
all probability from the latter's wish to restore heaven to its place
in politics, whence Machiavelli had excluded it.[5] A Frenchman put it
more moderately, but with the same point: Machiavelli's character
was not one to be touched by this prophetic tone, nor by all this Old
Testament rhetoric. 'Il avait étudié l'histoire de la Rome républicaine, et il prouvera plus tard dans ses écrits qu'il en admirait trop la
politique réaliste pour éprouver aucune sympathie envers la théocratie chimérique du dominicain.'[6]

We have yet to turn to the *Discorsi* for Machiavelli's major statement, but in the meantime we may be impressed by this unanimity
of conclusion with regard to him and Savonarola. Can there be any
point in challenging what has been so generally accepted? It is when
we pause to ask the question that we shall recall that some of these
very statements have fallen in the consideration of Machiavelli's
temperament; and that though their authors saw the contrast between
the pair as clear-cut and absolute, yet when they looked to Machiavelli they hesitated plainly about his nature. Indeed, we may feel
justified in turning once again, though with a different purpose, to
those closing passages of the *Prince*, where Machiavelli used with

[1] Russo, 11.   [2] Villari, *G.Sav.*, I, 319–22; II, 107.
[3] Russo, 10 and 102–5.   [4] Toffanin, *M. e il Tacit.*, 13 and 29.
[5] Janni, vii, 7 and 176.   [6] Gautier Vignal, 48.

great naturalness, and with obvious conviction the same prophetic fervour, and the same Old Testament rhetoric, which have just strenuously been denied him. For there is at least one particular here on which attention has not so far rested. It is the moment when Machiavelli has stated the need of Italy, the exaltation of the House of Medici which makes the opportunity, and the ideas of justice and necessity. He goes on: 'Oltre di questo, qui si veggano estraordinarii sanza esempio condotti da Dio: el mare si è aperto; una nube vi ha scorto el cammino; la pietra ha versato acqua; qui è piovuto la manna.'[1] Now it is already sufficiently indicative of a formative period in Machiavelli that excitement should bring him to such biblical language, rather than to something different. But not the least remarkable thing here is the 'condotti da Dio'. It throws us back to Philippe de Commines, with his repeated statements that Charles VIII's expedition was plainly God's doing, and not human achievement; but it throws us also back to Savonarola, who was the authority behind Commines's reiterations. Nor, oddly enough, does Machiavelli's continuation to this passage strike a note alien to Savonarola. He goes on: '. . . ogni cosa è concorsa nella vostra grandezza. El rimanente dovete fare voi. Dio non vuole fare ogni cosa, per non ci torre el libero arbitrio e parte di quella gloria che tocca a noi.' Had not Savonarola preached in 1495, when Charles VIII was approaching Florence on his return from Naples, and Piero de'Medici was in his train, on the need to arm as well as to pray? 'Fate orazione, ma non tralasciate i provvedimenti umani; bisogna aiutarsi in ogni modo, con tutti i mezzi, ché allora il Signore sarà con voi.'[2] If before the 'condotti da Dio' surprised us, perhaps equally here this insistence on using all the means available may give us pause. Both Savonarola and Machiavelli could here appeal equally to texts of Livy, or of Sallust.[3] This is a concurrence which does something to undermine the gap that Toffanin wished to establish between the two. He quoted Savonarola's saying that there was no remedy for the princes of Italy other than repentance ('E dicoti, o Firenze, che i principi dell'Italia non hanno rimedio se non penitenza'[4]), which would indeed separate him from Machiavelli. But that was what Savonarola had said in 1494. He does not always

---

[1] *P.* XXVI, 50, 2.   [2] Villari, *G.Sav.*, I, 378.
[3] Livy, XXII, 14: 'Stultitia est, sedendo aut votis debellari credere posse,' etc. Sallust, *Con. Cat.*, 21: 'Sed inertia et mollitia animi, alius alium expectantes cunctamini, videlicet Diis immortalibus confisi, qui hanc Rempublicam in maximis saepe periculis servavere. Non votis neque suppliciis muliebribus, auxilia deorum parantur, vigilando, agendo, bene consulendo, prospere omnia cedunt.'
[4] Toffanin, *op. cit.*, 29.

speak the same language. And in 1513 is it not Machiavelli's conviction that the penance of Italy has been sufficient?

It looks, then, possible to examine Machiavelli and Savonarola and find points of contact. Naturally, they will not amount to an establishment of identity. Even, it may seem that there is an essential duality in Savonarola himself which might give new light on Machiavelli's judgments with regard to him. There is in Savonarola the legacy of medieval Christianity with its nihilism. St. Thomas à Kempis asked what use it was to know all the Bible and all the opinions of the philosophers, and answered that a humble peasant serving God was certainly more than a philosopher. And Savonarola on mental prayer was not afraid of reaching an equally logical extreme: the ignorant man can reach the heights in this as easily as the learned one—'*anzi* spesso avviene che colui il quale recita i Salmi senza comprenderli, fa una preghiera assai più accetta del dotto che saprebbe spiegarli'.[1] No one who follows in the wake of humanism could sympathize with such a statement.[2] And was not Savonarola enmeshed (it was an embarrassment to his well-wisher Villari) in a dantesque interpretation of the Bible according to five senses, which left him free to twist authority as he pleased, while Machiavelli casually dropped a hint on those who read the Bible 'sensatamente'.[3] Savonarola at one moment says it is better to have no answer to the problems of this world; at another he allows himself the option, on divine inspiration, of any answer his interpretation may wrest from the Bible; and at still another he attempts a practical answer based on an understanding of the Florentine situation. But perhaps it is precisely this discrepancy of treatment by Savonarola that provokes Machiavelli's adverb 'sensatamente', so that the latter, as well as serving to differentiate him from Savonarola, might also serve as a proof of a preoccupation with him. Was there not some justification for Machiavelli's double comment in *Discorsi* I, Chapter XLV? There he praised first Savonarola's qualities, 'la dottrina, la prudenza, e la virtú dello animo suo', and it is after that he goes on to note 'l'animo suo ambizioso e partigiano'. It is not necessary for the first to be sarcasm, even if the second is where Machiavelli comes to rest. It is not obligatory to accept all in order to approve of something. Does not Guicciardini, in spite of considerable sympathy for Savonarola, halt with an ambiguous judgment on him?[4] And if Savonarola was incoherent in his attitude then distrust follows inevitably.

[1] Villari, *G.Sav.*, I, 117.   [2] Cf. Whitfield, *Petr. and the Ren.*, 81.
[3] *D.* III, XXX, 404–5.   [4] Guicciardini, *St. F.*, 181.

Now that we have entered our caveat, let us see what the contacts amount to. And here it is apparent first that some occurred to Villari, and that if he had not been prevented by his general thesis he might have drawn conclusions from them. It was, indeed, Villari who noticed the reawakening of political spirit in Florence under the popular government instituted by Savonarola, and said quite rightly that thinkers like Machiavelli, Guicciardini, and Giannotti were the fruits of this awakening.[1] It was Villari who observed the unanimous answer of the political theorists to the question: What is the perfect government? in the quest for it begun after the expulsion of Piero de'Medici. All answered that it was the one in which a tyrant could not rise, and where the nobles' desire for honour and the people's cry for liberty was combined. This is the theory later minutely propounded by Giannotti, and established by Machiavelli and Guicciardini; it is frequent in the contemporaries of Savonarola, and the latter formulated it clearly in his treatise on the *Reggimento e Governo della Città di Firenze*.[2] And later Villari came back to dwell on this uniformity: Machiavelli, Guicciardini, and Giannotti, writing when Florentine liberty had fallen, meditated on all of Roman history, as well as on that of Florence and Italy, to find a fitting form of government for Florence; and they all concluded that there was nothing better than the Consiglio Maggiore of 1494, to which they merely proposed modifications that would adapt that constitution to changed times. 'And it is wonderful to consider how even in the modifications they proposed these great men did not depart from the ideas of the monk. They wanted a life-Gonfaloniere, and he before he died had counselled it more than once; they wanted a new tribunal for criminal offences, and he had preached in favour of it; they proposed free discussion in the Consigli, and nothing had he recommended more constantly.'[3] Is it not already evident that if Machiavelli had meditated on Savonarola, he had not only sneered or palely smiled as a conclusion to his meditation?

Villari could not go further, or advance to any deduction such as this. He did not seem to imagine that he had opened a door, and so it was the opposition that remained conclusive for him, not this influence which he had himself established. But we need not be so limited, and we shall still find, ironically enough, that Villari is of service in making further comparison: for, alongside the points that he did not miss, there are those also which his blinkers prevented him from seeing. First though, since we may need proof that Machiavelli

---

[1] *G.Sav.*, I, 455.   [2] *ibid.*, I, 268.   [3] *ibid.*, I, 315-6.

listened to Savonarola at all (apart from the letter on the sermons of 1497, or the statement in *Discorsi* III, Chapter XXX, on his sermons as full of invective against his political opponents—which posit a familiarity with him), we may note that the cautious annotation of Lisio to Chapter XII of the *Prince* can be taken as a certainty. 'E chi diceva come e'n'erano cagione e'peccati nostri. . . .' Lisio said, he was alluding *perhaps* to Savonarola.[1] Who else but Savonarola had said this so persistently? 'In verità, sono i vostri peccati, i peccati d'Italia, che mi fanno per forza profeta, e che dovrebbero far profeta ognun di voi. . . .'[2] It is, like the matter of the interpretation of the Bible anagogically or sensibly, an indication of a preoccupation on Machiavelli's part. But in these two cases Machiavelli dissents from the opinion of Savonarola, even if in the second one he uses still his terminology. Elsewhere he is curiously in accordance. Russo made a statement on both of them as being, both, but in opposite ways, extremist in their logic. But Villari affords us an example of Savonarola on the same extreme as Machiavelli. We have seen already Savonarola's attitude in 1495 on the approaching danger from Charles VIII and Piero de'Medici. Villari noted that Savonarola's language changed from irony to grow terrible. He knows no half measures when Florence is in danger. In church, in the pulpit, with the crucifix in hand, he counsels openly the putting to death of those who wish to re-establish tyranny in Florence, of those who want the return of the Medici. 'Bisogna usare con costoro, come fecero i Romani contro quelli che volevano rimettere Tarquinio. Tu che non vuoi avere riguardo a Cristo, vuoi averne ai privati cittadini? Fa'giustizia, ti dico io. Tagliali il capo, e sia pure il maggiore della casa sua quanto si voglia: tagliali il capo. . . .'[3] Two things are especially notable in this pronunciation of Savonarola: one is the advice, the other is the authority for the advice. Here in Florence there are the major citizens who look for a restricted form of rule in which there will be scope for them: they look to the return of the Medici as an outlet for themselves. And Savonarola says that one must kill them to preserve the popular form of government. Not only this, but he appeals to Livy for his example. Who were those who wished to restore the Tarquins, and who suffered death so that the new liberties of Rome might be secure? Were they not the *sons of Brutus*? and is there not a notorious chapter in the *Discorsi* which says precisely that a new liberty cannot last unless one disposes of the partisans of the old tyranny? that you cannot have

---

[1] P. ed. Lisio, 77. [2] G.Sav., I, 333. [3] *ibid.*, I, 387.

democracy in Germany unless you destroy the Nazi bosses and so forth?[1]

Well, it may only be a coincidence, and nothing more. But Savonarola has not finished being Machiavellian. He finds Florentine justice too lenient against certain kinds of vice. To be thus piteous is a form of cruelty. 'Vedi, adunque, Firenze, tu che vuoi essere cosí pietosa, vedi quello che fece fare Iddio. Sei tu piú savia di Dio? sei tu piú misericordiosa di Dio? sei tu piú d'assai di Dio, tu?' . . . 'O Firenze! tu vuoi essere piú clemente di Dio; ma la tua clemenza è una demenza: tu hai una pietà crudele; fa'giustizia, ti dico io, di quel vizio nefario.'[2] To be merciful, and by being merciful to be also cruel, to arrive at a *pietà crudele*, it is an arresting paradox. But it will not baffle the student of Machiavelli long, for it is one of the first paradoxes one associates with his name. And if we turn back to that chapter in the *Prince* where Machiavelli studies the question, we find that he does so in identical terms: it is a chapter *De Crudelitate et Pietate*. All princes must desire to be held *pietoso*, not *crudele*, but they must not use their *pietà* amiss. Caesar Borgia was cruel, yet what did he do for Romagna? And if we consider rightly his amendment there we shall see that he was 'molto piú pietoso che il populo fiorentino, il quale, per fuggire el nome di crudele, lasciò destruggere Pistoia'.[3] This time does it not look as if Machiavelli may have been more influenced by Savonarola, or at least more akin to him, than prejudice had thought?

To confirm this suspicion there is a further place where they speak the same language. Savonarola, as is sufficiently known, was the fierce adversary of Roman corruption. It is an invective which finds its echo in many an honest Florentine diarist or chronicler, as in Giovanni Cambi.[4] 'Ora è spenta ogni religione, e si costuma; oggi in teatro, e domani nella cattedra episcopale; oggi in teatro, e domani canonico in coro; oggi soldato, e domani prete'—so Savonarola inveighs.[5] And the burden of his accusation is very much the same as will be that of Machiavelli against the warrior-priest Julius II. Did he not rebuke such as Julius in the *Discorsi*, 'quanto sia da stimare poco chi vive e regna come loro'.[6] And the whole judgment of Savonarola on the corruption of Rome is closely related to the famous remark of Machiavelli in an earlier chapter of the *Discorsi*, where he is specifically discussing the question of religion; and where he puts as a first obligation of Italy towards the Roman Church 'di essere

---

[1] *D.* III, III.
[4] Cambi, II, 167, 170, e.g.
[2] *G.Sav.*, I, 396.
[5] *G.Sav.*, I, 467.
[3] *P.* XVII, 32, 2.
[6] *D.* I, XXVII.

diventati sanza religione e cattivi'.¹ Now, it may be that Machiavelli is only concerned with the problem of religion as an essential part in preserving morality: that he considers it as a *religio*, something that bonds men together and keeps them good, and not as a *fides*, with a supernatural goal as its main business. If he does so, of course, it is once more a development of the practical concern of humanism, to which movement he most properly belongs. I do not, before considering the *Discorsi*, wish to make any further examination of this matter. It is sufficient here to show how close the Florentine reformer Savonarola is in his disapproval of Rome to the Florentine politician Machiavelli. And we can make one other parallel, in this matter of religion, which is striking. Savonarola, in his assault on the vices of Rome ('O vaccae pingues . . .'), lashed the trumpery of Catholicism, the superficial religion of saints and ceremonies: 'Va di qua, va di là; bacia san Pietro, san Paolo, quel Santo, quell'altro. Venite, venite, sonate campane, apparecchiate altari, ornate le chiese, venite tutti quei tre giorni innanzi Pasqua, ma non poi piú là. Dio se ne ride dei fatti vostri, e non si cura di vostre cerimonie . . . perché voi sarete dopo Pasqua peggior di prima. Tutto è vanità, tutto è ipocrisia nei nostri tempi; la vera religione è spenta.'² Like all reformers, Savonarola desires a return to the origins: and we shall find that this has coloured largely Machiavelli's view, and has overflowed with him from the religious to the political field. But that question of the return to the *principio* (the word which Machiavelli will hand on to Montesquieu) is something that will force itself upon us later. Just for one moment we may pause to notice that even this word *spenta*, which is Savonarola's word, is Machiavelli's word also. Turn to the first chapter of the last book of the *Discorsi*, where he discusses the role of St. Francis and St. Dominic, and there you will find it, twice.³ But there is something even more important than that coincidence. This of Savonarola is dramatic language: yet it could not quite be used *tel quel* in a drama, because Savonarola's pulpit oratory does not stop at an ironic statement. It has to proceed unambiguously to the moral lesson, for fear the audience does not take the point, or it has to drive the latter home by iteration. But if someone were to use the situation dramatically? Then he would, would he not? have to content himself with taking the irony, and leaving the moral statement to be guessed. Is it not Machiavelli who does so, in the first comedy which deals with contemporary material? At least, there is a notable soliloquy of Fra Timoteo which lashes with its irony this

¹ *D.* I, XII.   ² *G.Sav.*, I, 428–9.   ³ *D.* III, I, 305–6.

same superficial devotion. It is in the fifth Act of the *Mandragola*, where perhaps I may leave the reader, who will not be without his knowledge of that play, though he may not have thought of it as containing anything Savonarolan, to look for it.[1]

It is in the light of these coincidences of statement (which must not be taken as being even in intention exhaustive, being offered as a preliminary investigation, and by a student of Machiavelli rather than by one of Savonarola), not in that of the fancied opposition set up by nineteenth-century criticism that we must consider Machiavelli's views of Savonarola himself. They range from instinctive distrust in 1497 (when it seemed to him that Savonarola was playing a political game, 'colouring his lies' to gain his ends) to the sincere tributes which he pays here and there to the learning, prudence, and virtue of the friar. Perhaps, since they are comments rising at widely differing dates, we do not need to eschew any of them, or to imagine that Machiavelli—any more than any other Florentine—was obliged to maintain an unvarying estimate of Savonarola's aims and achievement. Have we not seen Guicciardini, in spite of sympathy, hesitating in his judgment? We might, then, even allow (though it does not seem very clear that we need to) the critics to be right in regarding the judgment of the *Primo Decennale* as being contemptuous.[2] We might even admit the adjective *versuto* in the letter to Francesco Guicciardini as a pejorative, that dismisses the Dominican friar from his memory.[3] Even then, though, we shall not have established a clear divorce between them: it will be Savonarola's sincerity that Machiavelli has dismissed, not his programme. There is a proof of that for those who have the patience to read on a few lines after coming to the sensational adjective *versuto*: 'Vedendo, oltre di questo, quanto credito ha un tristo che sotto il mantello della religione si nasconda, si può fare sua coniettura facilmente, quanto ne arebbe un buono che andasse in verità e non in simulazione, pestando i fanghi di san Francesco.'[4] Can it be that Niccolò, malignant Niccolò, has dared to judge Savonarola from some more lofty stance than we had expected? It may be so; but at least it is the fact of certain sympathies, certain identities, which we must bear in mind. Neither Machiavelli nor Savonarola stand to lose by being at certain points on the same platform. It is by way of being a certificate of realism for the latter (on one side, at least, of his personality); it is by way of being part of the certificate of respectability for the former.

---

[1] Act V, sc. 1, in M.C., 721, 2.   [2] *D.P.*, M.C., 803, vv. 154–65.
[3] *L.F.*, M.C., 901, 1.   [4] *ibid.*

VI

THE ANATOMY OF VIRTUE

THE coupling of Machiavelli's name with that of Savonarola led, as we saw, to a surprising close, in which the former sighs, or seems to sigh, for someone who should be more genuinely good than Savonarola. But had Machiavelli the right to think in such a way? Has he not pinned his faith to something different, something that has seemed indissolubly attached to his name and writings: to a doctrine of *virtù*? Now in English we have reduced the word *virtue* to one main sense, and to this sense of conformity to moral principles all other senses are subordinate (as when we say *by virtue of . . .*), or else are obsolescent. This simplicity of use, which is not affected by differences between abstract and concrete, makes us perhaps a little insensitive to the possibility of other employment for the word. We can distinguish with ease between virtue and virtuosity, because the words no longer seem connected. Nor do objects of vertu (a monopoly of sale catalogues) disturb us. But the spectacle of the word *virtue* with an obviously divergent sense from our own is enough to cause misgiving. And, indeed, no word in Machiavelli's vocabulary has aroused more excitement, or more indignation, than the simple word *virtù*. For those who have known no more of this author than his reputation the notion that he abandoned virtue to put in its place some pagan conception of *virtù* has replaced the need for documentation on his qualities as a writer: it has represented concrete, and detailed, proof of his wickedness. An author who has no concern for virtue must be immoral or amoral (the former being the old-fashioned, the latter the modern, view of Machiavelli). And for many there has seemed no need to consider the case of Machiavelli more closely when he had revealed his colours so clearly. There have been, of course, excuses for such an attitude. Although many have written on Machiavelli, few have examined the values he attaches to words; and in consequence some traps have lain ready for the unwary. Benoist, who was ready to find some excuse for Machiavelli in his patriotism, remarked on a sentence in the *Legations*, 'Le grand mot y est en toutes lettres: *la patria*.'[1] It was there indeed,

[1] Benoist, 129.

92

but it was not, and never became, a *grand mot* for Machiavelli. It was one's birthplace, therefore, one's native city: it never expanded in his use, or in his mind, to reach the concept of patriotism. Machiavelli never has the nineteenth-century Risorgimento idea of the unity of Italy, any more than anyone else of his own time. That is why we have seen the ambiguous term *provincia* as his use for a whole country. And if Benoist caught a crab with *patria*, anyone who jumped at *nazione* in Machiavelli's pages and tried to link it with its reappearance in France at the end of the eighteenth century would go similarly astray: *nazione*, and it is the regular Florentine use, is the identification of where one is born, so that a man may be of the Florentine, though he cannot be of the Italian, nation.

There are, then, snags; and Ercole, who (apart from the useful, though not impeccable, annotations of editors such as Lisio) stands almost alone in this examination of terms, has shown that there is much to learn on Machiavelli's vocabulary generally. But his work is fairly recent, and in the matter of *virtù* it does not offer much help. As a basis of consideration for this latter word perhaps Ercole's conclusions on the Machiavellian use of *stato* are the most helpful. *Stato* has a whole gamut of meanings, ranging from the Latin one of *state, condition*, to something very near the modern conception of the *State*; but with a general tendency to convey something less than this last, *power, those that hold it, government*, rather than *territory*—though this last is not absent.[1] In any given passage the word *stato*—such is the uncertainty of Machiavelli's use of it—may have any one of this range of shades. And this unscientific use of terms is not untypical of Machiavelli. He is so much more concerned with things than with words that his symbols may be inadequate. His vision of things is, as has been generally recognized, astonishingly sharp; and even as a consequence of that very sharpness, his notation of them is at times misleading.

Such a point of departure for the consideration of the word *virtù* would not seem to lead to a doctrine based on this word. Yet it has been a fairly general belief that such a doctrine existed, and that to the exclusion of the meaning *virtue*. Even, this certainty as to the existence of a blind spot in Machiavelli's make-up (and, by one of those inviting side-steps, in the Renascence as well. Is it not the Age of Machiavelli, or of Peter Aretine?) has seemed sufficiently well known to need only a passing allusion to it. Lanson expresses, and dismisses, it in a

[1] Ercole, *La Pol. di M.*, 65.

bare sentence which may give us clearly the usual definition of it:
'La théorie de la *virtù*, d'où toute notion morale est exclue, fait de
l'individu même l'oeuvre où l'individu travaille à réaliser la plénitude
de la force et de la beauté.'[1] And a trail of others, more or less
authoritative, but all unanimous, keep Lanson company. Thus
Woodward, in his novel about Caesar Borgia, wrote: 'For what in
the days of the Borgia was legitimacy in comparison with force,
with personal distinction, with *virtù*?'[2] It is clear, from such a question, that the individuality of the word is taken for granted, and
felt as giving a dubious air not only to its author, but to his times as
well. One does not call the Renascence 'the days of the Borgia'
without conveying a slur of some sort; and this slur spreads from the
conception of *virtù*. *Elena* was the unsuccessful divagation of a scholar;
but other scholars than Lanson have said the same in their own field.
Einstein remarked on Elizabethan borrowing from Machiavelli,
noting it as often from the pseudo-Machiavelli: 'Nevertheless, it
can scarcely be doubted that Machiavelli's doctrine of *virtù* fitted in
with the ideas of the age.'[3] Praz wrote of 'that pagan doctrine of
virtù'.[4] Gentile quoted Burckhardt's definition of the Machiavellian
virtù as a union of force and ability, something that can be summed
up in force alone, if by force one means human, not mechanical,
force: will, and therefore force of ability.[5] Ercole himself, in spite of
his habit of examining the variations in Machiavelli's use of words,
talked of the rise of 'il concetto della virtú machiavellesca',[6] so strongly
was this current flowing; and in a later work, where his criticism of
Machiavelli has been wholly overlaid by a Fascist gloss (was not
Mussolini's so-called thesis on Machiavelli merely a crib from
Ercole's earlier work?), he presents the definition of the word in
two stages. I have already made my comment on the swollen
idiom which has passed for literary criticism in Italy in recent times,
and I leave Ercole's definition to stand in the words he used himself.
Basically, *virtù* is the 'esercizio concreto della libertà propria dell'uomo
di energico e conscio volere, non già di fermare a sua posta o di
deviare a suo arbitrio il corso della realtà, tra cui vive e che lo circonda,
ma di piegarlo in modo da imporgli l'impronta della propria azione
. . . non soltanto a volere un fine, ma anche ad agire per tradurlo
nella realtà'.[7] This, then, is purely utilitarian if it is made to serve
private ends, the good of the individual; it becomes moral, at least for

[1] Lanson, 224.
[2] W. H. Woodward, *Elena* (1929), 18.
[3] Lewis Einstein, *Ital. Ren. in England*, 368.
[4] Praz, *St. d. lett. ing.*, 61.
[5] Gentile, *Studi sul Rinascim.*, 108.
[6] Ercole, *op. cit.*, 20.
[7] Ercole, *Pensatori*, etc., 169.

Machiavelli, when it serves something transcending this, not for mere 'proprio libito, ma per un dovere che annulla ogni libito'—that is, for one's country. Hence *virtú* is either good or bad according to its application; but in any case it is the privilege of the very few.[1] Such language is more ambitious, it presupposes the existence of a modern conception of patriotism in Machiavelli, and it has the vice of building a general theory on a particular statement of his; but it is only in this rider that it modifies accepted ideas.

I do not know of anyone after Ercole who has seen fit to examine the problem. The first necessary step is to dismiss the casual statements which imply a doctrine or theory of *virtú* individual to Machiavelli, and seek to characterize him, or even the Renascence, thereby. There is no doctrine of *virtú* in Machiavelli. If there were it would be easy to discover in his works; but Machiavelli was not given to such theorizing, and he himself would have been the first to be surprised at the stir the word has caused. The second point is that even if Machiavelli were always to use *virtú* as something poles apart from *virtue* that particular would not, in itself, permit the deduction that he was oblivious of the claims, or ignorant of the existence, of virtue. To say that Machiavelli uses *virtú* always in an odd sense of his own is a linguistic observation only, unless it is accompanied by a certificate that he has no other word for virtue. Then we should have a surprising, and an incriminating, omission. But it is quite clear that Machiavelli is not short of words, and normally *buono, onesto* with their opposites *cattivo, tristo* replace *virtuous* and *vicious*. They are adjectives which accord straitly with contemporary Florentine usage, so that Landucci remarks on the fate of Savonarola that 'hanno potuto piú e tristi ch'e buoni'.[2] One can hardly be preoccupied with goodness and badness without having some conception of virtue; and there is no moral case that can be based against Machiavelli on the use he makes of *virtú*.

But one can go further than this: Machiavelli has not only other words for virtue, he does not even exclusively reserve *virtú* for a pagan (*scilicet*, a Latin) sense. It is exactly here as it was with *stato*: his use of terms is imprecise, and he employs them as they come to cover any of their several acceptations—beginning with what he found in his Latin authors, and ending with current meanings. Tommasini, in noting the influence of Galen on Machiavelli, with a consequent tendency to use medical metaphors, observed that his use of *virtú* was medical also, and that it represented a 'potestas quaedam

[1] Ercole, *ibid.*, 170–1.   [2] Landucci, 124.

efficiendi'.[1] That I believe to be a more helpful annotation than the elaborated theorizing of Ercole. But it is only a single facet of the word, and Tommasini probably exaggerated this medical connection. Machiavelli was only using the metaphors that the historians and moralists of Rome had found to hand. And for *virtú* itself, there are passages, and by no means solitary ones, in which its acceptation must perforce be that of virtue. To begin with the *Prince*, and with a passage which we have met already, it is plain that here there is no twist to virtue: 'Perché, se si considerrà bene tutto, si troverrà qualche cosa che parrà virtú, e seguendola sarebbe la ruina sua, e qualcuna altra che parrà vizio, e seguendola ne riesce la securtà et il bene essere suo.'[2] Equally plain are two examples from the *Discorsi*. In the passage contrasting the Roman Empire under a good and a bad emperor Machiavelli sees in the first state of things 'la nobilità e la virtú esaltata'; in the second he sees innumerable cruelties in Rome 'e la nobilità, le ricchezze, i passati onori, o sopra tutto la virtú, essere imputate a peccato capitale'.[3] Later on, in demonstrating that good laws may become bad in changed conditions, he notes that originally in Rome those who deserved magistratures demanded them; but with the passage of time, and the growth of effrontery, the good stood on one side, the bad grasped out for office: 'Non quelli che avevano piú virtú, ma quelli che avevano piú potenza, domandavano i magistrati; e gl'impotenti, comecché virtuosi, se ne astenevano di domandarli, per paura.'[4] This observation is worth noting, because it completely precludes any interpretation of *virtú* in terms of force, energy of the will, or what-have-you. It is unmistakably plain virtue that Machiavelli means.

I do not put forward those few quotations as all in which *virtú* and virtue are synonymous; but as sufficient in themselves to show incontrovertibly that Machiavelli, apart from other words which have the same meaning (as *bontà*), is not ignorant of virtue under its own label. Nor, naturally, do I put them forward either as preventing him from using the word elsewhere (even in close proximity) in a different sense. Just as he juxtaposes verb-forms from the stem *poss-* by others from the stem *pot-*, so that *posseva* follows *poteva*, etc., with no concern for the discrepancy, so it is with the senses of *stato*, or of *virtú*. Indeed, it is quite obvious that the idea of a theory of *virtú* could not have arisen were there not conspicuous examples in which *virtú* has a sense akin to, or derived from, that of Galen. Nor are

---

[1] Tommasini, II, 39. Cf. Dante's use of *virtú* in *Purg.*, XXV, 41.
[2] P. XV. 31, 1.   [3] *D.* I, X, 47.   [4] *D.* I, XVIII, 72.

other Latin senses unrepresented. Thus in 'Cose tutte da maravigliarsi come in un esercito cosí fattó fusse tanta virtú che sapesse vincere, e come nello inimico fusse tanta viltà che da sí disordinate genti potesse essere vinto',[1] the word is defined by its opposite to give the sense of valour and bravery which Machiavelli found most frequently given to it in his author, Livy. And the *surprise* over a victory by 'disordinate genti' shows that Machiavelli had in mind as well the contrast between barbaric *furor* and Latin *virtus*. Other opposites, besides *vizio* and *viltà*, stand with *virtú*, and give relief to it in specific passages. Thus *ozio* gives a sharp definition in a passage of the *Discorsi*.[2] Perhaps more frequent still is the opposition with *fortuna*, a pair which Machiavelli had obviously learnt from the Latin historians, from whom so much of his idiom comes. Quintus Curtius, for example, had discussed the question whether Alexander the Great owed more to *virtus* or to *fortuna*;[3] a question which Machiavelli repeats for Caesar Borgia in Chapter VII of the *Prince*. And it is the same Quintus Curtius, if it is not Sallust, who defined the word most sharply in the sense that has been proclaimed essentially Machiavellian. When Alexander's soldiers quail before their leader's appetite for conquests, and for jungle penetration, their spokesman says, 'Virtus enim tua semper in incremento erit, nostra vis in fine iam est.'[4] And Sallust makes that quite explicit by debating whether military success depends more on the *vis* of the body, or on the *virtus* of the mind.[5] We may see once more a comparable use a few pages earlier in Quintus Curtius, where Porus uses his last weapon to transfix his brother Taxilis (who had urged on him surrender to Alexander): 'Hoc ultimo opere virtutis edito fugere acrius coepit.'[6] The force of his mind being spent, he turned to the force of his legs. In cases such as these virtue is already an energy of the will, transcending mere force. It is a regular Latin sense, and one which is surely implicit still in Cicero's contribution of virtue as moral perfection:[7] it represents, that is to say, one avenue of development towards ·a perfection. Where Machiavelli is so often indebted to his Latin authors for construction and vocabulary there is nothing odd in his taking also the various Latin uses of *virtus*, and leaving them concurrent, as he did with the senses of *stato*.

In the case of *virtú* there is a further check on the process. I do not think the dictionary recognizes it quite explicitly, but there is in Latin

[1] *I.F.*, ed. P. Carli, V, XXXIV, 57. [2] *D.* II, II, 189.
[3] Quintus Curtius, X, 160. [4] *ibid.*, IX, 138.
[5] Sallust, *Con. Cat.*, 1. [6] Quintus Curtius, VIII, 132.
[7] *De Legibus*, I, VIII, 25.

a gap between *virtus* and *virtutes*. It is the first one only that admits the sense of energy of the will, or bravery; the second is already concerned only with good actions, or good qualities. In Valerius Maximus there is *virtus* in the anecdote of Xenophon's continuing his sacrifice, and replacing of his wreath, when learning that his son had died in battle, but had died with valour.[1] But Valerius Maximus uses the plural *virtutes* differently. Marcus Brutus is 'suarum prius virtutum, quam patriae parentis parricida'.[2] The ancient Roman who killed his wife because she had drunk wine found no accuser, for the use of wine for women shuts the door to all the virtues, and opens it to all the vices—'et virtutibus omnibus ianuam claudit et delictis aperit'.[3] We could trace this opposition between singular and plural in other Latin authors, who may be, perhaps, closer to Machiavelli, as in Tacitus, or in Suetonius (who, for Domitian, talks of a mixture of *virtutes* and *vitia*, which makes it quite clear).[4] But probably this illustration is already sufficient. Machiavelli retains this plural when, for instance, he speaks of the prince's duty to show himself 'amatore delle virtú'.[5] And this coincidence with the Latin use is sufficient to resolve the ambiguity which Lisio recognized— though he spoke for the good interpretation—in the passage on Hannibal in the *Prince*. When Machiavelli writes of 'quella sua inumana crudeltà, la quale insieme con infinite sua virtú lo fece sempre nel conspetto de'sua soldati venerando e terribile',[6] there is implied a contrast between the qualities, as there is explicit one between the epithets resulting from them. Hannibal is not venerable because of his inhuman cruelty, or terrible because of his virtues. This plural is, I think, rarely used by Machiavelli: there is at least one case where he has replaced a Latin plural by the singular, with the sense of virtue, and this in the passage I quoted on Rome under the bad emperors.[7] But if it is a rare use, at least it is stable in sense, as it was in Latin.[8] The singular is more volatile. This ambiguity, however, which leaves the reader with the task of fitting one of the several Latin senses, the medical one, that of energy of the will, of bravery, of Ciceronian virtue, or the post-classical sense of Christian virtue, can involve no reflection on Machiavelli. Rather, it is clear, as it was in our consideration of the *Prince*, that there are other elements in Machiavelli's theory of the prince, or of the republic, than mere go-getting; and it is not profitable to consider him as a writer without taking them fully into account. Machiavelli is no

[1] Val. Max., V, X, 5.   [2] *ibid.*, VI, IV, 8.   [3] *ibid.*, VI, III, 10.
[4] Tacitus, *Hist.* (ed. Davanzati), II, 269; Suetonius, *Domit.*, 172 v.   [5] P. XXI, 45, I.
[6] P. XVII, 100, n. 15, ed. Lisio.   [7] D. I, X, 47.   [8] Cf. the end of P. XI.

more the standard-bearer of *virtù* than the Renascence is the age of the Borgias.

That does not mean, of course, that we should neglect consideration of this particular aspect of the word when Machiavelli uses it. Not only does it appear to me that Machiavelli cannot easily be dismissed from the moral field, in that he did not only know this sense, but that he finds himself in irreproachable company at this point precisely where he has been most vilified. Let us go back to this *virtù* which records respect of some sort for the energy of achievement without regard to the moral nature of the achievement. It is this that has stuck in people's throats; it is this that had least right to do so. For Machiavelli is, I imagine, merely treading here on the same ground as Dante; and Dante at this point speaks the same language as does either Cicero before him, or La Rochefoucauld after him. One could, by looking harder, probably see more; but I hope that such citation will be enough to put Machiavelli, on this point at least, in better light. While before in this chapter I have been concerned to show that there is no consistent doctrine of *virtù* in Machiavelli's writings, it is my purpose now to prove that where he touches some such doctrine fleetingly it is a common (and I would add, a common-sense) inheritance.

Let us begin with Dante. Quite palpably Dante hesitates at the outset of his journey. He stands in danger of showing pusillanimity, and in the effort of separating himself from this *viltà* (the recurrences of the word itself are worth noting in the first few cantos of the *Inferno*) he writes the finely savage episode of the nameless crew who rush for ever naked after a blank banner, with the admirable biting lines against the nameless pope who runs with them. As soon, says Dante, as I saw him there, *at once* I knew the nature of the throng. They do not speak (what could they have to say?), there is no name given to their category; and Dante looks away. So far, by this tremendous scorn, is he himself removed from the *viltà* with which Virgil had reproached him at the beginning of the canto.[1] And these sinners, whether originally angels who took no part as between God and Lucifer, or men who had the courage neither for good nor ill, are outside hell, and yet, by Dante's scorn for them, beneath its lowest depths:

> 'Caccianli i ciel per non esser men belli,
> né lo profondo inferno li riceve,
> ch'alcuna gloria i rei avrebber d'elli.'[2]

[1] *Inf.*, III, 15.   [2] *ibid.*, 40–2.

That is theologically wrong, and psychologically right. These are
the vile, the spineless, the aimless; and even those below,

> Ausi omnes immane nefas, ausoque potiti,

have some claim on our regard which these have not.

This attitude of Dante, and its relation to his temperament, is
sufficiently known for there to be no point in my labouring it; but
surprisingly enough it has not been related (perhaps because of this
fact that it has its roots in Dante's nature) to a passage in a work
which Dante knew well, the *De Officiis* of Cicero. At least, I do not
find the connection made by Dr. Edward Moore, nor have I noted it
elsewhere. Yet this passage in Cicero is germain to Dante's conception of *ignavia*, and is not uninteresting for Machiavelli—who also,
as we have seen, was well acquainted with his *De Officiis*. I give it *in
extenso* because of its importance as a link between the three of them:
'For men generally admire all those things which they observe as
great, and outside their expectation; separately in individuals if they
see some unexpected good quality. And thus they exalt with the
highest praises those men in whom they think they see certain
excellent and outstanding virtues. But they despise and contemn
those in whom they think there is no capacity (*nihil virtutis*), no spirit,
and no vigour. For they do not despise everyone of whom they think
ill. They think ill of those who are wicked, slanderous, fraudulent,
ready to commit injustices, without indeed despising them. Where-
fore, as I said, those are despised who, as the saying goes, are of no use
either to themselves or others, in whom there is no exertion, no
activity, no care for anything.'[1] That text is abundantly clear: one
may say, if one likes, that Dante's view of *ignavia* derives from it;
or that it does not need to. The identity, at any rate, will remain a
constant.

Similarly, if we look beyond Machiavelli to La Rochefoucauld,
we shall find that this very natural idea has occurred to him as well.
Two or three maxims are worth quoting, and they will not take up
the room of Cicero: 'La foiblesse est plus opposée à la vertu que le
vice.' 'On ne méprise pas tous ceux qui ont des vices, mais on méprise
tous ceux qui n'ont aucune vertu'—that is almost literally Ciceronian.
'Nul ne mérite le titre de bon, s'il n'a pas la force et la hardiesse
d'être méchant: toute autre bonté n'est le plus souvent qu'une paresse
ou une impuissance de la volonté'—which we may relate to the *alcuna
gloria* of Dante's text. And finally, to clinch the series, 'Il y a des

---

[1] *De Off.*, II, X, 320.

Héros en mal comme en bien.' Now, although many have labelled La Rochefoucauld as a cynic (a little rashly, perhaps—but that is none of our business here), no one would care to maintain that he intended equal applause for both sorts of *heroes*. He implies approval for those who do good, and disapproval for those who do bad (you cannot, after all, use the words *good* and *bad* in more than one way); and there remains contempt for those who are in between, who are without the means to do either. Despise Alexander, or Napoleon? No, but condemn them if you like.

Now let us think of Machiavelli, and his so-called admiration for *virtù*. I think we may do so suitably in terms of one of the most telling shafts of Pascal in his third *Lettre Provinciale*. What is most orthodox in others became heresy in M. Arnauld's use, and could only become orthodox again if others took it over from him. How so? 'Ce ne sont pas les sentiments de M. Arnauld qui sont hérétiques: ce n'est que sa personne. C'est une hérésie personnelle. Il n'est pas hérétique pour ce qu'il a dit ou écrit, mais seulement pour ce qu'il est M. Arnauld.' And in precisely the same way, we know how wicked Machiavelli is, so therefore what was righteous indignation in Dante, or moral analysis in Cicero, or social reflection in La Rochefoucauld, becomes repulsive cynicism in Machiavelli. One cannot, it seems, bear a name like his with impunity. If we need an instance, first, of the label, let us turn to Professor Toffanin, whose chapter in his survey *Il Cinquecento* can be taken as one stopping-point for modern views of Machiavelli. The episode for use as a touchstone is obviously that on the conduct of G.-P. Baglioni at Perugia on the occasion of Julius II's imprudent putting of himself at the mercy of this petty tyrant whom he had come to oust. It is an episode that inspired, says Toffanin, 'one of the most cynically stupendous pages in the *Discorsi*'.[1] Those are strong words; but usual ones, for, as we may expect, this page is also one of those black-listed by the estimable Burd as worthy of perusal by those who might wish to convince themselves that the 'methods suggested in the *Discorsi* are quite as thorough and as unscrupulous and quite as little determined by moral considerations as those of the *Prince*'.[2]

When we are just about to turn to the *Discorsi* for their contribution to Machiavelli's general attitude, it is very good that we should have the opportunity of a preliminary investigation at an incriminated point. But alas! it looks as if poor Machiavelli must have given himself badly away; and after such advertisement as Burd and

---

[1] Toffanin, *Il Cinquecento*, 302.   [2] Burd, 42, n. 1.

Toffanin supply we may expect the worst. What, if we turn now to *Discorsi* I, Chapter XXVII, do we find? As the particulars of this expedition of Julius II are well known I may legitimately limit myself to quoting the comments of Machiavelli. First, there is his judgment on (that is, against) Julius II. The fall of Julius, at any hands, would serve for Machiavelli as a moral lesson to the Church, showing what estimate one should have of those who live and reign like Julius.[1] One cannot easily retain a flair for moral lessons when one has washed one's hands entirely of moral considerations. And in this case we have very excellent corroboration for Machiavelli's judgment on Julius in two blunt passages in the *Legations*. They both date from 1510, and they both think of Julius (with admirable cause) as one who may bring Italy to ruin. 'Dispiace a chiunque è qui questo movimento del Papa, parendo ad ciascuno che cerchi di ruinare la cristianità, e fornire di consumare l'Italia,' so Machiavelli wrote from Blois on the 26th July; and only a few days later he confirmed this with a statement of 'that diabolical spirit' which was reported to have entered into Julius, so that he might well 'cause Florence to be trampled on, and bring himself to the grave'.[2] If there was reason for such views, can one doubt whether Machiavelli was justified in passing condemnation on Julius? Perhaps, however, it is the comment on Giovampagolo Baglioni which betrays the cloven hoof? 'Fu notata, dagli uomini prudenti che col papa erano, la temerità del papa e la viltà di Giovampagolo. . . . Né si poteva credere si fusse astenuto o per bontà o per conscienza che lo ritenesse (because, as Machiavelli proceeds to state circumstantially, it was well assured that he had neither) . . . ma si conchiuse, nascesse che gli uomini non sanno essere onorevolmente cattivi, o perfettamente buoni; e, come una malizia ha in sé grandezza, o è in alcuna parte generosa, e'non vi sanno entrare.'[3] If we reduce that to its essential elements we find G.-P. Baglioni despised for his pusillanimity (and Machiavelli uses Dante's word—*viltà*), his badness being stated as beyond question; while the matter itself is stated in terms of a Machiavellian *aut-aut* (be *honourably wicked*, that is, qualify for the *alcuna gloria*, be a Capaneus or a Mahomet; or else, be perfectly good—a Trajan, shall we say?). And in between remains that condemnation of most men who have the energy for neither course, a condemnation by contempt. 'Il y a des Héros en mal comme en bien.' No doubt there are: but Giovampagolo is in no danger of belonging with them.

---

[1] *D.* I, XXVII, 89.   [2] *Opp.*, P.M., VI, 30 and 71.   [3] *D.* I, XXVII, 89.

If we are just to Machiavelli we must admit, I think, that there is an absolute identity here of views with Cicero, Dante, and La Rochefoucauld. We do not imagine that Dante liked Mahomet because he despised Celestine V. We only imagine that Machiavelli would have approved more highly of a more wicked Baglioni because we have been told by responsible historians like Villari that such was Machiavelli's strange attitude of mind. And there have always been the Maritains to offer their assent absolutely *a priori* to Villari's words on Machiavelli's supposed admiration for brigand chiefs who upset a country and his lack of alarm at 'any sanguinary and cruel action'. 'Puisque je vous dis que Machiavel ne croyait pas en Dieu! ni en l'église de Rome!' as an unkind reviewer summed up Maritain's expostulations.[1] But if we look honestly at the two texts I quoted from the *Legations* on Julius II whose policy is feared as one calculated to bring ruin on Christendom and to consummate the downfall of Italy, on Julius whom Machiavelli sees as possessed with a diabolic spirit, then the situation wears a different air. M. Maritain appeals to the idea of what the papacy ought to be, and therefore must have been; so Machiavelli's revolt from it can only have been occasioned by his own wickedness. Machiavelli looked at what it was, which does not happen to have been identical with what it must have been. And perhaps it is the place here to refer the reader to the words of Laurent which Tommasini rescued from that author's short section on machiavellianism. 'Ce qui nuit à la réputation de Machiavel, ce sont les illusions que l'on se fait sur le christianisme et sur la chevalerie. L'on s'imagine qu'il y a eu au moyen âge une politique chrétienne, dont les papes étaient les organes; et que pouvait être cette politique, sinon l'expression de la morale pure de l'Evangile? L'on s'imagine encore que la chevalerie avait introduit dans les relations de la féodalité tout ce qu'il y a de sentiments nobles et délicats, et on fait également honneur de ces sentiments au christianisme. Puis l'on suppose que Machiavel a remplacé l'idéal chrétien par la vile doctrine de l'intérêt. Il y a dans ces illusions autant d'erreurs que de mots.'[2] Not everything that Laurent says on Machiavelli in his section is still acceptable, but could one more genially bring back M. Maritain to consider what Machiavelli's attitude should have been to the *diabolical* policy of Julius II? Here we have a Machiavelli taking alarm at sanguinary action. It is the Machiavelli whose distress at the plight of Italy in the first quarter of the sixteenth century led him

---

[1] I quote from the South American review *Lettres françaises*, fév. 1943, in a *compte rendu* of Jacques Maritain, *La fin du machiavélisme*, 1941.

[2] Laurent, *Etudes sur l'Humanité*, X, 307. Cf. Tommasini, II, 727.

to pen, a year before his death, that anguished phrase to Guicciardini.[1]
This is the man who has, to use the frivolous words of Toffanin,
the Renascence admiration for the *facinus*.[2]

It is well to remember too that this whole chapter of Julius II
and Baglioni is introduced as an illustration to a theme stated in the
previous chapter; and the second half of this Chapter XXVI is very
pertinent to us here. Machiavelli mentions as a model Philip of
Macedon, and quotes on him the bitter words of Justin.[3] Here
surely, if the Villaris are to have any justification for their language,
will be the brigand chief whose *virtù* Machiavelli is bound to admire:
this man who made himself, from being a petty ruler, monarch of
all Greece! This man who, in the words of Justin and Machiavelli
himself, transferred whole peoples as herdsmen do their cattle. Here
is the *facinus* in this forerunner of Hitler: where is the admiration for
it? Alas! Machiavelli turns away from the model he has proposed,
as he did before from Agathocles. 'Sono questi modi crudelissimi, e
nimici d'ogni vivere, non solamente cristiano, ma umano; e debbegli
qualunque uomo fuggire, e volere piuttosto vivere privato, che re
con tanta rovina degli uomini.'[4] That is a most revealing sentence
for the mentality of Machiavelli; only it does not reveal anything
we might have expected from the statements of Villari or Toffanin;
or from any acquaintance with Maritain and machiavellianism.
But in this case Philip of Macedon is not a *model*? No, the word is
misleading—he is a *pattern* which conduct will assume if it goes one
way, and which needs stating for completeness (just as Dante states
hell, while he desires paradise). Again, you must be one thing or
the other, or something in between; and Machiavelli states the
problem starkly, and in terms of good and ill: 'Nondimeno, colui che
non vuole pigliare quella prima via del bene, quando si voglia mantenere conviene che entri in questo male. Ma gli uomini pigliono
certe vie del mezzo, che sono dannosissime; perché non sanno essere
né tutti cattivi né tutti buoni: come nel seguente capitolo, per esemplo
(the example of Julius and Baglioni), si mosterrà.'[5] That makes
Machiavelli's attitude to G.-P. Baglioni perfectly plain before he is
introduced: he is a bad man, and having started on a bad course he
could maintain himself by being wholly bad (and parenthetically, his
badness might even prove of benefit if it cancelled that of Julius II);
but he ends by being merely despicable because he has not personality
to do that. Is it not clear that he stands condemned by Machiavelli

---

[1] VIII, 202: 'Liberate diuturna cura Italiam, extirpate has immanes belluas, quae hominis
praeter faciem et vocem nihil habent.'
[2] Toffanin, *op. cit.*, 376, etc.   [3] Justin, VIII, 5.   [4] *D.* I, XXVI, 88.   [5] *ibid.*

in any case? And that Machiavelli's objectivity dóes not mean
cutting himself adrift from moral considerations?

Nor does it make the matter different that Machiavelli has both
Livy and Tacitus behind him in this objection to the 'vie del mezzo'.
It was a phrase that first came under his pen in that short discourse
of 1503 on the rebellion a year before in the Valdichiana. That was
Machiavelli's initiation to the idea of a full eradication of one's
troubles. It was enthusiastic and unrealistic, and we cannot take it
as anything final. Rather, his Livian connection is one to be examined
next when we turn to its main expression in the *Discourses*. For the
moment, let us content ourselves with looking to Tacitus, who also
concurs with Machiavelli and with the other authors who have
expressed contempt for spinelessness. Thus Tacitus wrote of Fabius
Valens, who dallied, wasting in consultation the time for action,
that in the end he rejected both counsels and did what is the worst of
things, he followed an ambiguous course, '*dum media sequitur*'.[1] Here
also then the middle way is rejected. But Tacitus is not indifferent
to which side a person takes, and his comment a little later on another
similar case makes his position clear. Claudius Apollinaris was
'neither constant in faith, nor strenuous in perfidy'.[2] It is, I hope,
visible that *strenuous in perfidy* is not a term of approval. The attitude
of Tacitus is the same one that Machiavelli adopts towards G.-P.
Baglioni. Machiavelli is in reasonable company, and we may con-
clude: firstly, that it never occurred to him that there was a theory
of *virtú*, so that he is innocent of any systematic use of the word
itself, as of any systematic exclusion of the idea of virtue; and secondly,
that in following Dante and the rest who prefer energy to the lack
of it, he still, with them, prefers a good use of it to a bad one. Have
we not already seen the statements of the *Prince*, and do we not know
from it that if one turns wholly with Philip of Macedon to the left,
not to the right, one will not maintain oneself for long? Once we
have realized that this matter of *virtú* rests largely on prejudice, and
not on reason, we are ready to approach Machiavelli's main statement of his political ideas in his commentary to Livy.

[1] Tacitus, *Hist.*, III, 312.   [2] *ibid.*, 318.

VII

THE *DISCOURSES UPON LIVY*

THE *Discorsi*, whose composition extends over the years 1513 to 1519, represent the capital book of Machiavelli; and it has been an embarrassment even to those who have proclaimed it as such, the majority always having preferred to draw their quotations for the statement of Machiavelli's political doctrine from the *Prince*, as being more handy and more sensational. The careful Burd only noted a score of pages in the *Discorsi* as proof of the fact that Machiavelli's methods here were as unscrupulous as the ones advocated in the *Prince*: though this very list of incriminated passages may lead us automatically to the conception that there is room for more, or other, than wickedness in the *Discorsi*. But proof that this work has been neglected by students of Machiavelli is not far to seek: there is, as of most of Machiavelli, a critically established text for the *Discorsi*; but there has been, as yet, no critical examination of the contents beyond the very partial, and often erroneous, list of sources compiled by Tommasini. Partly, it is the fragmentary and unsystematic nature of Machiavelli's thought that has been blamed for this neglect. Such was the judgment of T. S. Eliot; and something very similar was applied specifically to the *Discorsi* by Mazzoni. You cannot easily summarize the *Discorsi*, and therefore it has seemed easier to abandon the attempt in favour of the *Prince*. Now, it may not be altogether an objection that the *Discorsi* are unsystematic. A Utopia fits everything together within itself, but may nevertheless have no point of contact with reality, or at the most an impractical one. And we may be grateful to Machiavelli for producing an intense local light, a coruscation round particular matters, rather than general theory for which there might be no particular use. It is dangerous to be only a theorist, even if it is baffling to be only a commentator. But does this latter state mean that it is impossible to discover what Machiavelli was doing in the *Discorsi*? that we cannot discern any points to which he attaches primary importance? Because if this were so it would naturally make his commentary less remunerative.

Now we have first Machiavelli's own statement, made plain and unequivocal in his dedication to the work: 'For in it I have set down

all I know, and all that I have learnt in a long conversancy and a
continual reading of affairs.'[1] *Quanto io so, e quanto io ho imparato—*
it is the exhaustive nature of the *Discorsi*, in Machiavelli's intention,
which we should note first. And to this we must add the passage
from the Proem to Book I which emphasizes his approach: the expression of his natural desire to do such things as he believes will
conduce to the common good of all.[2] If we were to analyse these
prefatory statements I think we might find that they derive in no small
measure from Sallust (everybody, Machiavelli will remark casually
later in the *Discorsi*, has read Sallust's *Catiline*) and from Cicero.
Must not Machiavelli have read Cicero's remarks on his enforced
leisure with the feeling that they applied equally to himself?[3] Cicero
and Sallust also turned to writing as a means of pursuing good when
action seemed out of reach. We, after the searchlights have played
on them, may be more critical of the personality of either. Is it not
nearly a hundred years since Taine referred to the latter in unflattering
terms as 'Salluste, qui veut paraître homme de bien faute de l'être'?[4]
But we shall do well to remember that Machiavelli had no such
disintegrating criticism to hand, and that in his time they represent
an honest company.

Quanto io so—if the *Discorsi* represent the whole of Machiavelli's
experience, they must include, or override, the *Prince*. How could
the *Prince* lie outside, or even counter to, the whole of Machiavelli's
experience? The preliminary assertions of the *Discorsi* bear the marks
of sincerity, and encourage us to test the connection between these
latter and the *Prince*. We saw that Machiavelli had tied down his
treatise to a particular context and a particular opportunity; but that
he wrote with such an impetus that the bases of his ideas are some-
times not expressed at all in the *Prince*. Thus in the last chapter there,
he invites his future prince to look at the present time and see in it
one more suited to a *principato nuovo* than any other; but the point
seems to him then so obvious that he describes the conditions without
theorizing. We shall find his conclusions on the need for a *mano
regia* in a chapter of the *Discorsi* which needs reading to complete the
Prince.[5] Similarly, we have seen already that his impetus is too great
in the *Prince* for him to consider at all the danger that might arise from
an initial acceptance of necessary violence. 'Nemo enim unquam
imperium flagitio quaesitum bonis artibus exercuit,' wrote Tacitus

---

[1] *D., Dedica*, 1.   [2] *D. I, Proem*, 5.
[3] *De Off.* III, I, 370: 'nam et a republica forensibusque negotiis, armis impiis vique prohibiti,
otium persequimur; et ob eam causam, urbe relicta, rura peragrantes, saepe soli sumus'.
[4] *Essai sur Tite Live*.   [5] *D. I, LV*.

sadly; and Machiavelli's commentary on this should be within the pages of the *Prince*, but is, instead, in the *Discorsi*.[1] We shall find other points of contact, and before we finish we shall see that there is no reason to think of these two works as antithetical. Only we must never forget that the *Prince* is written sharply, built on a current opportunity, while the *Discorsi* are a musing set against the same contemporary background, but with no idea of an immediate solution.

But, in the meantime, are we to accept those statements of Machiavelli's intentions at their full face value? Well, not all have done so. Out of Taine's discovery of an opposition (if it was the work of Taine, for we might easily push it back to Ginguené, or beyond) between the *Prince* and the *Discorsi* arose a feeling in others of an indifference in Machiavelli to the matter he was analysing, an indifference which was interpreted as cynicism. Others, as Flamini and Burd, chose rather to draw the books together again, but the link they saw lay in an abiding immorality and unscrupulousness. Neither of these conclusions is particularly consonant with an acceptance of Machiavelli's claim to be concerned with the common good. Let us take for a moment a sample reaction from a moderate viewpoint: 'A close student of the realistic policy of ancient Rome, he constantly paralleled current events with the data of Roman history, particularly as they were told by the pessimistic Tacitus; and he was divided between his theoretical tendency to democracy and his practical realization of the necessity of despotism. So that he could illustrate Livy in his *Discorsi* in the light of contemporary events, and draw a picture of the possibilities of despotism in *Il Principe* practically at the same time (1513).'[2] That would establish a different reason for the division between the two works; but it would nevertheless leave a division. It is, however, a statement which has been already in part invalidated by what we have seen. If one tries to derive a theory of despotism from the *Prince* one will find it a much harder task than the title of the book has led its onlookers to suppose: in reality, as we have seen, it looked at external dangers, and insisted strenuously, and uniformly, that internal ones could only be conjured by having the favour of the people. As Machiavelli had learnt already from Livy in 1503, in his first essay on political affairs, and as he will repeat years after in a long quotation in the second book of the *Discorsi*, *Certe id firmissimum imperium est, quo obedientes gaudent*.[3] It is a continuity which is not to be disregarded.

---

[1] D. I, XVIII.
[2] *Italy, a Companion to Italian Studies*, 98. This section is due to Prof. Foligno.
[3] Livy, VIII, 13; cf. *Del metodo di trattare*, etc., II, 386, and D. II, XXIII, 263.

But there are other points in the moderate judgment of Professor Foligno which need examination, and which are scarcely able to survive reflection. Does it not strike an odd note that Tacitus should be put forward as the favourite pasture of Machiavelli, when he chose instead to write his commentary on Livy? Yet, here again, there is not lack of company. Perhaps, indeed, the authors of the *Antimachiavel* led the procession (to go no further back than the eighteenth century) when they cited Tacitus at every turn apropos of the *Prince*. It was a case, they thought, of birds of a feather. And in our own time this supposed bias to Tacitus has been developed into a curiously paradoxical thesis.[1] According to this, the *Discorsi* spring from discussions in the Orti Oricellari, they are dedicated to Buondelmonti and Rucellai, and these latter are by temperament and upbringing Piagnoni, adherents of Savonarola, believers in the republic. Out of this arises the necessity for Machiavelli to cloak his thoughts. If he had had his own way, of course he would have written a commentary on Tacitus: does he not really believe in absolutism? It is only because he has to humour his audience that he chooses Livy. Now, if we were to accept such a theory, it would cancel those phrases of the Dedication and the Proem. How could Machiavelli put in *all* he knew under such circumscribing conditions? But this argument, which suited Toffanin solely because he wanted to discount the *Discorsi* in favour of the *Prince*, runs against a mass of evidence. Was it not, as I have just reminded the reader, Livy, not Tacitus, who sprang naturally to Machiavelli's mind in 1502 on the occasion of the rebellion of Arezzo? Count the times that he draws on Tacitus in the *Discorsi*, and they may reach a dozen, though I do not think they will. But count his debts to Livy, and they run into hundreds. Is not that by itself conclusive? Furthermore, Toffanin took advantage of his discovery to see irony in Machiavelli's words at a few points where he seemed to wax eloquent in favour of democracy, and this *ex hypothesi*; but what he should have found, to make his point acceptable, was a sustained irony throughout, a lack of genuine interest in the matter and the author that Machiavelli was treating against his inclinations. Nobody can discover that, for the very simple reason that it is not there. Whatever other discoveries the candid reader will make about the *Discorsi* he will find that they are honest, transparently so. Machiavelli's Muse is enthusiasm, not irony; and we shall find ourselves much nearer to accepting his own statement of his intentions and performance than the distortion of them advanced

[1] Toffanin, *Machiavelli e il Tacitismo*.

by Toffanin. If we do, is it not clear that we are helped in doing so by what we have found already with regard to Machiavelli's temperament, and his relation to Savonarola? If Buondelmonti and Rucellai are *piagnoni* or republicans, and yet are the friends to whom Machiavelli dedicates his major work, is there not here a straightforward testimony of which we must take stock?

Then it is apparent that we are approaching another important point. What should we think, and what did Machiavelli think, of these Romans to whom he looked back? and what does it signify that he should go back to one author of Roman history rather than to another, especially when that other has been accounted liker to himself in style and temperament? Once more, we must begin with the little treatise of 1503 and with the expression in it of the humanist view of history as 'la maestra delle azioni nostre e massime de'principi, e il mondo fu sempre ad un modo abitato'.[1] What had been a point of rest for Boccaccio, when he made a similar discovery in point of space in the consolatory letter to Pino de'Rossi, becomes an impetus for Machiavelli when it is applied to time. We can look back, he thinks, from our own unsuccessful times, to ones that were better managed, confident that there will be lessons that can be learnt, and that can be applied, since the elements are stated to be the same in all times. But naturally, it follows from such a theory that one must look back to times that were well managed, not to ones which represent a period of decay or dissolution? Of course, inevitably: but if that is so, and it is confirmed by the constant preoccupation of Machiavelli with stability and duration, then equally inevitably it follows that the matter of Tacitus's histories is of much less use to him than is that of Livy. What stability is there in the *Annals* or the *Histories*? It follows, then, that the commentary on Livy is by definition what Machiavelli must desire to write, and that a commentary on Tacitus will be inhibited from developing. So much, for the moment, we may accept as being axiomatic. But there is another point in the judgment that I quoted from the symposium *Italy* which demands some scrutiny, since it will not have escaped notice, and carries with it some odium. It was the opening statement: the one making Machiavelli a 'close student of the realistic policy of ancient Rome'. Now we have our own connotation for that realism, and it is often able to generate more highly-coloured views than appear with Professor Foligno. Let us put it at its most damaging, so that we may see where we stand: 'Machiavel adopte, selon le principe de la République romaine,

1 Cf. *Petr. and the Ren.*, 101.

la prospérité de l'Etat aux dépens de l'individu, et l'on sait que Rome n'a renoncé à aucune ruse et a eu recours à toutes les injustices et aux pires cruautés pour fonder son pouvoir et l'étendre.'[1] We think, then, of the Romans as ruthless in their adherence to the *ragion di Stato*, as machiavellian in their realism: therefore, we argue, this is what Machiavelli had in mind in looking back to them, and their machiavellianism is a proof of his. Such reasoning is very natural, and the mind listens to it very readily. But it is more facile than it is sound, and the fact that it has passed without some scrutiny or some challenge shows that simple directives are necessary for dealing with the subject of the *Discorsi*.

There is, in reality, a clear and interesting curve in the assessment of the ancient Romans, and it is necessary before we evaluate Machiavelli to place him somewhere on its path, and not right at the end of it along with ourselves. Nor is there any need for me to enter into any excess of detail in establishing the curve. Dante saw the Roman Empire as the culminating achievement of human reason operating without grace, and as the essential prerequisite of the Redemption. Petrarch saw also a Christian destiny to Rome: the prize of victory in the contest with Carthage was the domination of the world, and it was not only his admiration for Scipio that made Petrarch sure where victory would lie. *Quid est omnis historia nisi Romana laus?* he asked somewhere in a moment of expansiveness. But in spite of this lead, with a growing knowledge of the Roman emperors, and a move away from the aprioristic arguments of Dante, the enthusiasm of the humanists is for the Roman republic, not for the Empire; and it was in Livy that the virtues of the Roman republic were admired, and accepted. Livy is the Roman historian for the fifteenth century, and the interest in him, and the editions of him, far outweighs the interest in what was known of Tacitus's text. We know that Machiavelli follows in the wake of this movement, and that he comes to ancient history not with the mission of the research student, to establish what had been, in the place of what was said by Livy to have been. Instead, he comes with the idealism of a temperament looking for what might still be, in his own time. There is a pretty instance of this uncritical nature of Machiavelli in a remark he makes about Herodian: 'E se non fosse la riverenza dello istorico, io non crederrei mai che fosse possibile quello che Erodiano dice di Plauziano . . .'[2] If he shows such respect for Herodian, then *a fortiori* he does not come scepticism in hand to his reading of Livy. And

---

[1] Gautier Vignal, 213.   [2] *D.* III, VI, 332.

everything, as we have seen, conspires to send him to Livy, not to
Tacitus. Livy is a constructive writer, and as well, his picture is one
that is very close to the purpose of Machiavelli. What is the Italy of
Machiavelli's time, but a pattern of city-states that stand in rivalry
among themselves? And what is Livy's Rome?—a city-state that
stands at first in the same case, and then by its adherence to certain
virtues and to certain *order* emerges to supremacy. Just as Machiavelli
always calls the inhabitants of France or Gaul equally *Franciosi*,
because of his principle of identity of elements in differing times,
so he sees a necessary identity between the political struggle of early
Roman times and that of his own age. Nor, and here I am brought
back to the question of the curve, does he suspect Livy's account of
being an idealized version, reflecting in its texture the Augustan age
of Rome. We are, with Machiavelli, before the emergence of the
absolute monarchies of Europe, which dates from the ascendancy
of Charles V, and it is only after that phenomenon that the preoccupation with Tacitus instead of Livy, so marked at the end of the sixteenth
century, will come. Even then, Livy is not so much debunked, as
demoded. We have only to look to the French dramatic writers of
the early seventeenth century, to Rotrou and Corneille for instance,
to see reflected the new interests of Europe:

> Sans rendre ni raison, ni compte de mes voeux,
> Je veux ce que je veux, parce que je le veux,

as Rotrou most elegantly expressed it.[1] Nor must it be thought that
such a couplet is unauthoritative because it is taken from a tragi-
comedy, and not (as would be fitting) from a tragedy. 'Sans cette
autorité absolue, le roi ne peut ni faire le bien, ni réprimer le mal,'
writes Bossuet,[2] and he and Racine are in accord in thinking that a
subject suffering oppression from his legitimate prince has no right
in any case to revolt, and can only ask justice of God 'qui seul a droit
de faire rendre compte aux rois de leurs actions'.[3] The path from this,
as Machiavelli would have seen, is straight to the French Revolution;
and the reverse of the medal will be shown in William Hone's slogan
on The Right Divine of Kings to Govern Wrong. Is it so much of
an inconvenience that the political thought of Machiavelli (and even
more explicitly, of his contemporary Guicciardini[4]) anticipates
Montesquieu by not positing any *legitimate* rule?

I have digressed a moment to look at a new trend of thought

---

[1] *Laure Persécutée*, I, x.   [2] Cf. Cherel, 222, as also 151–4.
[3] Racine, *Abrégé de l'Histoire de Port-Royal*, in *Oeuvres*, éd. Mesnard, IV, 476, q.v.
[4] Cf. the most important passage in *Reggimento*, 163.

which grows up in Europe after the establishment of the concentrated monarchy, but it is a digression which we shall not regret later when we see more clearly in what way Machiavelli stands outside this movement. At present it is enough to note that the new tendency is to look to absolutism, rather than a looking against republicanism. That is why Livy recedes from view without being called very much in question. It is by one of those precursors of the eighteenth century that the first stones are thrown against Livy: read Saint-Evremond's *Réflexions* on the Roman people, and you will feel, slight as is this unsystematic and unfinished work, that a new spirit of irreverence towards the old republican virtues breathes through it. In Machiavelli's pages we shall find the venerable figure of Brutus put forward as a pattern. Saint-Evremond has a very different argument about him. The success of Rome, for him, made its origins appear respectable (just as we are unready to imagine that the man we see in the palace began life in the gutter). But how do we know that Brutus put his sons to death through virtue sternly followed? Might not ambition be the motive power? Perhaps he calculated that the choice lay between establishing his own power by this horrible example, or else retiring from the scene?[1] Such an attitude is most corrosive. It may be only a resumption of the scepticism that made its appearance with Valla in the fifteenth century, but which in the earnestness of humanism did not then have its effect. At least, when it is born anew it can bear fruit. And already it permeates Saint-Evremond. Do you remember how long old Cincinnatus had masqueraded as the pattern of the frugal mind in his passage from the plough to the Dictatorship, then back once more to the plough? But this, said Saint-Evremond, was not a frugal virtue reposing on choice: it was merely the reflection of a primitive way of life.[2] Where else should a ploughman go back, than to his plough? With this there is a natural revaluation of such old favourites as the geese that saved the Capitol, greeted now by a smile of polite derision—they trusted to geese and dogs for safe guard! A somewhat childish art of war! But, more significant still, there is in Saint-Evremond as there is in his contemporary Fénelon what will be given supreme expression with Montesquieu, the idea of these early Romans not only as uncouth barbarians, but also as troublesome aggressors: 'A proprement parler, les Romains étoient des voisins fâcheux et violens, qui vouloient chasser les justes possesseurs de leurs maisons, et labourer, la force à la main, les champs des autres.'[3] That begs the question without the reader really noticing

---

[1] *Réflexions sur les Divers Génies*, etc., 10.   [2] *ibid.*, 12.   [3] *ibid.*, 11.

it: we register the label for the Romans in our minds, without the certificate of moral superiority for their neighbours, on which the badness of the first depends for its effectiveness, receiving any attention. But Fénelon says the same, and the modern attitude to the Romans is initiated.[1]

Now we shall find later that there are a few links to be discussed between Machiavelli's statements on aggression in *Discorsi* II and these views of Saint-Evremond. But nevertheless this is in reality a revolution in outlook which has been accomplished. Partly, it represents a greater use of historians other than Livy, as, for example, Polybius and Florus (who, though like Livy he speaks of the ancient Romans as being powerful by their respect for law and treaties, yet is much franker in speaking of Roman aggression, as in the matter of the defence of Messina which was only an excuse for the First Punic War, the real cause being covetous eyes cast upon Sicily). But partly, also, it is the prelude to the disrespect of the eighteenth century, to the spirit of Montesquieu and Voltaire. And it is when we follow on to Montesquieu's account that we first find an exposé of Roman conduct that might easily have served for a copybook for Hitler, with treaties meant to be violated, the yielding of an adversary at one point merely an earnest for a series of yieldings, tribute imposed to make rulers unpopular, and so forth.[2] Montesquieu thus systematized a new view of the Romans which Machiavelli in his simplicity never dreamt of. Then, finally, to add the coping-stone, when that revision in values had been long digested, there came another great French critic to systematize it in its relation to Livy himself. It was Taine who declared that Livy had never understood the barbaric ages of Rome: in the speeches (where Livy's ideas are to be found) primitive characters speak with the polish of contemporaries of Augustus. Only too occasionally is there a window back on to the primitive past. And from that classic viewpoint of Taine the way is clear to the judgment of a Ferrero, who contrasted all the useless monuments of Rome with the useful achievements of the peaceful English in building half the railways of Europe. Thus from a Livy who was quasi-infallible, in that first flush of humanist enthusiasm, there has developed a new Livy who is largely a failure. And perhaps his reputation has never quite recovered from the blow which Taine had dealt him. At least, it is in our own time only that there is a backwards movement of the pendulum; and certainly it is not my business to concern myself with that now.

[1] *Dialogues des Morts*, VIII, 28, for Tatius's charges against Romulus.   [2] *Grandeur et Décadence*.

But in the meantime, to go back to the argument of Gautier Vignal, it is clear from this account how little right we have to say: We know the tricks of the Romans, and Machiavelli admired them because he wanted to be tarred with their brush. We have removed, then, one obstacle; and, once again, it acts retrospectively. 'Il avait étudié l'histoire de la Rome républicaine, et il prouvera plus tard dans ses écrits qu'il en admirait trop la politique réaliste pour éprouver aucune sympathie envers la théocratie chimérique du dominicain.'[1] That is to say, Machiavelli may not at this point either be necessarily an opposite to Savonarola, and certainly, since he had Livy's view, he did not have a realistic view of Roman policy, in the sense that we interpret the adjective after Montesquieu and Taine. He had, then, an idealized view, not only that of Livy, but that of Livy uncritically accepted. Now it might appear from this that the *Discorsi* are going to be to a great extent invalidated before we get to them. If they are an idealistic gloss to an idealized history, what contact with realism, or even with reality, will they retain? or what contact with Machiavelli? For in the latter's case we know how often the critic's eye has been arrested by the plain speaking in which Machiavelli indulged at the beginning of Chapter XV in the *Prince*: there where he mocked at imaginary republics, and spoke what seemed the decisive words about the *verità effettuale* which he preferred to follow himself.[2] Now perhaps not the least piquant thing about that passage is that Machiavelli may have had Livy himself in the back of his mind in making it. For it was Livy who anticipated it by remarking pessimistically, 'si qua sit sapientium civitas, quam docti fingunt magis, quam norunt'.[3] And Livy, like Machiavelli after him, makes the comment in good faith. But that did not prevent him from joining the doctors, and fashioning early Rome as such a city. Are we, then, obliged to accept it for Machiavelli, as everyone has readily done, at its face value? I think it is largely a misleading remark.

But perhaps, if we were to make such an admission, it would involve a destruction of confidence in the value of the *Discorsi*, comparable to that which Taine effected for the *Decades* of Livy himself? Take truth out of history, said Polybius, at the outset of his own narrative, and it will be as though you had cancelled the light of the eye from a body: all that is left is useless, and so also will the narrative become. But if this may be true when we limit ourselves to the consideration of what did happen, it is not necessarily the same when we turn instead to consider what we may achieve. The whole

---

[1] Gautier Vignal, 48. [2] *P.* XV, 30. [3] Livy, XXVI, 22.

scope of Machiavelli's *Discourses* is intended to be constructive. We may class him amongst those whom he calls, in a picturesque phrase from this same book, 'questi scrittori della civiltà'. Civilization is a construction, not a destruction. Is it not apparent that, however much people may hanker for an attachment between Machiavelli and Tacitus, it is Livy who inevitably provides a base? and for the precise reason that he is going in the right *direction*? Suppose we were to accept the pessimistic conclusion of the Spanish poet, that this life is a pack of cards, badly shuffled, and subject to hazards which we can in no wise control?

> Toda esta vida es jugar
> Una carteta imperfeta,
> Mal barajada, y sujeta
> A desdichas y a pesares;
> Que es toda en cientos y azares
> Como juego de carteta.

What is left, after the adoption of such an attitude, but the gesture of despair and resignation? But supposing we modify that only slightly, and answer still in very similar coin with Terence that we must use our skill to make the game come right?

> Ita vita est hominum, quasi, cum ludas tesseris;
> Si illud, quod maxumo opus est jactu, non cadit,
> Illud, quod cecidit forte, id arte ut corrigas.

Or if we preferred a more modern idiom (for this is a serious matter, and we must get it right), we might give ear to Boileau:

> Le vrai peut quelquefois n'être pas vraisemblable.

Does it not follow that we must build it as we want it to be? And is not Livy automatically Machiavelli's author, not only because of the background of humanism (though this is moving also towards Boileau's statement), but because Livy's conscious or unconscious building of a façade to early Roman history can be the basis for a *lesson*, as distinct from a *warning*? It is here too that we must grapple, as Boileau with the terms *vrai* and *vraisemblable* (and this is the reason that I introduced Boileau into the argument), with the misleading word *realism*. It cannot be only what is real that is realistic: for it may be only (and, indeed, it most often will be) the mess that men have made of what was and of what might have been. To be concerned with what may be will then prove more realistic than to be concerned only with what is. Just as the *vrai* in its cruel and disappointing statement may turn out to be very different from the *vraisemblable*, so the *real* may often prove most *unrealistic*. Does not, with Boileau, the principle of classical art, which is progress from what was to what should be because it can be, hang on this issue? Nor if we give assent to such an argument are we re-establishing the *dover essere* of De Sanctis's Middle Ages in place of the *essere* of the new age of Machiavelli. What *ought to be* has no obligatory coincidence with what *can be*, and the statements of the two are normally as far apart as chalk from cheese. The first leads us, does it not? to Dante and to Bossuet: to the monarch who should have everything within his grasp, so that he may be above cupidity of anything;[1] to the king who must be absolute in order to be paternal.[2] The second is the genuine discovery of Machiavelli, and is the one that leads us on to Montesquieu and to the modern world, which has no longer any use for the political ideas of either Bossuet or Dante. Indeed, we shall discover the specific rebuttal of these postulates of both before we finish with the *Discorsi*. It follows, then, from this that we may feel the *Discorsi* have their value, even if they are on very different ground from that chosen for Machiavelli by many of his expositors.

It is with this in mind that we should turn to read the main chapter where Machiavelli shows his acquaintance with Tacitus—the tenth chapter of Book I. It is something fundamental for Machiavelli's intentions and his outlook. Nor, if the reader has given me any credence so far, will he be misled by Toffanin's ingenious thesis of Machiavelli buttering his republican friends, and therefore writing here exaggeratedly, somewhat rhetorically or theatrically. It begins with the establishment of two categories of men, the one most praised, the other most infamous: those who build, and those who destroy, the fabric of civilization. Perhaps, again, in establishing the descending hierarchy of these infamous undoers of civilization Machiavelli echoes consciously the comment of Cicero on such men as Catiline, Caesar, Antony, the Gracchi.[3] But such a coincidence will not lessen the value of his attitude; and for him it is something axiomatic and incontrovertible. 'E nessuno sarà mai sí pazzo o sí savio, sí tristo o sí buono, che, prepostagli la elezione delle due qualità d'uomini, non laudi quella che è da laudare, e biasimi quella che è da biasimare.'[4] Such certainty springs from no pessimistic view of the nature of man: the good, by definition, is what we desire; and it is only by a mistake in its discernment that men go wrong. That is not very far from the great principle of Thomas Aquinas, *Malum nihil agit nisi virtute boni.*

[1] Dante, *De Mon.*, I, XIII. Cf. A. H. Gilbert, *Dante's Conception of Justice*, 48 and 55.
[2] Cf. Cherel, 151–4.   [3] *De Off.*, I, XVII, 214.   [4] *D.* I, X, 44.

Nor need we be surprised, says Machiavelli, that writers, corrupted by his good fortune, have praised Caesar: look what they said of Catiline, when there was no need to spare his feelings, for a truer estimate of Caesar—Caesar, who is worse because he did what Catiline only hoped to do. And it is after this that Machiavelli paints the picture of Rome under its few good emperors to contrast it with the horrors under the bad. No one who comes with an open ear to these passages of Chapter X could possibly mistake their lyrical note for anything but rapture, or give credence to the misguided view that there was a lurking sarcasm beneath their surface. 'Perché, in quelli governati da'buoni, vedrà un principe sicuro in mezzo de'suoi sicuri cittadini; ripieno di pace e di giustizia il mondo: vedrà il Senato con la sua autorità, i magistrati co'suoi onori; godersi i cittadini ricchi le loro ricchezze; la nobilità e la virtú esaltata: vedrà ogni quiete ed ogni bene; e, dall'altra parte, ogni rancore, ogni licenza, corruzione e ambizione spenta: vedrà i tempi aurei, dove ciascuno può tenere e difendere quella opinione che vuole. Vedrà, in fine, trionfare il mondo; pieno di riverenza e di gloria il principe, d'amore e sicurtà i popoli.'[1] Does not such a passage echo obviously the fervour we have seen in the last chapter of the *Prince*? Only, there is this difference: that there Machiavelli was fervent in the statement of something regrettable, and is fervent here over something to be desired.

From that picture Machiavelli turns to the opposing one, and nothing is more significant, or more conclusive, than the fact that here is his most extensive debt to Tacitus. Here, in this very chapter which was rhetorical because it was false, because it diverged from Machiavelli's interest in the world of Tacitus, Machiavelli is found paraphrasing Tacitus's own summary of the theme of his *Histories*! 'Italy afflicted, and full of new misfortunes, its towns ruined and sacked. . . . He will see Rome burnt, the Capitol undone by Rome's own citizens. . . . He will see innumerable acts of cruelty in Rome. . . .'[2] It is as clear as anything ever can be that it is because of this theme of the 'pessimistic Tacitus' that Machiavelli must find Livy to be his author. And this expression of opposites is followed, as I indicated in discussing the temperament of Machiavelli, by the inspiring affirmation: 'E sanza dubbio, se e'sarà nato d'uomo, si sbigottirà da ogni imitazione de'tempi cattivi, ed accenderassi d'uno immenso desiderio di seguire i buoni.'[3] That carries Machiavelli on to something reminiscent of Petrarch, in a *canzone* which Machiavelli knew

---

[1] *D.* I, X, 47.   [2] *ibid.* and cf. Tacitus, *Hist.*, I, II.   [3] *D.* I, X, 47.

well, since he quotes it in the *Istorie Fiorentine* at a point only a line
or so away:

> Quanta gloria ti fia
> Dir: Gli altri l'aitâr giovene e forte,
> Questi in vecchiezza la scampò da morte.[1]

If one were a prince, one should desire corruption to reorder, as a
lasting monument to oneself; and Machiavelli concludes his chapter
by observing that if the ordering aright a city (we must note the
word, for it will be useful again soon) involved of necessity the re-
nunciation of rule, then there would be some excuse for not perform-
ing it. But since rule may be retained, and yet government ordered
aright, then there is no excuse. Men must consider that there are two
ways before them: one leading to security, and to posthumous glory;
the other to continual fear, with after death the portion of eternal
infamy. There is no dissonance here from what we have already
found within the pages of the *Prince*. This option does not mean that
Machiavelli can be thinking of a despot as useful for himself, or for
anyone else; but he may still be thinking of a prince. We shall find
that in much of the *Discorsi* a balance is maintained: does Machiavelli
recommend a monarchy, or a republic? The answer to the question
has varied according to the prejudice of the critic, so that from Taine's
affirmation of the *Discorsi* as the theory of republicanism we have
advanced to a denial of such interests in Machiavelli on the part of
Fascist, or crypto-Fascist, criticism. If there were not some room for
hesitation then it would be hard for the back to be turned on the part
that is not wanted. And, indeed, we may find Machiavelli answering
the question by saying (and more than once) that the general look
no further than to public order. In other words, we shall find that
he is not absolutely preoccupied with the question in those terms.
But we must not forget what this chapter reveals so plainly: that he
looks to no absolute rule. There is never anything to cancel the
categorical statement at the end of *D.* I, XXXV, that an absolute
authority corrupts in the shortest space of time.

Well, what would Machiavelli like best? It may surprise the
reader, though the measure in which it does so will be the measure
also of prejudices still lurking with regard to Machiavelli's intentions.
He would like a Florence, at rest, unaggressive, but active and strong
enough to defend herself. That is the root of his preoccupation with
the *city*—that term we have seen replacing the concept of native land
for Machiavelli. Was not a *patria* always a city, not a country for

---

[1] Petrarch, *Rime*, LIII, 96–8.

him? so much so that he was at a loss for the latter word, employing
usually *provincia*, which might seem to mean something quite
different. The statement of this political ideal, very strong, though
it might seem casually introduced, is at the end of *D. I, VI.* The best
thing would be a city well ordered for defence, without ambitions
externally, and all the better if this lack of ambition has official seal
in the constitution by a provision against expansion. 'E sanza dubbio
credo, che, potendosi tenere la cosa bilanciata in questo modo, che
e'sarebbe il vero vivere politico, e la vera quiete d'una città.'[1] How
affectionately those two *vero* cling round their nouns ! It is easy to see
from them how local are Machiavelli's interests, how modest, and
especially, how honest. And should we not note too how this
Machiavelli who was stated to be pessimistic, all 'doubt and searching',
has a habit of plunging forward into an affirmative with an 'E sanza
dubbio credo'? He would like, then, a Florence unmolesting and un-
molested. Yes, but this last is not what he has seen? And, then,
perhaps, such bliss is not practicable? It is here that the external
considerations force themselves across Machiavelli's inclinations, and
lead him on to conclusions alien to his temperament, and to the observation of flux in human affairs; and this, perhaps, as we can see where
Machiavelli comes back to it, leads in turn to too geometrical an
assumption, the basis of an error in Machiavelli's account, the idea,
that is, of a balance to be struck between the ups and downs so that
the elements are always numerically, as well as potentially, the same.
On the contrary, it is because all are free to move in any direction
that the combinations are so colossal and so incalculable. Meanwhile,
the statement of flux is characteristic: 'Ma sendo tutte le cose degli
uomini in moto, e non potendo stare salde, conviene che le salghino,
o che le scendino; e a molte cose che la ragione non t'induce, t'induce
la necessità. . . .'[2] Reason, and inclination, says Florence; *necessity* says
something else,

> La raison dit Virgile, et la rime dit Quinaut.

This is something which strikes an answering chord. Count this
theme of necessity in its several occurrences, as noun or adjective, on
this one page: they add up to no less than five. It means that, when we
test it cautiously, the book of the *Discorsi* turns out to be cognate to
the *Prince*, in spite of that old opposition which Taine formulated
between them.

Where, then, does necessity lead? It leads first, not without rela-

---

[1] *D. I, VI,* 31.   [2] *ibid.,* 32.

tion to the *Prince* itself (though we must not forget that we are starting with a city-state, not with a nation), to the conclusion that one
should prefer in this world of ups and downs—as may be self-
apparent—to *go up*, rather than to *come down*. It is the key, once again,
to his choice of early Rome as theme for his discussion. For here, as I
have observed elsewhere in a different context, Machiavelli's anxiety
to learn a lesson from history causes an innocent betrayal. The history
of Rome represents the rise of an obscure colony till it becomes the
head of a vast empire co-extensive with the known world. Machiavelli therefore draws a line through what took place, starting from
the assumption that this progress was foreseen, and so provided for.
Had he been able to read Livy XLI (still unfound when he was
writing) he would have noted its opening passage, and accepted its
statement on Rome's moderation in her expansion: when things
went well, Rome was powerful by authority rather than by rule;
and she made it her boast to conduct affairs with other peoples
more by counsel than by force and terror.[1] And he would have
accepted, as something noted before in earlier books (in the matter of
Greece, for instance), the idea of Rome as having preserved the laws
and liberties of conquered races. But he would perhaps have halted
at the idea that the rise of Rome was something accidental and un-
foreseen, springing from the rivalry of others, rather than attendant
on any set course pursued by Rome.[2] It is a matter on which we
shall not find Machiavelli speaking with an undivided voice, when
we come finally to the main discussion of it in the second book of his
Discorsi. But for the moment, at least, it is clear that Machiavelli
needs to recommend the Romans as having been conscious of what
they were doing for the preservation (and therefore for the expansion)
of their State.

We may take it, then, as clear why Machiavelli goes back to Rome,
and why he goes back to Livy. The resolution of this problem, however, leaves us confronted with another important question which we
cannot shelve. It will be remembered that Petrarch appealed to
Charles IV with words that were a presentiment of Machiavelli:
'Believe me, Caesar, the world is the same it was, the sun the same,
the elements the same: virtue alone is diminished.' Nor will it have
been forgotten that the heirs of Petrarch thought the same: 'As if
character and gravity of life were not the same then as they are now !'[3]

---

[1] Livy, XLI, 1: 'Sed in tanta fluentium,' etc.
[2] *ibid.* 'Augendae dominationi causam materiamque praebuit potius inconsulta hostium et
aemulorum pravitas, quam ipsius ambitio.'
[3] Cf. *Petr. and the Ren.*, 29 and 102.

In this matter of going back Machiavelli is indisputably, as he felt himself to be, in the humanist tradition. But is he justified in his assumption when it is applied to the scene of history? The basis is plain enough: the elements of the political scene are the same in every age, their combination only is different. Hence the possibility of learning from the right combinations that have been. The objection, however, is plain also: Machiavelli lacks the idea of a historical evolution, a theory which emerges only much later than the sixteenth century. Is not this something which invalidates the *Discorsi* at the outset? That, of course, is the objection which Guicciardini made, without him having formulated the theory of historical development itself: it was no longer time to be having the Romans always on one's lips! It is Guicciardini who raises the objection first, and ironically enough we may appeal, amongst many texts, to Guicciardini himself against the objection. Are we not now, with all the developments of modern science and of modern thought, entirely outside the range of the fifteenth century? Could we apply any situation of that time, by a mere transposition of names, to make it fit, or nearly fit, our own times? If we can find so much contact over so wide a gap, then there will be nothing odd in Machiavelli finding it over what was a lesser gap.

There is in one of Guicciardini's most interesting, and most important, lesser works an account of the situation of Florence in the fifteenth century *vis-à-vis* the desire of Filippo-Maria Visconti to recover domains that had been lost. 'He sought to lull our city with the request for a peace most honourable for us, and as secure as could be desired if it had lasted. This deceit was seen through by Nicolò da Uzzano and a few other prudent ones, who saw how he did not desire peace and friendship with us, but by this means to remove the obstacle we made to the establishment of his affairs in Lombardy and the acquisition of Genoa, then after he could turn to extinguish us; and though in committee and council they pointed out this danger, nevertheless the name of peace was so pleasant to both merchants and people that, refusing the advice of the prudent, they accepted what he proposed. And where safely and with slight expenditure they could have stopped the rise of his power, they had to enter on very long and very dangerous wars, in which they used up infinite wealth and compromised a great deal of the dignity of the city; for Florence was compelled to ally herself with Venice on such terms as the Venetians saw fit to grant; nor was it possible to escape this danger without creating another one, that is, by aggrandizing the

Venetians, who have been ever since redoubtable for Florence.'[1]
That is, no doubt, a longer quotation than I ought to make from
anybody else than Machiavelli; nor do I wish to run on into the
dismal prognostications which might be suggested by its close. But
without doing that, is it not clear that if we were to use this as a
palimpsest, in order to transfer its concern from Florence and Milan
in the fifteenth century to England and Germany in the period before
1939, we should have little to cancel beyond the proper names, and
that we should find it still apt and illuminating? If there is anything
to be altered, it is in the scale of the transactions, not in their nature.

That, to us, may represent a depressing impotence of human affairs
to lift themselves out of a state only too familiar. In a way it may
seem that in progressing from the stage of constant and inevitable
warfare (of each against each, and all against all)—a time when the
margin over brute life is either non-existent or else negligible—
the intervals which have allowed that margin to be established or
even elaborated have only magnified the basic factors at work in
human relationships, but have never really altered them. How else
could the pattern of Hitler correspond so closely to that of Filippo-
Maria Visconti? It may appear that mankind has always been faced
with the unfortunate lot of those unhappy Byzantines of Polybius's
account—who lived peaceably in the fertile Bosphorus; and just as
they had tilled their fields and prepared for the rich harvest of corn
and fruit, the Thracians from outside came down in war to make
the most of it. Any stoppage in the basic human trade of war means
two things: it means a lack of appetite for carnage in those engaged
in building up the margin which we know as civilization; it means
playing for higher stakes or with larger counters when the burst
comes. And if we can discover not only a fundamental likeness
between the scene of fifteenth-century Italy and part of our own time,
but even an identity in substance, then the historical progression must
not be exaggerated. Nor, indeed, has it been felt by historians to have
made any unbridgeable gulf, or to have prevented Machiavelli's
commentary from having a range of applicability over subsequent
events. 'The authentic interpreter of Machiavelli, the *Commentarius
Perpetuus* of the *Discorsi* and the *Prince*, is the whole of later history,'
wrote Lord Acton; and nobody who has experienced Machiavelli's
acumen, and observed the light that falls on matters contemporary
with himself from Machiavelli's account of ones in his own day, or in
antiquity, will venture to dispute so authoritative a dictum. How

[1] Guicciardini, *Reggimento*, 61-2.

could such a remark be possible if the process of historical evolution led us from one scale of values to another that was quite different? In between Machiavelli and Lord Acton there comes Montesquieu, who appeals to the same principle as Machiavelli: 'L'histoire moderne nous fournit un exemple de ce qui arriva pour lors à Rome, et ceci est bien remarquable; car, comme les hommes ont eu dans tous les temps les mêmes passions, les occasions qui produisent les grands changemens sont différentes, mais les causes sont toujours les mêmes.'[1]

The acute vision of Machiavelli is, then, not necessarily at fault in looking back to Roman times; nor will Livy's conscious or unconscious organization of Rome's own past be a liability. Does not that already show the intelligence of man ordering the chaos of political phenomena? It has a future relevance, if not a past accuracy. For to establish the past merely as it was is a work of archaeological importance primarily: to establish it as it might have been is both a suggestion, and a furtherance, of achievement. Nor, as we have seen, does this mean a return to the political world of Dante. There the endeavour was to look for the theory first, and to assume that human affairs should adjust themselves to it, and that if they did not do so totally then they were doomed for ever to be wrong; this following the principle of Dante for affairs in general,

Che di su prendono e di sotto fanno.[2]

Here the procedure is the reverse, and derives from Petrarch's search for a solution out of possibilities; and what has been done as a play of the intelligence may be done again as a play of the intelligence, but this time operating over similar factors as they occur, instead of when they have occurred. In it the concern of Machiavelli will be with *stability*, with *durability*. One critic, at least, has put together Machiavelli's references to this idea of stability, and the accumulation shows unmistakably his preoccupation with it.[3] But it is perhaps here, then, that we have him, and that the *Discorsi* will be invalidated? For we have seen that Machiavelli starts with a very different idea from stability in his mind: 'Ma sendo tutte le cose degli uomini in moto, e non potendo stare salde, conviene che le salghino, o che le scendino. . . .' If human affairs cannot, by definition, ever be stable, what will it profit Machiavelli to have taken from Cicero the basis of political life as security, since, in the nature of things, there can be no security? Yet this last is what Machiavelli has done; and if we look at his statement in *D*. I, XVI, we shall find it to have an

---

[1] Montesquieu, *Grandeur et Déc.*, I, 354.   [2] *Parad.*, II, 123.   [3] Collotti, 25.

indubitably Ciceronian air: 'quella comune utilità che del vivere libero si trae . . . la quale è di potere godere liberamente le cose sue sanza alcuno sospetto, non dubitare dell'onore delle donne, di quel de'figliuoli, non temere di sé . . .'[1] Can this be made to fit in with the *ups* and *downs*—a theme which is also neo-classical, as we can see by its appearance in its starkest form in *D*. I, XLVI, where what looks like (and is) Machiavelli at his most pregnant, turns out to be a direct translation from Livy. 'E l'ordine di questi accidenti è che, mentre che gli uomini cercono di non temere, cominciono a fare temere altrui; e quella ingiuria che gli scacciano da loro, la pongono sopra un altro; come se fusse necessario offendere o essere offeso.'[2] That is, indeed, a depressing sequence, and a pessimistic conclusion. Apply it to private affairs, and we shall not feel secure in the possession of anything; apply it to public matters, and it may lead us on to such melancholy wonderings as whether the end of one imperialism can be anything than the birth of another; or to the reflections of the poets.

> Great *Carthage* low in Ashes cold doth lie,
> Her Ruines poor the Herbs in height scant pass,
> So Cities fall, so perish Kingdoms hie,
> Their Pride and Pomp lies hid in Sand and Grass:
> Then why should Mortal Man repine to die,
> Whose Life, is Air; Breath, Wind; and Body, Glass?

What can be more melancholy, or more appropriate, than the younger Scipio's observations on the dismal end of Carthage, falling like Troy, and following the lot of the kingdoms of the Assyrians, the Medes and Persians, who before had risen to the peak of their prosperity?[3] *Difficilis mora in summo est*: we may be approaching it, or receding from it; we may be offending, or we may be offended; but we shall not be still. Once more, if I may pause to point the parallel, Montesquieu speaks the language of Machiavelli, or of Livy: 'Mais, par une maladie éternelle des hommes, les plébeiens, qui avaient obtenu des tribuns pour se défendre, s'en servirent pour attaquer.'[4] Nor, if we wished to do so, should we find much difficulty in transferring his observation to our own day.

All this is very true; but far from invalidating the *Discorsi*, it predetermines them. Let us look at the matter once again. In the general

[1] *De Off.*, II, XXI, 354: 'Hanc enim ob causam maxime, ut sua tenerent respublicae civitatesque constitutae sunt.'

[2] Livy, III, 65: '. . . cavendoque ne metuant homines, metuendos ultro se efficiunt: et iniuriam a nobis repulsam, tanquam aut facere aut pati necesse sit, iniungimus aliis.'

[3] See the moving account in Appian, who is, with Florus, among the least used of the historians to whom Machiavelli had access.

[4] Montesquieu, *Grandeur et Décad.*, VIII, 406.

flux of political forms, Machiavelli seeks the formula of stability.
He found not only Livy's Rome, but he found alongside Livy a
reasoned exposé of the causes for Rome's endurance. I think it is
plain that the fragments of Polybius's sixth book were known to
Machiavelli, though they were not in Perotti's Latin translation that
had been in print since 1473. I have no means to solve this puzzle,
and no wish to open here again the question of Machiavelli's knowledge of Greek. Rather, I take it as quite plain that he did not know
Greek. But all the vital leads in *D.* I, II, are to be found in the fragments of Polybius, and I think that we may accept as certain that this
rationalization of Rome was known to Machiavelli; that he learnt
from it the weakness of the three simple forms of government, their
tendency to degenerate into their adjacent pejoratives; and the
resourcefulness of Lycurgus, who sought to prevent that cycle of
recurrent forms because he saw the process of decay generated by
the vices inherent in each simple form. Lycurgus made an equipoise—
just as on ship the cargo is distributed so that its weight falls evenly
throughout. The proof of his success? Look to the length of duration
of the state he ordered, to the eight hundred years which caught
Machiavelli's eye. Then following Lycurgus, in Polybius's account,
to make doubly sure that Machiavelli is listening to the tale, there
come the Romans, who reached the same goal as Lycurgus, but by
chance, by the way events developed. But in any case, however it
came to pass, they more excellently than all others ordered their
estate. In its three parts (with consuls, senate, and tribunes speaking
for the people) it was so evenly poised that it would be hard to decide
to which of the three orthodox forms of government it belonged.
And because of this it was a form of state unconquered, and invincible:
nothing was too hard for Rome in time of war; and in peace,
when ease leads on to wantonness, the remedy lay within Rome's
constitution.[1]

I have set out the gist of Polybius's observations, and I refer the
reader to Machiavelli's use of them, and of the cycle theme, in the
admirable Chapter II of *Discorsi* I. Not a crumb has fallen unheeded
there (or if the last one has fallen elsewhere, it is none the less grate-
fully accepted by Machiavelli: it is the wisdom of having remedies
to hand from within, not from outside, a constitution, and his
nomenclature we shall find to be a distinction of *ordinary* and *extraordinary* remedies—the first which heal, the second which disrupt,
the State). What will be most striking, I think, to the reader who

---

[1] I have used the translation of Domenichi, Giolito, 1564, 323–48.

makes the comparison between Polybius and Machiavelli is not so much that the latter has copied his ideas, as the ease with which he handles his material, and the genuinity of his intellectual assent to the thesis which Polybius expounded. With Machiavelli we must never forget the noble words he wrote in the most eloquent of all his letters, the one prefixed usually to editions of the *Prince*, in which he gave details to his friend Francesco Vettori of his life after the break in 1513, and in which he speaks of his putting off the muddy clothes of day to commune in the evening with the writers of the past: 'e rivestito condecentemente, entro nelle antique corti delli antiqui uomini dove, da loro ricevuto amorevolmente, mi pasco di quel cibo, che *solum* è mio, e che io nacqui per lui; dove io non mi vergogno parlare con loro e domandarli della ragione delle loro azioni. E quelli per loro umanità mi rispondono. . . .'[1] There is never any need for Machiavelli to be ashamed: he is as strong, or stronger than what he has taken. In particular, he can more easily look down upon Polybius than Polybius could on him, though it is clear that he had this account in mind in the *Prince* also: as when he made the statement in Chapter IX (which is fundamental for him) of the two humours which are always present in every city—the people's desire neither to be commanded nor oppressed by the grandees, the grandees' desire to command and oppress the people. Out of which two appetites there springs one of three effects, 'o principato, o libertà o licenzia'.[2] But also, in this intrusion into Machiavelli's commentary on Livy of a whole initial section from Polybius (and we can see in the latter's passage to the praise of the Roman constitution why Machiavelli has been attracted sidewards even before his book has begun; and this not towards a Tacitus), we can test still further the criteria employed in this consideration of politics.

Supposing we were to compare this sort of analysis with Dante's case in the *De Monarchia*? Could we not say that here we have an opposite procedure? It starts, not by appeal to a transcendental truth to which the earthly scene must be accommodated (or is doomed for ever to be wrong), but by an explanation, conjectural if you like, yet plausible, of the evolution of a polity out of nothing. For Machiavelli, as there had been for Polybius, there is a casual origin: 'Nacquono queste variazioni de'governi a caso intra gli uomini. . . . Da questo nacque la cognizione delle cose oneste e buone, differenti dalle perniziose e ree.'[3] That is again, if you like, a looking at things as they are, not as they ought to be, because the ultimate sanction of

---

[1] *P*. ed. Lisio, 5.   [2] *P*. IX, 20.   [3] *D*. I, II, 14–15.

the imperative does not enter into the question. Or, if there is an imperative, it originates in the nature of things themselves, and is not to be sought elsewhere. But are we led, therefore, on to a cynical use of the material factors of the situation in order to impose some ruler who knows how to calculate on the adding-machine for his own benefit and aggrandizement? That was the presupposition of nineteenth-century thought. Let me quote it for a moment in a twentieth-century echo of it: 'The cynical frankness with which Machiavelli disregards all moral scruples in his treatises on the art of government are without parallel in the history of political literature.'[1] But the sense of such a sentence is as defective as its grammar. Most obviously the discovery is, for both Polybius and Machiavelli, something valuable. And we are still concerned with things as they may be, as well as with things as they are. If this *as they may be* replaces the old *as they ought to be*, it does so with no sinister intent: is not the goal in view, to forestall the vices inherent in the simple forms of government, to arrest the worm in the wood and the rust on the iron? If man discovered casually moral values, yet this addition to the primitive texture of life is none the less valuable or honoured for being man's achievement (and, one might add with Polybius, what distinguishes man from all the other animals). And the aim of Machiavelli is the discovery of some form of equipoise which can reconcile the conflicting humours of men, in order to achieve a stability that may rival Sparta's eight hundred years under the constitution of Lycurgus, or the greater duration of Rome itself. Is not that a very moral state of affairs, very different in its character from the Desanctisian picture of Machiavelli's realism? or from the judgment of Niebuhr which Tommasini saw fit to prefix as the epigraph to his chapter on the *Discorsi*: 'The Romans whose policy was completely Machiavellian'? Yet one has only to read the *Discorsi* with this theme in mind to see how much they are a commentary on the details and the psychology of its working.

There is a very simple, and a very necessary, method of testing Machiavelli in the *Discorsi*, one suggested already perhaps by the mention of the name Lycurgus: if Machiavelli really has a latent admiration for the PRINCE rather than the legislator, then surely he will betray himself during the pages of the book. Are there no Caesar Borgias waiting to be recommended or extolled? Let us recall again Villari's clear indication of what he took to be Machiavelli's preference: 'Even if a brigand chief had had the daring and

[1] A. H. Johnson, 14. The page deserves a reading.

dexterity to upset a country and subject it to his rule, Machiavelli
would have admired his ability and courage without taking alarm at
any sanguinary and cruel action.' That is a statement made with all
the assurance of conviction, and without any trace of a feeling that it
might meet with disapproval. If it is right, then somewhere in his
main work Machiavelli must have been true to himself and looked
with an admiring eye towards some brigand chief. *Sans doute*, but
which one is it, and in which corner does he lurk? Ought it by
rights to be Catiline, the central figure of a historical account which
Machiavelli thought everyone must know?[1] Alas! it is Sallust whom
he admires, and Catiline whom he condemns. Two references,
and neither kind, and he is gone, scaled up against Caesar: the latter
(in spite of adulation born under awe of his success) all the more
detestable in that he did what Catiline desired to do.[2] Then it is not
Caesar either,

Cesare armato con gli occhî grifagni?[3]

The passage at the end of the same chapter is sufficient indication: 'E
veramente, cercando un principe la gloria del mondo, doverrebbe
desiderare di possedere una città corrotta, non per guastarla in tutto
come Cesare, ma per riordinarla come Romolo.'[4] The references to
Caesar are somewhat more numerous than those to Catiline, though
they hardly exceed a dozen in the course of 450 pages; and when one
has the patience to trace them it is to find that they in no case belie
that unflattering start, and that three of them couple with him the
disagreeable epithet *tiranno* or speak of his *tirannide*.

That is not an encouraging beginning, at least in one way. And
we have seen earlier how little he admires Philip of Macedon, who,
as Justin said, drove men from province to province, as herdsmen
drive their flocks. 'Sono questi modi crudelissimi, e nimici d'ogni
vivere, non solamente cristiano, ma umano; e debbegli qualunque
uomo fuggire, e volere piuttosto vivere privato, che re con tanta
rovina degli uomini.'[5] How un-machiavellian this is of Machiavelli,
to be taking alarm at sanguinary and cruel actions! Ought not Villari
to have taken him to task, or it to heart? Then Machiavelli seems
allergic to the charm of Quintus Curtius's romantic narrative. His
references to Alexander are few, and mainly insignificant (as in the
anecdote on the founding of Alexandria, centring round the bright
idea of Dinocrates). Where he has something to say about Alexander
(apart from coupling him with his father Philip, which implies no

[1] *D.* III, VI, 336.   [2] *ibid.* and *D.* I, X, 45.   [3] *Inf.*, IV, 123.
[4] *D.* I, X, 48.   [5] *D.* I, XXVI, 88.

good) he puts him, apropos of Cleitus—whom he killed, look you, in
his cups—amongst the *uomini infuriati e sciolti*.[1] That is not very reassuring, I mean, for Alexander; and we may contrast it with the
soothing words of Anaxarchus, who consoled Alexander in his
remorse by proving that since he had done it the fates had willed it
and it was just. 'Do you not know,' he asked his master, 'that duty
and reason are in Jove's hands, so that you may know that all that
Kings do is just and lawful?' Or, if we wish to listen again to another
than Anaxarchus,

> Sans rendre ni raison, ni compte de mes voeux,
> Je veux ce que je veux, parce que je le veux.

But that belongs to the seventeenth century, the first naïve stating of
the theme *L'Etat, c'est moi*; and in spite of the use critics have made of
the title of the *Prince* it bears no relation to the thesis of Machiavelli.

Let me give one more example of this argument from Machiavelli's indifference. In his own lifetime, in his own city, one who
was himself a colleague, and who could style himself even more
legitimately by that appellation which has stuck for some reason to
Niccolò, *Secretario Fiorentino*, translated one of the most attractive
of the historians of Rome, not from the Greek original (that had
been done already by the well-known scholar Pier Candido Decembrio in 1472), but from Latin into Italian; and Alessandro Bracci
made of Appian a very happy rendering into the purest Florentine.
The *External Wars* were printed at Rome in 1502, the Civil ones not
until 1519 at Florence, though Machiavelli might have known them
in MS., or in Decembrio's Latin. Here surely at last, with Mithridates,
Marius, Sylla, there should be brigand chiefs enough? Did not the
former shake the Roman world for forty years? And honest Bracci
in his translation introduces him as one who did his utmost: 'Certa-
mente questo Re pare che non lasciasse intentata alcuna cosa possibile
alle forze e ingegno humano, cosí nel fare, come nel pensare.'[2] It is,
is it not? the perfect maximum of *virtú* in its old and sinister sense.
Yet, to confirm our doubts upon that matter, so little interest does
Machiavelli take in him and in his wars that the sole reference to him
in the *Discorsi* is not about him, but about Lucullus; and what he says
about Lucullus is all wrong. He says Lucullus was without experience
when sent against Mithridates, and that his army formed him: it is
part of the discussion on armies and captains.[3] But the truth is (though
Appian only mentions Lucullus's successes, not the reason for his

---

[1] *D.* I, LVIII, 167.   [2] Appian, *Guerra di Mithrid.*, 130 v.   [3] In *D.* III, XIII.

being sent) that Lucullus before he went was rated with the greatest captains of his age, with Pompey, busy in Spain, and with Metellus, then retired, and that he was sent out by general consent as the man most likely to succeed. Machiavelli has confused him with Flaccus, a creature of no experience a few pages earlier in Appian; but he came to an unhappy end, being cut to pieces by a colleague who found him hiding.[1] It is not the only time Machiavelli has joined, by a slip of his strong memory (and I would take the opportunity of adding, against the commentators, that his slips in quotation are a proof of how much and how well he knew, without needing to look up), the beginning of one's history to the latter end of another's, and drawn a moral from it by oversight.[2] But at least we may take it that it dissociates him as neatly as anything could do from any substantial interest in Mithridates. As for the other two, they are not entirely without mention in the *Discorsi*; but we have only to turn to the first reference to Marius to see the judgment Machiavelli passes on them: 'donde nacque la potenza di Mario, e la rovina di Roma'.[3] They represent the dissolution, the final seal on which is set by Julius Caesar; and Machiavelli, who, we have seen, was concerned with the duration of Rome, not with its collapse, does not pretend to like them. Even so, as a close to the epoch in which he is interested, they receive more mention in the *Discorsi* than does the Emperor Augustus, who belongs to an epoch in which Machiavelli evinces no interest at all. We may contrast the wistfulness of Dante's line,

e vissi a Roma sotto il buon Augusto,[4]

with the couple of bare mentions Octavian (*tout court*) receives in the *Discorsi*. For Machiavelli is interested in a *vivere libero*, and once more Montesquieu's attitude lies alongside, and his comment illuminates, Machiavelli's view: 'Auguste (c'est le nom que la flatterie donna à Octave) établit l'ordre, c'est-à-dire, une servitude durable: car dans un état libre où l'on vient d'usurper la souveraineté, on appelle règle tout ce qui peut fonder l'autorité sans bornes d'un seul; et on nomme trouble, dissension, mauvais gouvernement, tout ce qui peut maintenir l'honnête liberté des sujets.'[5] That adjective *good* which Dante prefixes to the emperors by definition from their office (does not Bossuet add explanatorily, 'Tout ce qui mérite le nom de puissance,

---

[1] Cf. Appian, 154–63; and Plutarch, *Life of Lucullus*.
[2] Cf. the account of Claudius Nero in the curious ch. D. III, XVII, where Marcus Livius owns half the episode.
[3] *D. I, V, 25.*   [4] *Inf.*, I, 71.   [5] *Gran. et Déc.*, XIII, 439.

naturellement, tend au bien'?[1]) has slipped from Machiavelli's, as from Montesquieu's, account. Perhaps if Machiavelli did read the Civil Wars in Appian it could not have survived that nightmare of the proscriptions by which the triumvirs laid hold on the power that they had shared out. But whether he read that or not, his interest lies elsewhere.

We can never do better than to take Machiavelli at his word; and if we turn to one of the most significant chapters of the *Discorsi*, to *D*. III, V, the prelude to the whole important, and protracted, treatment of the theme of conspiracies, we shall find repeated the warning that punctuates the pages of the *Prince* and precludes it from being a manual for tyrants: 'Sappino adunque i principi come a quell'ora e'cominciano a perder lo Stato, che cominciano a romper le leggi, e quelli modi e quelle consuetudini che sono antiche, e sotto le quali gli uomini lungo tempo sono vivuti.'[2] Was not this the reason why the hereditary prince should find his maintenance an easy matter?[3] Far from being consumed with admiration for the brigand chiefs who upset the State, Machiavelli's whole concern is with those who, and those things which, preserve it. Test him at this point again: first there is the example that he has to recommend, which is that a ruler should take as his looking-glass the life of good princes, for instance, Timoleon of Corinth or Aratus Sicioneus, and in their lives he will find so much security and so much satisfaction both of ruler and of ruled, 'che doverrebbe venirgli voglia di imitargli'.[4] Note how once again his estimate of human nature is not so low as to provide for the worst choice only being made. Instead he takes it for granted that if the best is set forth it will be naturally acceptable; which is what we found as far away as in *D*. I, X. There also Timoleon was to be found, and with him this same idea, that if one read history it would be impossible, being a private individual, not to wish to be a Scipio rather than a Caesar, and, being a ruler, not to prefer to be Agesilaus, Timoleon, Dion rather than to be a tyrant such as Nabis, Phalaris, or Dionysius. If we wish to know what role Machiavelli associates with such men as Timoleon, then we may see it in his comment elsewhere on him and Dion as ones whose personality (*virtù* well used) kept their native Syracuse free during their lifetime.[5] And here we might do worse than have recourse to Plutarch's life of Aratus for the opposition between prince and tyrant, in their life and in their latter end. The first statement there identifies him with

---

[1] Cherel, 151.   [2] *D*. III, V, 313.   [3] *P*. II, 5, 2.

[4] *D*. III, V, 314.   [5] *D*. I, XVII, 68.

a natural hatred against tyranny, and his whole life was spent in service of what Machiavelli would call a *vivere civile*; while he is specifically contrasted with Aristippus, the same who went up the ladder to bed and had it removed and locked up by his mistress's mother, who called him out in the morning like a snake out of its hole. But Aratus, without force of arms, and clad in a wretched cloak, acquired unshakable rule; and Plutarch contrasts him with those who seize castles, keep guards, provide themselves with arms to defend themselves. Few of these (like hares) have shunned a violent death, or left either a monument worthy of memory for their descendants, or even any descendants. Is it right for me to follow Machiavelli off to Plutarch, whence he drew his example? It would be wrong if Machiavelli spoke any different language himself. But this is the conclusion that he makes apropos of tyrants, and which he illustrates by the lines from Juvenal,

> Ad generum Cereris sine caede et vulnere pauci
> Descendunt reges, et sicca morte tiranni,

preceded by his own wise recommendation, 'Né può, da questo omore, alcuno tiranno guardarsi, se non con diporre la tirannide.'[1] There is nothing anywhere in the *Discorsi* to whittle away these plain statements, and this obvious division of categories.

There is, however, just one name received with approval by Machiavelli which has been boggled at, and though I have glanced at the matter already, it is right that I should return to it here. The page in which Machiavelli excuses Romulus for the death of his brother and of Titus Tatius (even when he has gone further than Livy seems to warrant, and made Romulus personally responsible) is one of those listed by Burd as being injurious; and others too have detected cynicism here. This business of killing brothers to become a king has seemed too near to the procedure of Hamlet's father's wife and her new husband. But how does Machiavelli judge Romulus? Not on the score of killing, but on a major count, which is closely linked with the theme we saw developed by Polybius: if the Roman constitution was so good a thing that when the Tarquins were driven out it needed no change other than the provision of two consuls with annual power in room of a king, then that is proof enough that the first *ordini* of Rome were closer to a 'vivere civile e libero' than to an 'assoluto e tirannico'.[2] (We must note how those adjectives pair off,

---

[1] D. III, VI, 317; and cf. Cicero, *De Off.*, II, VII, 317, where also Phalaris and Dionysius are alleged.
[2] D. I, IX, 42.

for they are typical of Machiavelli's idiom, and of his interests, and we shall find this second couple again.) But this, with the establishment of a senate, is a proof of Romulus's goodness, of his lack of personal ambition; and it is in the full light of this that Machiavelli is willing to regard Romulus's actions before as being tolerable, and speaks the words that have given offence: 'Conviene bene, che, accusandolo il fatto, lo effetto lo scusi; e quando sia buono, come quello di Romolo, sempre lo scuserà: perché colui che è violento per guastare, non quello che è per racconciare, si debbe riprendere.'[1] In spite, that is, of the casualness both Polybius and Machiavelli associated with the origins of Rome's constitution, the latter cannot resist the link with his theory of *one* legislator; and it is, significantly, on this very page that he confirms his requirements of the legislator.[2] He is certainly not setting up for his prince, or for us, the precept of murdering our relatives in order to take over rule; and I have observed earlier that he pairs here rather (in this somewhat naïve satisfaction at the example falling pat) with a Father of the Church than with any encourager to vice.

If that is not a theory, but a perhaps over-enthusiastic illustration of a case, what recipe is Machiavelli going to propose to achieve duration? In a way, his ideas here could be summed up in a phrase which derives immediately from Livy, though the psychological gloss to it, which cannot be so easily summed up, is, as always, Machiavelli's own work. The kernel is in a phrase occurring early in *Discorsi* I: 'Quelli che prudentemente hanno constituita una republica, in tra le piú necessarie cose ordinate da loro, è stato constituire una guardia alla libertà.'[3] The phrase echoes directly Livy, but in the latter it is concerned with a specific point, the reduction in the term of office of the censors.[4] Machiavelli accepts that point of short periods of office, but he does not stop at it, and this leads us on to a divergence from Livy, as to ideas that are fundamental with Machiavelli. Granted the two opposite humours we have seen in men, where shall we entrust our guard to liberty?—to those who have, or to those who have not? Or, as Machiavelli expresses the question, which are most ambitious, those who desire to acquire what they have not got, or those who desire to maintain the position they have already? It is in this form of analysis that Machiavelli excels, and

[1] D. I, IX., 41.
[2] *ibid.*: 'Però, uno prudente ordinatore d'una republica, e che abbia questo animo, di volere giovare non a sé ma al bene comune . . .'
[3] D. I, V, 23.
[4] Livy, IV, 24: 'se . . . libertati populi Romani consulturum. Maximam autem eius custodiam esse, si magna imperia diuturna non essent.'

his answers can lead us, by an adjustment only of the scale on which they are made, to the solution of such problems as why it should take rivers of blood to attempt (only attempt) the establishment of a republic in Spain, while a Hitler could seat himself in the German saddle with relatively little opposition or bloodshed. The discussion is at the end of *D*. I, V: Both of these appetites can give rise to tumults. Yet for the most part the latter are caused by those who possess, for the fear of losing breeds the same desires in them as are in those who desire to acquire. For men do not deem their possession secure unless they continue to acquire. And moreover, there is the fact that, possessing more, they can with greater power and effect make innovations. 'E di piú vi è, che, possedendo molto, possono con maggiore potenza e maggiore moto fare alterazione.' It is a luminous phrase, one that springs perhaps from the modesty of his own personal circumstances, and attests the moderation of his political ideas; and once we have digested this chapter we shall have little difficulty in finding reminders of it elsewhere in the book. Or if we wish to use what we have learnt here outside Machiavelli and his time, shall we come to inquire why Louis XVI and Necker failed? The reason is as Machiavelli put it: 'Dans l'oeuvre de réparation qu'il devait entreprendre, il allait heurter de nombreux intérêts et rencontrer une résistance d'autant plus grave qu'elle partirait de ceux-là mêmes qui vivaient du désordre, c'est-à-dire des hommes les plus puissants et les plus accrédités.'[1]

This analysis has other applications. For instance, it may be true that a prince must beware of the resentment of any subject (for nobody can be so despoiled that a knife is not within his means), but it is not here that the main danger lies. Those who have conspired against princes have all been 'uomini grandi, o familiari, del principe; de'quali molti hanno congiurato, mossi cosí da'troppi beneficii, come dalle troppe ingiurie'.[2] It is a sensitive observation, one that was later to be crystallized as a maxim by La Rochefoucauld: 'Il n'est pas si dangereux de faire du mal à la plupart des hommes, que de leur faire trop de bien.' And Machiavelli a page later supports it in terms that are reminiscent of his chapter in Book I. The prince, in fearing conspiracies, must fear rather those to whom he has been over-kind, than those to whom he has been over-harsh. 'For the latter lack the means, the former have them in abundance; and the desire is equal, because the wish to rule is as great or greater than the wish to be revenged.'[3] Fear Wolsey, not John Ball. We see the sense in

---

[1] Rocquain, 316.   [2] *D*. III, VI, 319.   [3] *ibid*., 320.

which Machiavelli makes these new psychological observations: it is obviously not in favour of the despot (whom we have seen him formally refuting). The whole long chapter on conspiracies—often misrepresented in spite of its clarity—begins with a double warning: the first, already quoted, to princes, that they begin to lose their state the moment they begin transgression of its laws and customs; the second to the people, expressed in Machiavelli's approval of a 'golden' saying of Tacitus, that men must honour the past, and obey the present; that they must desire good princes, and, whatever they are, put up with them. Is not that a mild sentiment for him to admire in Tacitus? Under these conditions the chapter on conspiracies becomes an essay in pathology: because, as we shall find elsewhere, if the state is rightly ordered there is no possibility of their arising.

Since there is this check—arising, as Machiavelli might say, from the order of things—upon the prince, it follows that there is a limitation to his idea of *one* legislator. This idea, which is an optimistic one, and perhaps the most theoretic part of Machiavelli's propositions, is perhaps also the one which is least interesting to us now. Not that we are entirely out of earshot: do we not delegate a Sir William Beveridge to draft a report covering matters of nation-wide importance under the impression that one man may be able to rise superior over party and partisan interests? That is the contention of Machiavelli. Is it not germane to the conception of the *Prince*? But just as in that treatise he took for granted an internal organization in terms of law, so also does he in the *Discorsi*. What other purpose could a *legislator* serve? Therefore he does not put forward a state that depends upon one man. If only Mussolini is right, then everybody else is wrong; which may not matter greatly while he lives. But since Mussolini's life is no longer than another's, it follows that the succession to him is a poor affair. 'Donde nasce che gli regni i quali dipendono solo dalla virtú d'uno uomo, sono poco durabili, perché quella virtú manca con la vita di quello.'[1] Is not that an interesting text for the student of Machiavelli and of the good old machiavellianism? Twice in one sentence he brings out his odious word *virtú*, and each time we could tie it down as having the use the critics wished to pin on it. Yes, and he damns it as something that is of no avail. And not only that, so little is he afraid

> (Inter oves locum praesta
> Et de haedis me sequestra,
> Statuens e parte dextra),

[1] *D*. I, XI, 51.

or so little does he anticipate his critics, that it is Dante who springs to his lips, not Dante

> pacer of the shore
> Where glutted hell disgorgeth filthiest gloom,

nor Dante disapproved; but Dante of the *Purgatorio*, and prefaced by an affectionate 'come prudentemente Dante dice'. It is not wisdom, then, merely to govern prudently while one lives, but to leave a constitution which on one's death may still maintain itself. Hence, the whole conception of *ordini*, the term he inherited from his author, Livy, and without which Machiavelli's book disappears. Hence, the idea (from which I have not departed far) of the *guard on liberty*: which applies from the other side as well as from that of the legislator. 'Il popolo debbe, quando egli ordina i magistrati, fargli in modo che gli abbino avere qualche rispetto a diventare scelerati'[1]— and the key-word *guard* follows immediately, so fundamental is it. This is what Fénelon will express in striking manner: 'Le suprême et le parfait gouvernement consiste à gouverner ceux qui gouvernent.'[2] And since I have emphasized Machiavelli's use of Dante (so well known to him), it is right to remind the reader again that the *rapprochement* was not intended to presume an identity in their political views. For it will not have been forgotten that both Dante and Bossuet, unlike Fénelon and Machiavelli, saw no need for any brakes on power, if only it was legitimate power.

It should, I think, be apparent from all the foregoing in which direction Machiavelli is moving: in spite of the old thesis on the glorification of the individual he stands modestly for an *aurea mediocritas*. Where others saw in the discord in Rome between plebs and aristocracy the cause of downfall, and regretted its existence, Machiavelli saw in it instead the principle that had preserved Rome free so long, and conditioned Rome's expansion. It is one of those cases of a choice of snags, and it is one of the parts that might with profit have been read by Mussolini. If you want a strong and numerous people, capable of empire, you will get one that you cannot handle as you will; but if you hold it down so as to be able to handle it, it will not acquire empire. Or, if it does, you cannot retain it, for your people will have become so cowardly that you will be the prey of whoever attacks you.[3] There was a precise function to be served by discord in Rome. What Machiavelli regretted was not the discord—that was inevitable from the opposing humours, and he contrasted the mildness of political strife in early Rome (without bloodshed and

---

[1] *D.* I, XL, 128.   [2] *Télémaque*, II, 371.   [3] *D.* I, VI, 30, and cf. *D.* II, II, 186.

almost without exiles) with that of Athens[1]—but its foreclosure to the detriment of the people. It is because of this attitude that one finds Machiavelli preoccupied with preventing the rise of any single citizen until he emerges from beneath the shadow of the public laws. Have we not seen what he thought of Marius, or of Caesar? This is one of those themes which occur in Book I, and recur in Book III. Now it is to be noted that in proposing the thesis that the reputation of citizens is the cause of tyranny,[2] Machiavelli does not intend to establish a state on that Turkish model which he had outlined at the beginning of the *Prince*. Indeed, he had stated in the sentence before that a republic without citizens of repute can neither subsist, nor govern itself well in any particular. 'L'égalité, c'est la chose la plus naturelle, et la plus chimérique,' wrote Voltaire; and naturally Montesquieu before him thought the same. 'Il y a toujours, dans un état, des gens distingués par la naissance, les richesses ou les honneurs; mais, s'ils étoient confondus parmi le peuple, et s'ils n'y avoient qu'une voix comme les autres, la liberté commune seroit leur esclavage.'[3] No humanist could dissent from such ideas. But that does not prevent Montesquieu feeling the same preoccupation as Machiavelli, as we can see by turning to a couple of sentences from the *Grandeur et Décadence*: 'Man, always more avid for power through having more, desirous of having all only because he possesses much.' 'Load a man with benefits, the first idea you rouse in him is that of seeking the means to preserve them: *ce sont de nouveaux intérêts que vous lui donnez à défendre*.'[4] That is precisely what we have seen Machiavelli stating with regard to his theories on conspiracies. Both have the same reasons for the same moderation. If in Montesquieu it finds expression in the idea of giving honour, and not power, in Machiavelli it is expressed in terms of the legitimacy of public favour and public honours, and of the pernicious effects of private ones. Spurius Maelius may have begun by meaning well, in attempting to relieve out of his private fortune the hunger of Rome, but out of his piety could arise a dangerous partisanship for him which might carry him to power.[5] So it happened with Cosimo de'Medici.[6] What would be left but for Machiavelli to give assent to the conclusion of Montesquieu? Let those who are distinguished in various ways form 'un corps qui ait droit d'arrêter les entreprises du peuple, comme le peuple a droit d'arrêter les leurs'.[7] And is this anything else than

---

[1] D. I, XXVIII, and, for its central statement, *De Off.*, II, VII, 312: 'Acriores autem morsus sunt intermissae libertatis, quam retentae.'
[2] D. III, XXVIII, 399.   [3] *Esprit des Lois*, XI, VI, 213.   [4] *Gr. et Déc.*, XI, 427, and XIII, 438.
[5] D. III, XXVIII.   [6] D. I, LII.   [7] *Esprit d. l.*, XI, VI, 213.

a formulation of what Machiavelli would regard as the specific virtue of the Roman constitution?

Meanwhile, in Machiavelli, this principle of equipoise modifies that original idea of the purpose of a community—the enjoyment in security of one's own property. Since with Spurius Maelius or Cosimo there comes a point at which private property may become a public menace, then the answer must lie in limitation. As proof of the formative elements for Machiavelli's way of thought, we have the identity of his view with that of so firm a believer in Florentine liberty as Rinuccini. We have seen what the latter said with reference to Piero de'Medici, on not letting, for liberty's sake, any citizen grow till he stood above the law; and he added: 'Perché lo insaziabile appetito delli uomini, quando può piú che non si conviene, piú anche vuole e desidera che non è licito.'[1] What Rinuccini said of Piero is what Machiavelli thought of Cosimo; and of course Livy, in his sentiments with regard to Scipio, is there for either to agree with.[2] Nor is Machiavelli's short concluding chapter on the whole episode of Appius and the decemvirs in Rome irrelevant to this matter: 'Il che esaminato bene, farà tanto piú pronti i latori di leggi delle republiche o de'regni a frenare gli appetiti umani, e torre loro ogni speranza di potere impune errare.'[3] It is this concern which brings us to a point at which the neo-classical thought of Machiavelli cuts across another neo-classical trend. Both derive from the Renascence equally, even if this means that the Renascence is not a simple phenomenon. Remember the theme of *magnificence* and *amplitude* as it emerges in the wake of Petrarch in the pages of Matteo Palmieri and Leon-Battista Alberti. It was a theme which went with the wealth of the commercial expansion of Italy. But no idea is more widespread in the Latin historians than that wealth breeds ease and ease breeds deterioration. Hannibal met his Waterloo, not on the field of battle, but in the delights of Capua. Or, as a contemporary (fellow-citizen?) of Machiavelli wrote in the margin of my 1513 Giunta copy of Sallust, *Pax atque otium omnium in republica malorum cause.*

This, I repeat, is nothing exclusive to Sallust. Would not Livy alone suffice to demonstrate the change which Montesquieu announced, and which forms the judgment of Machiavelli? 'A mesure que le luxe s'établit dans une république, l'esprit se tourne vers l'intérêt particulier',[4] away, that is, from the *bene comune* which is

---

[1] Rinuccini, ciii.
[2] Livy, XXXVIII, 50: 'Neminem unum civem tantum eminere debere, ut legibus interrogari non possit.'
[3] D. I, XLII, 129–30.   [4] *Esprit d. l.*, VII, II, 131.

Machiavelli's concern. But it is Sallust, as we shall see, who formulates an answer in terms which Machiavelli echoes; it is Sallust who furnishes at almost every turn ideas and expressions which pass into Machiavelli's idiom, and we may do well to look towards him at this point. If Machiavelli had no use for Catiline, the anti-hero of Sallust's book, the same is not true of its author, whom Machiavelli has thoroughly absorbed. After Livy, who is naturally *hors pair*, there is perhaps only Justin who vies with Sallust in this matter of the frequency of echoes. Nor must we underrate Justin, who is so frequently Machiavellian in expression.[1] Indeed, if one were to collate the idiom of the historians of Rome (as Sallust, Justin, Livy, Tacitus) one might be surprised to find how unanimous they are in certain ideas; their variations arising rather in their subject-matter (what they are looking at) than in any wide divergency of outlook. Did not even M. Cherel make the discovery that Amelot de la Houssaye was rude to Tacitus in thinking of Machiavelli's tacitism? 'Mais qu'est-ce, chez Amelot, que la "politique de Tacite"? Au vrai, c'est celle des personnages de Tacite.'[2] Tacitus himself was the enemy of absolute power. Well, it opens a new field of comment for us if Machiavelli could look to these and find a homogeneous attitude; but I have not the competence to press the point, and instead I turn back to Sallust in order to go ahead.

Perhaps even, if Machiavelli grasped quickly Polybius's idea of a cycle, it might be because it was something in embryo in Sallust, and in connection with this degeneration through success and idleness. The fear of Carthage kept Rome *in bonis artibus*. When it ceased there came wantonness and pride in the nobles, licence in the people.[3] The idea of the two humours could be traced in Sallust.[4] From him, or (it matters not which, so little is there need to think of Machiavelli as inferior when he imitates or agrees) in accord with him, comes the *superbia paucorum*, crystallized in a brilliant phrase by Machiavelli. Entering on the theme of the necessity for opportunities to accuse, so as to forestall calumnies (part of the idea that ordinary remedies prevent extraordinary ones), he remarks, 'Bisogna che i giudici siano assai, perché i pochi sempre fanno a modo de'pochi.'[5]

---

[1] E.g. Justin, V, V, 52: 'apud quem plus prior offensa valuisset, quam recentia beneficia.' Or the pair *contemnendus* and *metuendus* balanced in XXI, II, 159, etc.

[2] Cherel, 160.

[3] *Bel. Jug.*, 43. 'Nanque coepere nobilitas dignitatem in superbiam, plebs libertatem in libidinem vertere, sibi quisque ducere, trahere, rapere.'

[4] *Bel. Jug.*, 40: 'Nam fidei quidem, et concordiae, quae spes est? dominari illi volunt, vos liberi esse, facere illi iniurias, vos prohibere.'

[5] *D.* I, VII, 35.

In Sallust, too, there is the idea of these *pauci* as leading to ruin as they emerge to pre-eminence, and the formula which Machiavelli is to make his own for characterizing the public welfare. It is in Cato's speech, with his statement of what is, and should not be: 'PUBLICE EGESTATEM, PRIVATIM OPULENTIAM, laudamus divitias, sequimur inertiam.'[1] What else is this but the basis for the phrase that Machiavelli repeats more than once in the *Discorsi*, 'tener ricco il publico, povero il privato'?[2] That is a theme dear to the neo-classic: will one not find a whole book (XXIII) dedicated to it in the *Avantures de Télémaque*? And in Sallust himself there is the entire speech of Marius which is directed firmly against civilization. 'Nam ex parente meo, et ex aliis sanctis viris, ita accepi, MUNDITIAS mulieribus, VIRIS laborem convenire, omnibusque bonis oportere plus gloriae, quam divitiarum esse, arma non suppellectilem decori esse.'[3] If we listened rigorously to Marius we should be led on to Alexander's comment on the bath of Darius ('So this is what it means to be a king'), or to his action in burning the baggage of his army with all the loot of all his conquests in order to march off unencumbered to conquer India.[4] We should destroy, that is, the passage from the nobleman to the gentleman which is the characteristic achievement of the Renascence. Nevertheless, in consequence of this attunement to Sallust and his like, here at the centre of the Renascence is a stern and simple note, creating a contradiction which Machiavelli does not resolve. Why does he give his ready enthusiasm to the idea of liberty as against servitude? It is because there is then the possibility of an expanding rhythm of prosperity: 'Veggonvisi le ricchezze multiplicare in maggiore numero, e quelle che vengono dalla cultura, e quelle che vengono dalle arti. Perché ciascuno volentieri multiplica in quella cosa, e cerca di acquistare quei beni, che crede, acquistati, potersi godere. Onde ne nasce che gli uomini a gara pensono a'privati e publici commodi; e l'uno e l'altro viene maravigliosamente a crescere.'[5] No doubt this enthusiasm for liberty is right: but if riches do multiply in these conditions, is not that a dangerous process? And where is Marius's warning? Would it not be better for the fear of Carthage to keep us all in civil modesty? Perhaps it is the difference in epoch between Machiavelli and Montesquieu that Machiavelli does not see the contradiction coming: he is too busy looking for the remedy to current disorder to be able to anticipate the theory of stability in prosperity. It is plain, though,

[1] *Cat.*, 21.   [2] *D.* I, XXXVII, 113, and *D.* II, XIX, 249.   [3] *Bel. Jug.*, 62 v.
[4] V. Plutarch.   [5] *D.* II, II, 190.

that his sympathies here are the ones which have led to his attitude
on the side of the people, as against the nobles.

From Sallust derived the terminology of *città corrotte* which accom-
panies Machiavelli's reactions to contemporary Italy. No chapter is
more important than the fifty-fifth of Book I, with its statement of a
lack of hope for Italy, as being more corrupt even than France and
Spain (a coupling together which hardly allows for the idea that
Italy's faults spring from new learning). In the latter two, the lack of
troubles is due to 'l'ordine di quegli regni, che ancora non sono
guasti'. Nevertheless, French, Spaniards, Italians are the 'corruttela
del mondo'. It is strong language, though it is to be observed that
it is neither condonation, nor indifference. Now, it is a passage which
has been generally quoted, only without the sweeping nature of the
charge being seen (so that it has seemed directed against Italy only,
and therefore an accusation of the Renascence); while at the other end,
what limits the statement with regard to Italy itself has usually been
omitted from the picture. For Machiavelli's strictures do not apply
to all Italy in the same way. There can be no *vivere politico* where
there are noblemen who live idly on their rents, without the need
either to cultivate land, or to perform any other labour for their
livelihood. Such men, says Machiavelli, are pernicious in any state:
they are doubly so if they have castles and retinue. But, 'di queste due
sorte d'uomini ne sono pieni il regno di Napoli, terra di Roma, la
Romagna e la Lombardia'.[1] By this Machiavelli comes close, for
instance, to the thesis of the pacifist Ferrero at the end of the nineteenth century: that an idle aristocracy supported on the back of the
producing-classes will justify itself by appeal to military glory.[2]
For Machiavelli 'tali generazioni di uomini sono al tutto nimici
d'ogni civiltà'. Is not that Florentine enough? There can be no
republic where they exist (and we may think again of the case of
Spain, with the combination of landowner plus army class against
the republicans). It is at this point that the theory of equipoise is
most emphatically stated, in one of those significant phrases that
Machiavelli finds so easily under his pen, and we must not forget that
he is speaking, not of all Italy, but of those noble-ridden regions
which he has just enumerated. To put them back in order there
could be no other way than to make them into a kingdom. 'La
ragione è questa, che dove è tanto la materia corrotta che le leggi
non bastano a frenarla, vi bisogna ordinare insieme con quelle maggior
forza; la quale è una mano regia, che con la potenza assoluta ed ecces-

---

[1] *D.* I, LV, 159.   [2] Cf. G. G. Ferrero, *Il Militarismo.*

siva ponga freno alla eccessiva ambizione e corruttela de'potenti.'[1]
Here is not only Petrarch's *regia manus*, but with it the idea of Montesquieu that all power goes forward till it meets its limit.[2] What, then,
can check the power of the nobility in those parts of Italy but the
imposition of a king? *Absolute* power brings with it here its own
epithet of *excessive*. That is something other than the pairing of
'absolue' and 'paternelle' that Bossuet believed in:[3] a coupling which
leaves room for a good deal of ineffectual preaching, but for no
effective restraint. It is, on the other hand, very like the 'tyrannique
et affreux' which go together in Montesquieu.[4] And from this it
follows that absolute power is the most local of remedies, not a
tendency of Machiavelli's; and from what we have found already,
it must be abrogated as soon as it has met its own emergency, or
else its holder will incur the penalties that we have seen lying in the
course of tyrants. That is something which reduces it, not to a
vanishing-point, but within strait, if optimistic, bounds.[5]

But for the moment we must note how many parts of Italy were
not inscribed on the list of those that can only be reordered through
a monarchy. Florence, Siena, Lucca, Venice—these are states that
receive a separate treatment. They have had all the pre-conditions
for a *vivere politico*, but they have lacked a legislator. This chapter is
other than a wholesale moral condemnation of the Italy which he
knew, and not because Machiavelli was without moral concerns, but
because he has valid distinctions to make. It is this disinclination both
to absolutism, and to the state of things which requires absolutism as a
necessary counter, that lies behind one of the most original attitudes of
Machiavelli. This attitude informs the whole close of Book I; but
it is nothing new in his thought. If it has not been usually insisted on
in the criticism of the *Prince* that is only because the critics have seen
(to borrow Lord Morley's phrase) half the *Prince*, and taken it for
the whole. Look back to its Chapter IX, and there is Machiavelli
repudiating the trite proverb that *to build upon the people is to build on
sand*; and perhaps, as Lisio's note suggests, his language echoes a
saying of Savonarola, only to depart from him, or at least to make a
valid distinction. Savonarola had spoken of the people as a fallacious
base to build on;[6] Machiavelli says, yes, if it is a private individual
who builds (shall we say, if it is a Savonarola?); but if it is a prince,
what better, or what other, foundation can he choose? 'Ma sendo

---

[1] *D*. I, LV, 159. [2] Cf. *Petr. and the Ren.*, 34–5.
[3] *Politique tirée de l'Ecriture Sainte.* [4] *L.P.*, CIII, 205.
[5] Cf. again *D*. I, XVIII, and the background to those doubts in Sallust and Tacitus.
[6] Cf. the note in Lisio, 66.

uno principe che vi fondi su, che possa comandare, e sia uomo di
core né si sbigottisca nelle avversità, e non manchi delle altre prepara-
zioni, e tenga con lo animo e ordini suoi animato lo universale, mai
si troverrà ingannato da lui; e li parrà avere fatti li suoi fonda-
menti buoni.'[1] (You see once more how affirmative Machiavelli is,
and how his convictions do not rest upon a pessimistic interpretation, either of possibilities, or of men in general.) That was the
leitmotiv of the *Prince* on one whole side; and here in the *Discorsi*,
where Machiavelli is neither inspired nor limited by the situation
which gave rise to the *Prince*, nor depressed by an Italy which he finds
wholly bad,[2] it is natural that it should receive stronger expression,
and have wider application. Here he is at variance with Livy and
Sallust, as he is with Savonarola. This is not because he disregards
their warnings: is not one of his most memorable sayings that men
are wont to lament their lot in time of trouble, and to be bored when
things go well? 'Come gli uomini sogliono affliggersi nel male e
stuccarsi nel bene; e come dall'una e dall'altra di queste due passioni
nascano i medesimi effetti.'[3] It is as brief, and as conclusive, as La
Rochefoucauld might be. But he is not bound by mere authority,
nor does the reverence we have seen for the historians of antiquity
as accurate in their account of events mean that he is to be intimidated
by their opinions. He speaks on this matter of the people the same
bold language as Valla had done when he inquired whether the
authority of reason was any less valid than the authority of an *ipse
dixit*. 'Ma, comunque si sia, io non giudico, né giudicherò mai
essere difetto difendere alcuna opinione con le ragioni, sanza volervi
usare o l'autorità o la forza.'[4] So in his view the bad that has been said
of the people can be extended to all men, but especially to princes, *e
massime i principi*. It is the penalty of being unrestrained by laws, and
the penalty will be worse for a prince than for a people. The former,
left to his own caprice, is shut off entirely from truth, his deviations
from reason are without correction and are cumulative: a people
will not elect to posts of dignity men who are infamous and corrupt
in life, but this may easily happen with a prince.[5] How many
favourites have been wholly base? A prince can be superior as a
legislator (subject to the qualifications we have found), a people
will be superior as a maintaining force.[6] Look for prudence and
stability—those very Machiavellian requirements—and it is in the
people you will find them: 'Ma quanto alla prudenza ed alla stabilità,

[1] P. IX, 21, 2.   [2] Cf. P. XXVI, 50: 'qui è virtú grande nelle membra . . .'
[3] D. I, XXXVII, 112.   [4] D. I, LVIII, 165. For Valla, cf. *Petr. and the Ren.*, 125.
[5] D. I, LVIII, 168.   [6] *ibid.*, 169.

dico, come un popolo è piú prudente, piú stabile e di migliore giu-
dizio che un principe.'¹ And in the next chapter, in the matter of
deciding whether confederation with a prince or with a people is
most stable, the decision is still for the latter. Here, reminding us of
that general Florentine pride we found in the good faith of their
city, Florence herself is among the examples.²

Machiavelli's conclusions to all this are explicit: better are the
governments of the people than those of princes.³ His comment on
it forestalls the dictum with which, for no better reason than that he
repeated it after a century or so of disuse, Lord Acton's name is
usually coupled: 'Perché un principe che può fare ciò che ei vuole, è
pazzo, un popolo che può fare ciò che vuole, non è savio.'⁴ There is a
nicety in that distinction which informs us fully where Machiavelli's
sympathy, and his judgment, lie. This reflection links him firmly to
Alberti, who anticipated Acton's dictum even more clearly: 'Onde,
potendo quello che tu vuoi, ne seguita che tu vuoi tutto ciò che tu
puoi, e ardisci e usiti a volere ancora piú che non si lice né si conviene.'⁵
Indeed, this was a commonplace in humanistic thought. Have we not
seen it only a little while back in the words of the honest, if not very
cultured, Rinuccini? We could find it again, in almost identical
terms, in Castiglione.⁶ We could find it also in Aeneas Sylvius Piccolomini, where its expression is in terms that show the link with
Petrarch, with the neo-classical view that putting water into vases is
the method of showing up their cracks, and in the same way *principatus detegit animum*.⁷ In this way we see not only how consistent
Machiavelli is with himself, but how little also the flower of humanism
has deteriorated from the prospects of the seed sown by Petrarch.
For we cannot come to the conclusion of a link between Petrarch,
Alberti, Aeneas Sylvius Piccolomini, Castiglione, and Machiavelli
without putting on one side the idea of a separate cynicism, or im-
moralism, in the latter. How could Burd's rash stricture ('He placed
on politics the stamp of irremediable immorality') fit in with such a
context?

It is in this light that we must consider the remedy of absolutism,
in which Machiavelli does not believe, which he did not write up in
the *Prince*, but provision for which he has made, in its capacity as
antidote, at a particular point. Human institutions (like men them-

¹ *ibid.*, 168.   ² *D*. I, LIX, 172.   ³ *D*. I, LVIII, 169.   ⁴ *ibid.*   ⁵ *De Iciarchia*, 9.
⁶ *Cortegiano*, 434: 'Aggiungendosi poi maggior potenza al mal volere, sí v'aggiunge ancora
maggior molestia; e quando il principe può ciò che vole, allor è gran periculo che non voglia
quello che non deve.'
⁷ *Epist.*, I, 605: 'Est autem principatus irritamentum quoddam vitiorum et admodum pauci
inveniuntur qui non aberrent, cum frenis omnibus sint soluti.'

selves) are either going up or down. The stability that Machiavelli desires to achieve may therefore be a constant, but it does not follow that there can be a constantly equal path to it. This is crystallized in a valuable remark: 'Perché altri ordini e modi di vivere si debbe ordinare in uno soggetto cattivo, che in uno buono; né può essere la forma simile in una materia al tutto contraria.'[1] Such an affirmation would by itself be sufficient to clear Machiavelli of the charges critics have sought to bring against him because of the gap they thought to see between the *Prince* and the *Discorsi* (that indifference to content as long as he was calculating political forces, etc.). The whole business of laws (*ordini*) should be to provide the counterchecks, the safety-valves: to reward publicly public achievements (think of young Horace, or of Manlius Capitolinus), and to punish misdemeanours, even in the same individuals (think again of young Horace and Manlius Capitolinus). But supposing they haven't done so? either have not existed, or have not fulfilled their function? Is one to renounce the contemplation of a political ideal? That would not be drawing good, or the least bad, from what is around us, as Machiavelli had recommended in the Ciceronian phrase of the *Prince*. And Machiavelli's prince is still an expression of idealism, not of pessimism. Violence may be necessary (as in the phrase of Neville Chamberlain, on the awful arbitrament of war), and when its authors proceed to establish order out of disorder, then, like Romulus, they will receive approval. But, in point of fact, if they begin with violence, will they have sufficient hold over themselves to eschew it afterwards? Will they not mount like Mussolini, or Hitler, rather than abrogate their power, like Romulus? I have quoted earlier the mournful saying of Tacitus ('Nemo enim unquam imperium flagitio quaesitum bonis artibus exercuit'), and linked it with the doubts that rise in Machiavelli's mind in *D*. I, XVIII. Alas, he may be right, for once, in this coincidence with the 'pessimistic Tacitus'. But such is the eagerness of Machiavelli's temperament that he is only held for a moment by such dismal forebodings. That is why he is led on to consider the various angles of approach which are rendered necessary (that Machiavellian term) by the situation as it is in its distortions. It is these which make possible the range of the *Discorsi* in spite of the simplicity of their central concern.

For the observation can be extended. Apply it to institutions, and it will result in the comment that ones valid and good at one moment may be pernicious at another: as in the case of the public petitioning

[1] *D*. I, XVIII, 73.

for office in Rome, which, while Rome was modest, kept the bad at bay, and encouraged the good. But when Rome had changed its spirit the same custom acted in reverse: it was the bad and bold who elbowed their way forward, while the good stood modestly apart. And at the end of that scale it means that the mere eclipse of a tyrant is not enough to restore a liberty, which leads Machiavelli to the brilliant remark that it is as difficult and dangerous to wish to make a people free that wishes to be enslaved, as it is to wish to enslave a people that wishes to be free.[1] Montesquieu is still available to add the commentary: 'Il étoit tellement impossible que la république pût se rétablir, qu'il arriva ce qu'on n'avoit jamais encore vu, qu'il n'y eut plus de tyran, et qu'il n'y eut pas de liberté; car les causes qui l'avoient détruite subsistoient toujours.'[2] Apply the observation to individuals, and it will show us the inability of one man to change his tactics to suit the times: as Fabius wanted to go on temporizing when the moment for temporizing was past, simply because that was his nature, now going with, now going against, the needs of the present time. Apply it to society in general, it will be the realization, characteristic of Machiavelli, that one may earn hatred by one's good qualities, quite as much as by one's bad ones; but it will be, of course, the hatred of different people. 'E qui si debbe notare, che l'odio s'acquista cosí mediante le buone opere, come le triste'—I quote it from the *Prince*, because Machiavelli's procedure is similar throughout; and it is his merit as a writer that these illuminating sentences punctuate his work so often. They naturally cannot be summarized, nor is any explanatory discourse on the *Discourses* going to string them all together. What reward would be left for the reader of Machiavelli if I had exhausted him in the process of explaining where he stands? Meanwhile, it is against all the accidents that are represented by the distortions that the constitution is to fortify itself, so that nothing takes it unawares, and all the remedies are found within itself, without disturbing its equilibrium. Here, and here alone, will be the golden age which that lyrical Chapter X evoked in Book I.

There is one element in the composition of the good state that we must consider further, though we may do so briefly because it is only through confusion with regard to Machiavelli's general position that it has seemed puzzling. This is religion; and along with good laws, good education (that is, upbringing), he puts religion as an essential. We can see in D. I, XII, the importance he attaches to it:

[1] *D.* III, VIII, 345; and cf. *D.* I, XVI, *ad initium.*   [2] G. et D., XII, 431.

'Perché, cosí come dove è religione si presuppone ogni bene, cosí dove quella manca, si presuppone il contrario.' There goes with that statement the attack, sharp as that of Dante or Petrarch (and in Machiavelli's time probably more necessary still), against the corruption of the papal curia. Had not this had double consequences: irreligion in Italy, and political division—the latter emphasized with particular clarity by Machiavelli, whose thesis is echoed by Guicciardini in his analysis of papal history. Nor has anybody ever ventured to dispute the case that Machiavelli here set out. Our obligation, he said, lies with the Church, and with no one else (so that Lodovico il Moro may have set in motion the final process, but the root cause lies further back, in Rome itself). What is Machiavelli, then, reformer, pre-protestant, or does he wish, as some have thought, to set up another religion altogether, that of antiquity? Or is he, as some have said, indifferent, accusing him of cynicism, or contrasting him with Savonarola, finding him leading devilwards, not heavenwards?

The charge of indifference we may perhaps skip over, as being improbable in view of the energy in the statement that I last quoted, an energy which flows through the whole chapter. Nor is indifference any key to Machiavelli: what is indifferent to him, he does not write about: as witness the often-cited observation of a letter to Francesco Vettori, 'che non sapendo ragionare né dell'arte della seta, né dell'arte della lana, né de'guadagni né delle perdite, e'mi conviene ragionare dello stato, e mi bisogna botarmi di star cheto, o ragionar di questo'.[1] And those who are sceptical with regard to Machiavelli might do worse than look at the formula with which he closes that particular letter. Does this statement of the dominant interest for him attach religion decisively to the theme of politics? Perhaps it does; and if it does it is in a way which Montesquieu revealed in a phrase (written apropos of a subject which receives consideration in the *Discorsi*, that of respect for one's oath) which Machiavelli would not have cast in any other form: 'Rome étoit un vaisseau tenu par deux ancres dans la tempête, la religion et les moeurs.'[2] Has it not been remarked that *fede* (I mean, in a religious use) is absent from Machiavelli's vocabulary, and that its place is held by the Roman term *religio*? That represents an extension of the practical concern of the humanist tradition. But these two anchors were conspicuously absent in the contemporary Rome of Sixtus IV to Julius II. Have we not seen the sharp condemnation which the latter earns from Machiavelli in the name of Italy and of Christendom? The situation is the

---

[1] *L.F.*, VIII, 36.   [2] *Esp. d. l.*, VIII, XIII, 163.

reverse of what Maritain supposed: it is not Machiavelli out of court already because he does not accept the Roman pontiff, but Machiavelli (like Guicciardini) who can pass scathing, and lasting, judgment on such as Julius. But though he is placed between the rottenness of the Catholic Church at its centre, with its effect on the political scene in Italy, and the world of Rome in the time of the republic, and has no difficulty in apportioning his praise and blame, he does not propose to leap back a thousand years. It is true that in a well-known chapter he draws a contrast between the glorification of doers in antiquity, as against the emphasis on sufferers in Christianity.[1] But in the sequel he talks in terms of a change in interpretation, not of an abandonment of the one for the other. In spite of some of the examples (Papirius Cursor and the rest) in the *Discorsi*, he has little patience with the manifestations of ancient religion. Were the ancients not a little over-credulous and superstitious? Look at the *Arte della Guerra*, and you will find no indications as to the meaning of swarms of bees on the eagles of the legions, or as to what to do when the victim has unfortunately misplaced, or lost entirely, some vital portion of its anatomy. Look through the corners of his works, at the places where he reveals his mentality unconsciously, and you will find, not Jupiter Stator, but the fellows and equivalents of the *Cristo ti guardi* of his letters to his kinsman Giovanni Vernacci. Did he not express the hope, so little to be realized, at Julius's election *che Iddio lo faccia utile papa alla cristianità*? If these are straws on the wind, at least there is a wind, and they are straws blowing one way. If the Roman religion bound men together and kept them good, should not Christianity, 'avendoci la nostra religione mostro la verità e la vera via,'[2] do the same, if it were not corrupted at its centre? Machiavelli is no theologian; he is probably also no Protestant. He stands rather alongside Savonarola in his condemnations and in his desire for a return to the beginnings (in which, by definition, the virtue lies) of Christianity. Does he not see the reform of St. Francis and St. Dominic, those two wheels of the chariot,[3] as being the restorative and preservative against the dishonesty of the prelates and heads of the Church? Dante, Savonarola, and Machiavelli here speak together; and the latter is the contemporary also of Erasmus. Indeed, that letter to Guicciardini which was mutilated in the old editions shows him reacting strongly (as did Guicciardini himself) against the hypocrisy and the *fainéantise* of the religious orders.[4] That is surely the commentary to the idea

---

[1] *D.* II, II, 188–9.
[3] *Par.*, XII, 106.
[2] *D.* II, II, 188.
[4] *L.F.*, ed. Alvisi, CLXXIX, 423.

from the chapter which I quoted with its objection to the 'viltà degli uomini, che hanno interpetrato la nostra religione secondo l'ozio, e non secondo la virtú'.[1] And Machiavelli's distrust of Savonarola was political, not religious. We might perhaps build on his statement in *D*. I, X, with its inclusion of liberty of opinion, a first claim for tolerance of religious convictions, a leaping past the *cuius regio, eius religio* that is to come; or a profiting by Alberti's enlightened views on punishing crimes against man, but of leaving crimes against God to be punished by God. If we do, we may be doing too much; and we might do well to remember that the phrase on opinion echoes Tacitus at the beginning of his *Histories*. But, now that the most recent thought on Rabelais, for instance, tends to stress the believing side of the sixteenth century ('un siècle qui veut croire'), we need have no scruple in accepting the sincerity of Machiavelli's repeated statements on the goodness, and the essential nature, of this tie between men. If we wish to see the difference between humanism at the beginning of the sixteenth century, and at the beginning of the eighteenth, we may turn to a page of Montesquieu, most like in some particulars, most dissimilar at others. The start is what Machiavelli feels: 'Car, dans quelque religion qu'on vive, l'observation des lois, l'amour pour les hommes, la piété envers les parents, sont toujours les premiers actes de la religion.'[2] But the close of the letter with its persiflage, like the reflections of the notorious Letter XXIV, is something quite outside Machiavelli's range.

If we have still doubts that lurk as to the nature of Machiavelli's intentions, it will be well to turn to the Proem of the second book of the *Discorsi*, which reconfirms in the most explicit terms both his intentions, and his assessment of himself. It is a discussion, conducted with all the energy characteristic of Machiavelli, of the theme *laudatores temporis acti*. He links it (and with a repetition of the keywords) to his conception of ups and downs: according to our place, and direction, on the scale we shall be right or wrong in looking wistfully back to the past. And Machiavelli himself, in looking back to the ancient Romans? For him, it is as clear as day: in the past there was something that made it marvellous; in the present there is nothing to redeem the misery and infamy, neither observance of religion, nor of laws, nor of soldiership, 'ma sono maculati d'ogni ragione bruttura'.[3] Is not this the language of a Savonarola, when it is uttered in the age of Leo X, of Raphael and Michaelangelo? *Mais non*, it is the language of Machiavelli. Only, it turns out not to be so very different. If we

---

[1] *D*. II, II, 189.   [2] *L.P.*, XLVI, 88.   [3] *D*. II, *Proem*, 178.

can obtain here, again, a confirmation of that kinship of temperament between reformer and political thinker, we have here also one of the conclusive cases for the use of *virtú* in a sense that implies moral approval: 'E veramente, se la virtú che allora regnava, ed il vizio che ora regna, non fussino piú chiari che il sole, andrei col parlare piú rattenuto'[1]—he would be less precipitous in speaking: is it not Machiavelli's confession of the nature of his genius? But it is manifest, and all can see it, and if Machiavelli cannot alter it by his own action, at least he can take Sallust's second choice: if not act, at least write what should be acted. 'For it is the office of a good man to teach to others the good which the malignity of his time or of his lot prevents him from accomplishing, so that some of them, being capable of it, more favoured by heaven, may carry it out.'[2] *The office of a good man*—how absurdly the phrase contrasts with a recent headline in *The Times* about an alleged plan (revealed in the course of the Nuremberg trials) of Hitler's to have his own ambassador at Prague assassinated so as to create an *incident*: A MACHIAVELLIAN SUGGESTION! That would hardly be the office of a very good man. Yet (perhaps as Machiavelli has been saying in this Proem, because of the very sharpness of the contrast) I venture to imagine that it is quite manifest where the truth lies. If it is too late now to detach the adjective *machiavellian* from the legendary taint it might be convenient to spell it with a capital when we wish to convey a connection with Machiavelli, and with a small letter when we merely wish to say that something is reprehensible.

This second book of the *Discorsi* (even if prepared for in Book I) is largely new, and homogeneous; though it is without the brilliancy of statement, and the range of applicability of the first. Just occasionally this flares up, as in the remarks on the credibility of exiles' promises: Never trust them, they will transfer their faith from you to anyone else who seems to promise return. So extreme is their desire to be back home that they believe naturally many things which are false, and they add knowingly to these, 'so that, between what they believe, and what they say they believe, they fill you with hopes' on which your enterprise will all go wrong.[3] That is wholly admirable, and not in any way limited to a particular situation. But there are fewer of these original flashes, which are the sign-manual of Machiavelli reading history, in Book II, and the subject-matter—the expansion of a city-state on the pattern of Rome—seems the least capable of adaptation to the needs of Machiavelli's own time. While the

---

[1] *ibid.*, 179.   [2] *ibid.*   [3] *D.* II, XXXI, 293.

Florentine prince, had he been ready to take Machiavelli's advice, might have had the chance to build upon the favour of Pope Leo X and of the Emperor until he was strong enough to stand on his own feet, Florence, or another city, was not able to play the part of Rome, since she did not start with equal rivals. Doubtless, the preoccupation is what it always is with him; and the result of not being in the Roman pattern is expressed in terms of Italy the prey of all who wish to traverse her;[1] an idea which he repeats a hundred pages later in that form which we have seen clinging to his pen: 'Vedesi ancora, per questo, ogni dí miracolose perdite e miracolosi acquisti.'[2] The phrase is in the *Prince*, and it is in the *Letters*: it is, then, still the root of the whole matter. Does it follow from this that the Romans, in going up, rather than down, were aware of the value of the formula that they used? Machiavelli would seem, in this same book, to oscillate, even to contradict himself. He turns a phrase of Sallust (*cum Gallis pro salute, non pro gloria certamen*) into a definition of the sorts of war.[3] The mainspring of the one sort (and it is the common kind) is ambition; the other arises when a whole people pours out, under duress, in search of living-space. It is here, in the consequences of this definition, that the charge of being merely a realist, and not an idealist, might most easily be brought against Machiavelli. How could he, being without a nationalism based on the realization of the oneness of Italy (and how, again, could he have that, when it did not exist?[4]), go beyond it to imagine as well an internationalism?—the extension of his system of equipoises and safeguards from the internal scene to the international, or interstatal, one? Naturally, Machiavelli has no conception of this, which is, of course, unfortunate for him, and for the world in which he lived. And we, to whom the idea has at least at last occurred, even if we have not yet succeeded in giving it any practical expression, are entitled to whatever superiority we wish to assume. Before we assume too much, we may suitably recall the doubting words of Faguet, written about the same problem in its relation to Montesquieu, at the very beginning of this century. Faguet observed that Montesquieu had seen this problem of perpetual war in Europe, 'dont il ne faut lui faire aucun reproche'; and Faguet added that there were only two remedies, and that both were chimerical: a confederated United States of Europe, or the conquest of all the States of Europe by one which should impose a new *pax romana*, disarming itself shortly after having disarmed all the rest.[5]

[1] *D.* II, IV, 199. [2] *D.* II, XXX, 292. [3] Sallust, *Bel. Jug.*, 74; *D.* II, VIII, 206.
[4] G. F.-H. Berkeley: 'Of course, the achievement of nationality is primarily a mental process.'
[5] Faguet, *Pol. Comp.*, 242–3.

Is it surprising that Machiavelli, towards the sad end of his life, in a pathetic passage of a letter to Francesco Guicciardini, wrote as follows: 'Sempre che io ho ricordo e'si fece guerra, o e'se ne ragionò; ora se ne ragiona, di qui a un poco si farà, e quando sarà finita si ragionerà di nuovo.'[1] There is a note of disillusionment in his letters towards those last years, which represents a tiring and a frustration.

In the meantime, he restates in Book II his and Livy's idea of that sequence forwards from defence to offence. It is impossible for a republic to succeed in remaining tranquil, enjoying its liberty and its small territory, 'perché, se lei non molesterà altrui, sarà molestata ella; e dallo essere molestata le nascerà la voglia e la necessità dello acquistare'.[2] This being so, then Machiavelli, with his conviction that the Romans acted with open eyes, concludes their policy was dictated by a desire to expand (*ampliare*) in the best manner. Their wars were undertaken offensively, not for defence.[3] On these grounds, then (and they are stated in the only chapter which the diligent Burd found wicked in its entirety), the Romans prepared deceit for the other cities of Italy with which they contended for mastery. Instead of subjecting them directly, they made them associates under their own laws, then used their help against those lying further off. As these last began to acknowledge Rome as their conqueror, not Rome's associates, so the intermediate cities awoke to find themselves enslaved before they knew it. Now this is stated by Machiavelli as an 'inganno', which is against the tenour of what he read in Livy, and is an extension of his practice of tying the finishing back to the beginning point in a straight and intentional line. It does not follow that the winning formula, because it won, was one that had been planned to work out in that way. Nor if we were to take Livy's side against Machiavelli on this, should we be at liberty to presume that he has here anticipated Saint-Evremond and his successors in a statement of Roman cynicism. As we have seen, there had not evolved in Machiavelli's time any check òn interstatal relations, and it is what he least anticipates. Even, for one statement ('E veramente, alcuna provincia non fu mai unita o felice, se la non viene tutta alla ubbidienza d'una republica o d'uno principe, come è avvenuto alla Francia ed alla Spagna'[4]) which anticipates the theory of national unities, there are scores which think in terms of the city-unit. Are not Pisa and Arezzo the constant enemies of Florence, not

---

[1] *L.F.*, VIII, 187 (the date is 1525).   [2] *D.* II, XIX, 249.
[3] *D.* II, XVII, 239: 'E veggendo come ei feciono quasi tutte le loro guerre per offendere altrui, e non per difendere loro.'
[4] *D.* I, XII, 55.

candidates for union with her? Machiavelli cannot transcend that
contemporary situation. It will be a logical development of the chain
of thought which he initiates that it should reach the idea of government for the benefit of the governed, and then go on to desire some
of the safeguards in international affairs which have become acceptable in national ones. But, once more, since we are still wrestling
painfully and elementarily with this type of problem it would be a
little excessive on our part to rail at Machiavelli for not having lived
in a stable enough world to anticipate it. In fact, if we look again
to the tentative ideas of Montesquieu on this point we can realize
how far there was, and is, to go. 'On diroit, Rhédi, qu'il y a deux
justices toutes différentes: l'une qui règle les affaires des particuliers,
qui règne dans le droit civil; l'autre qui règle les différends qui sur-
viennent de peuple à peuple, qui tyrannise dans le droit public:
comme si le droit public n'étoit pas lui-même un droit civil; non pas,
à la vérité, d'un pays particulier, mais du monde.'[1] That is admirable,
and is what we are waiting for: but the forgetting that it was not
even formulable as an aspiration in the time of Machiavelli has led to
inaccurate judgments about what he said, and what he meant. For
instance, that Chapter XVIII of the *Prince* on faith in rulers—how
often is it remembered that it has an external application? is part of
this difficulty of manoeuvring in a world of Ferdinands (*ce bon roi
parjure Ferdinand*)? Machiavelli's concern with the keeping of faith
within the State is constant and general: what other reason has he for
rejecting mercenaries than that you can place no reliance on them?
and is not a large part of the importance of religion in that it implies
the sanctity of one's word? There is no shortage of testimony for
this; but because of the distinction never having been made, it has
not been called, or else it has been entered with his cynicism.

But to return to the Romans and their *ambition*. It can easily be
shown that Machiavelli is really following a theoretic bent. For he
has already attributed another cause to the incessant wars of Rome
(that series so disconcerting when it is presented in epitome, as by
Florus). 'Questo medesimo omore si levò in Roma contro al nome
de'Consoli; perché veggendo quello popolo nascere l'una guerra
dall'altra, e non poter mai riposarsi; dove e'dovevano pensare che la
nascessi dall'ambizione de'vicini, che gli volevano opprimere, pen-
savano nascessi dall'ambizione de'nobili.'[2] As I observed in passing
earlier, the new view of Saint-Evremond handed a certificate to
Rome's neighbours which was not obviously justifiable. And if in

---

[1] *L.P.*, XCIV, 187-8.   [2] *D.* I, XXX, 121.

Book I Machiavelli talks of the ambition of others, not the ambition of Rome, in Book II itself he denies even the policy of ambition to the Romans! In fact, their policy, maintained while they were confined to Italy, of leaving local jurisdiction intact here appears as a virtue, not as a trick. The first Praetor they sent out was to Capua, at Capua's special entreaty—'il quale vi mandarono, non per loro ambizione, ma perché e'ne furono ricerchi dai Capovani'.[1] From this there comes the reminder of Livy's insistence on the virtues of the Roman republic as an observer of legality, and the quotation (as so often with Machiavelli's quotations, made from a full memory, and thus just coquetting with the actual words of Livy): 'Quod jam non solum arma, sed iura romana pollebant.'[2] It is true that this is followed a page later by the idea that men will cast themselves all the more readily into one's lap the more one seems unlikely to subdue them, which suggests the trick. But it does not transpire from Livy's account that he regarded the process in that light, and we might take Mictio's answer to Antioch as indicative of Livy's conviction.[3] Was it not Sallust's view as well that the origin of Rome's wars lay in her neighbours' envy? And when the Romans had repelled the danger, they helped their friends, 'magisque dandis quam accipiendis beneficiis amicitias parabant'.[4] Nor did Taine, perhaps, remember sufficiently that Greek praise for the Roman concern for law, their struggle 'ne quod toto orbe terrarum iniustum imperium sit, et ubique ius, fas, lex potentissima sint'.[5] Naturally, I do not put forward those few observations as any contribution to the history of Rome, but as points which stood in Machiavelli's way when he looked at that history. And it is sufficiently clear from the conflicting elements of his presentation in this same Book II what has happened in this passing from the answer to a pressing need to the erection of a system.

As well, there is in Book II, right at its outset, a chapter which dissociates Machiavelli from the very matter of the book itself. Chapter II debates the theme of liberty versus servitude, and I have quoted from it already the statement on liberty as a prerequisite to any expansion in power or wealth. Look at the rise of Athens after the death of Pisistratus, of Rome after the expulsion of the kings. Lose liberty, and gain an energetic tyrant (*virtuoso*), whatever progress

---

[1] D. II, XXI, 256.   [2] Livy, IX, 20.

[3] Livy, XXXV, 46: 'Mirari se, dixit, ad quos liberandos Antiochus, relicto regno suo, in Europam traiecisset. Nullam enim civitatem se in Graecia nosse, quae aut praesidium habeat, aut stipendium Romanis pendat, aut foedere iniquo alligata, quas nolit, leges patiatur.'

[4] Sallust, *Cat.*, 3.   [5] Livy, XXXIII, 32.

is made after will be for his benefit only. It is a chapter which Mussolini should have read. Here with the difference in temperament between ancient and modern religious thought comes the examination of why the love for liberty seems now absent, whereas formerly there was the strenuous resistance of a legion of city-republics to the Roman progress. It is at this point that he denies, as it were, the theme of his second book. 'Ancora che io creda piú tosto essere cagione di questo, che lo Imperio romano con le sue arme e sua grandezza spense tutte le republiche e tutti e'viveri civili.'[1] Even when the Roman Empire had fallen into dissolution, these were unable to reconstitute themselves. Is it not plain that if the impetus of his reverence for the Roman republic in its ascending course had not been so great, if he himself had been of a more sceptical turn of mind, a new and embarrassing train of reflections might have arisen in the wake of this realization? Can *ampliare* when it includes so self-stultificatory an end be any remedy? Are we not back on the cycle, and without the brakes? This, then, on the surface, may be the most 'machiavellian' part of the *Discorsi*, but the contradictions and limitations imposed on it by Machiavelli himself show that he has not lost the interests we have seen established elsewhere. Although Tommasini opined that Machiavelli followed Valla in the rejection of Aristotle's idea of virtue as a mean, and in spite of that surface tendency to like whole remedies and to eschew the middle path, Machiavelli is inevitably and resolutely moderate. Could he, who speaks constantly of one *inconveniente* springing from the resolution of another, have denied Montesquieu, that other great moderate, when he said: 'Ainsi, comme les monarques doivent avoir de la sagesse pour augmenter leur puissance, ils ne doivent pas avoir moins de prudence afin de la borner. En faisant cesser les inconvéniens de la petitesse, il faut qu'ils aient toujours l'oeil sur les inconvéniens de la grandeur'?[2] Rather, that is a wholly Machiavellian way of speaking.

It will have been noticed that I have only detached the second book of the *Discorsi* for separate discussion. The third has not a separate theme from the first (as the second had): it considers the same themes, only starting from the idea of individual influence on them. The central concern, and the pattern of Machiavelli's suggestions for the solution of political problems, do not change. So far is his thought from being fragmentary, as Eliot said, or *vaste et ondoyant*

[1] *D.* II, II, 189.
[2] *Esp. d. l.*, IX, VI, 178; and cf. *G. et D.*, XVIII, 481: '. . . et les inconvéniens ont fait naître les inconvéniens.'

(like Montaigne) as Mazzoni averred,[1] that it is rooted to one conception: and this is less perhaps the picture of Rome which he found in Livy, than the key to it which he borrowed from Polybius. Do we want a last proof? Let us look at the recurrence of the idea, the *guard on liberty*, which we found at the root of Roman stability. It is in the initial chapter to Book III, with the necessity of going back to the *principio*. And what language could be closer than this to that of Montesquieu, of Montesquieu to whom he handed this word *principe*? 'Quand une république est corrompue, on ne peut remédier à aucun des maux qui naissent, qu'en ôtant la corruption, et en rappelant les principes: toute autre correction est ou inutile, ou un nouveau mal.'[2] Or, as Machiavelli put it: in the origins lies the vitality (remember Sallust, 'Omnia mala exempla bonis initiis orta sunt'[3]). And according to the old, nor entirely exploded, medical doctrine, we add daily to our system poisons which accrue and must some day be purged out, if health is to be restored: so it is politically. Hence the reforms of St. Francis and St. Dominic; hence the reversion to early Rome. Machiavelli has not travelled, then, away from his preoccupations in Book I. Even the mentor at his ear is a familiar one. How does this last book open?—'Egli è cosa verissima, come tutte le cose del mondo hanno il termine della vita loro.' It sounds like a quotation, surely it is still Sallust ringing in his mind? 'Omnia orta crescunt, auctaque senescunt.' There can be no perpetual state then, that is a chimera: but Sparta with its eight hundred years, and Rome with a longer span? Do they not point the way to something that is worth aiming at, by contrast with the political instability of the period 1494 to 1519, the period from the first coming of Charles VIII to the finish of the *Discorsi*? We, who live in a world which has endorsed (for internal affairs) a large part of what Machiavelli desired, may suitably answer in the affirmative.

---

[1] Mazzoni said, 'La materia dei *Discorsi* è vasta e diversa,' or was it *infinita e varia*?—it matters not greatly which we choose.

[2] *Esp. d. l.*, VIII, XII, 161.   [3] Sallust, *Cat.*, 19; *D.* I, XLVI, 136.

VIII

CONCLUSION

THERE is an old story, put about, I think, by Bandello, of
Machiavelli being called upon to demonstrate his abilities as a
military expert. All through the morning he toiled away to make the
troops thus committed to his charge perform the correct evolutions
according to his theories, but he proved incapable of accomplishing
anything. Then Giovanni delle Bande Nere stepped forth from
watching him, and blew a whistle, and in a twinkling all were in
their proper place. *Se non è vero, è ben trovato*; and it puts the *Arte
della Guerra* neatly out of the way. Just as Burd did, by studying its
sources, and showing that Machiavelli was largely echoing people
like Vegetius; and when we add also that well-known lack on
Machiavelli's part of a proper appreciation of the merits, and the
future, of gunpowder, the hopeful reader ('mon semblable, mon
frère!') may feel that this work has an archaeological interest only,
and that I, who had promised not to be exhaustive, may let the book
rest on its shelf. And I protest that *almost* I will. For Machiavelli's
theories on how one should wage war have little applicability now,
when we can do it so much more professionally. But yet it is the
same Machiavelli who plunged into this theory of the art of war,
and there is much in this book which is not listed in the sources, and
which is confirmatory of what we have seen. One thing I mentioned
earlier which is not here, the interpretation of the omens; and if the
reader has the patience to reach Book VI he will find a specific renun-
ciation of this part of antiquity. Those were things that cannot
happen in our times, 'sí per non essere i nostri uomini tanto superstiziosi, sí perché la nostra Religione rimuove in tutto da sé tali
opinioni'.[1] Is that not interesting both in what it repudiates, and in
what it accepts? And the concluding passages of Book VII are to be
noted. But it is in the opening of the book that the most important
expressions of opinion will be found. If I may adopt, in reverse,
the procedure that Burd used for the immoral passages of the *Discorsi*,
and indicate the whereabouts of the most valuable statements of the
Arte della Guerra, it will prove expeditious. It is a matter of reading
the first twenty-five pages, starting with the Proem, in the Italia

[1] *A. d. G.*, VI, 387.

edition. And, indeed, it might be preferable for the reader approaching Machiavelli for the first time to begin with these pages in order to have a clear, and a reasonable idea of where he stood. Of course, he writes of war because (as Villari would say) he likes it? and admires those who use it ruthlessly for their own ends? Well, no: he writes of war because he dislikes it, but because he thinks of it as the necessary defence for those who are good from those who are bad. Was it not the classic comment of Bacon? 'For without this, virtue lieth open and unfenced.' And the basis for that is in the Proem here: 'Perché tutte l'arti che si ordinano in una civiltà per cagione del bene comune degli uomini, tutti gli ordini fatti in quella per vivere con timore delle leggi e d'Iddio, sarebbono vani se non fussono preparate le difese loro; le quali, bene ordinate mantengono quegli, ancora che non bene ordinati.'[1] Is it surprising after that that at the foot of the same page Machiavelli calls for men who are 'faithful, peaceful, and full of the fear of God,' even if, and even especially if, they are soldiers? It is well known that Machiavelli disliked mercenaries, and abhorred auxiliaries, in war. Who are to be his soldiers, then? They are citizens who will be ready to return to their professions when the emergency is gone, not professionals who desire continuance of turmoil. The end and object of war is peace, and Machiavelli comes here to the same statement, applied to the ordinary soldier, as I have quoted earlier from Castiglione against rulers who desire to live by war.[2] Let the reader add the reflections which he will find on pages 203–10, and he will find the valuable continuance to this same theme. There can be no more creditable, or credit-worthy, certificate of Machiavelli's intentions than these initial pages of the *Art of War*.

There is one more major work of Machiavelli, and I shall call upon it least: not because it goes against my purpose, or my argument, but because it has been already agreed that the *Istorie Fiorentine*, which initiate Europe so worthily into the art of writing history and no longer chronicle, are (to quote Tommasini's words) the 'riepilogo di tutte l'altre opere sue'. That means, does it not, that in the *Istorie Fiorentine* we can all find enough to confirm the views we hold of Machiavelli? How, for instance, does Florence differ in her history from Rome? In Rome, when the two humours led to discord, the nobility gave ground and compromised; in Florence they defended themselves, and hence there rose the series, bloodshed, exiles, laws 'non a comune utilità, ma tutte in favore del vincitore'.[3]

[1] *A. d. G., Proemio*, 186.   [2] *A. d. G.*, I, 199.   [3] *I.F.*, ed. Plinio Carli, I, 133.

Such a passage defines adequately for us the role of the *Istorie Fioren-tine* alongside that of the *Discorsi*. Nor will it have escaped the prudent reader that this is the final rejection of the idea of *virtú*: laws that are all in favour of a victor are the ones that lead to the history of Florence, not to that of Rome. And Machiavelli appeals from the former, which is a warning, to the latter, which is a lesson. There is still room for virtue to be a mean, not an extremity. Nor need we stop at such a demonstration if we wished to continue. It is because I feel that by now Machiavelli's ideas do not need confirmation, and am chary of mere repetition, that I leave them on one side. Besides, have I not already written enough? If the reader agrees with me, then he will be ready to proceed himself to the enjoyment of the *Istorie Fiorentine*; if, however, he disagrees, then there is plenty in the *Discourses*, the *Legations*, and the *Prince* that he will be anxious to turn back to. For myself, since this is a book that has in a way been a score of years a-writing, since first I was introduced into the company of Machiavelli, I may plead with him as Dante did with Virgil,

> vagliami il lungo studio e'l grande amore
> che m'ha fatto cercar lo tuo volume.

SUMMARY LIST OF EDITIONS
AND PRINCIPAL WORKS QUOTED

(N.B.—This is not intended to be a bibliography of Machiavelli)

Alberti, L. B., *Opere Volgari*, ed. Bonucci, 5 vols., 1843–9.
Alfieri, V., *Del Principe e delle Lettere*, in *Opere*, vol. II, 1828.
Appian, *Delle Guerre Civili et Esterne de Romani*, tr. Alessandro Bracci, Venice, 1550.
Artaud, A. F., *Machiavel, son génie et ses erreurs*, 2 vols., Paris, 1833.
Barbagallo, C., *Storia Universale*, vol. IV, Torino, UTET, 1936.
Bayle, P., *Dictionnaire Historique et Critique*, vol. III, ed. 1720.
Benoist, C., *Le Machiavélisme*, 3 vols., Paris, 1907.
Binchy, D. A., *Church and State in Fascist Italy*, London, 1941.
Boccalini, T., *Advertisements from Parnassus*, tr. Henry Cary, 1669.
Buonaccorsi, B., *Diario*, Florence, 1568.
Burd, L. A.—
    Le Fonti Letterarie di Machiavelli nell'Arte della Guerra, Rome, 1897.
    v. under Machiavelli.
Caggese, R., *Firenze dalla decadenza di Roma al Risorgimento d'Italia*, 3 vols., Florence, 1912–21.
Cambi, G., *Istorie in Delizie degli Eruditi Toscani*, tom. xx–xxiii, Florence, 1785–6.
Castiglione, B., *Il Cortegiano*, ed. Cian.
Chabod, F., *Sulla Composizione de 'Il Principe' di Niccolò Machiavelli*, in *Archivum Romanicum*, XI, 1927.
Chamard, H., *Les Origines de la Poésie Française de la Renaissance*, 1920.
Charbonnel, J. R., *La Pensée Italienne au XVIe Siècle*, Paris, 1919.
Cherel, A., *La Pensée de Machiavel en France*, 1935.
Cicero, *De Officiis*, ed. Ch. Appuhn, Paris, Garnier.
Collotti, F., *Machiavelli—Lo Stato*, Messina, 1939.
Commines, P. de, *Mémoires . . .*, ed. Buchon, Paris, 1836.
Croce, B., *Teoria e Storia della Storiografia*, 2a ed., Bari, 1920.
Curtius, Quintus, *Historia Alexandri Magni*, Aldus, 1520.
Ercole, F.—
    La Politica di Machiavelli, 1926.
    Pensatori e Uomini d'Azione, 1935.
Dante—
    La Divina Commedia, ed. Casini-Barbi, 3 vols.
    De Monarchia, ed. Fraticelli, in *Opere Minori*, vol. II, 1906.
Eliot, T. S., *For Lancelot Andrewes*.
Faguet, *La Politique Comparée de Montesquieu, Rousseau, et Voltaire*, 1902.
Fénelon—
    Dialogues des Morts, Amsterdam, 1727.
    Les Avantures de Télémaque, 2 vols., Paris, 1729.
Flamini, F., *Il Cinquecento*.
Florus, *Epitome Rerum Romanarum*, ed. P. Hainsselin and H. Watelet.

Frederick II, *L'Antimachiavel*, Geneva, 1759.

Gentile, G., *Studî sul Rinascimento*, 1923.

Gilson, E., *Dante et la Philosophie*, Paris, 1939.

Giovio, P., *Istorie del suo Tempo*, tr. L. Domenichi, Venice, 1556.

Guicciardini, F.—
>   *Istoria d'Italia*, 10 vols., Milan, 1803.
>   *Storia Fiorentina*, Florence, 1859.
>   *Dialogo e Discorsi del Reggimento di Firenze*, ed. Palmarocchi, Bari, 1932.

Jamison, E. M., Ady, C. M., Vernon, K. D., and Terry, C. S., *Italy Medieval and Modern*, Oxford, 1917.

Janni, E., *Machiavelli*, Milan, 1927.

Johnson, A. H., *Europe in the Sixteenth Century*, 7th ed., 1925.

Jovius, P., *v.* under Giovio.

Justin, *Historiarum ex Trogo Pompeio*, Oxonii, 1705.

Landucci, *Diario Fiorentino*, Florence, 1883.

Lanson, *Histoire de la Littérature française*, 12e éd.

Laurent, F., *Etudes sur l'Humanité*, 1865, vol. X for *Le Machiavélisme*.

Livy, ed. Travers Twiss, 4 vols., Oxford, 1840.

Machiavelli, N.—
>   *Opere*, 8 vols., Italia, 1813. (Still the most attractive edition of Machiavelli. I quote from it except for the *Prince*, and unless a contrary indication is given; but for the *Discorsi* while I quote the page of this edition I have accepted the readings of the Mazzoni-Casella edition.)
>   *Il Principe, e Discorsi* . . . premessevi le considerazioni del Prof. Andrea Zambelli.
>   *Le Opere* . . . per cura di L. Passerini e G. Milanesi, 6 vols. only, Florence, 1875. (Abbr. P.M.)
>   *Il Principe*, ed. Burd, Oxford, 1891. (Abbr. Burd.)
>   *Tutte le Opere Storiche e Letterarie*, ed. Mazzoni-Casella, Florence, 1929. (Abbr. M.C.) (The best text in an illegible format. In spite of the *all*, the Letters are a selection, and the Legations are omitted.)
>   *Il Principe*, ed. Lisio, Florence, 1927.
>   *Istorie Fiorentine*, ed. Plinio Carli, 2 vols., Florence, 1927.
>   *Lettere Familiari*, ed. Alvisi, Florence, 1883.
>   *Scritti Inediti*, ed. Canestrini, Florence, 1857.
>   *Pagine Scelte*, ed. V. A. Ruiz, Milan, 1929. (Abbr. Ruiz.)
>   Throughout I have abbreviated the titles of Machiavelli's works for the purpose of the notes to their initials (e.g. *P.* = *Principe*, *D.* = *Discorsi*, *L.F.* = *Lettere Familiari*, etc.).

Masi, B., *Ricordanze di B. Masi Calderaio*, Florence, 1906.

Montesquieu, *Oeuvres*, 3 vols., London, Nourse, 1767.

Morley, J., *Machiavelli* (Romanes Lecture), 1897.

Muir, D. Erskine, *Machiavelli and his Times*, 1936.

Mussolini, B., *Scritti e Discorsi*, vol. IV.

Nerli, F. de', *Commentarj dei Fatti Civili* . . ., 2 vols., Trieste, 1859.

Oro, I. dell', *Il Segreto dei Borgia*, Milan, 1938.

Paoli, Paolo, in the volume, F. Rinuccini, q.v., clxxi–cci.

Plutarch (I have used Domenichi's translation in the Giolito series).

Polybius, *Dell'Imprese de' Greci*, etc., tr. L. Domenichi, Venice, 1564.

Rinuccini, Alamanno, in the volume, F. Rinuccini, lxxxix–clxii.
Rinuccini, F., *Ricordi Storici*, ed. Aiazzi, Florence, 1840.
Rinuccini, Neri, in the volume, F. Rinuccini, clxii–clxxi.
Rocquain, *L'Esprit révolutionnaire avant la Révolution*, 1878.
Russo, L., *Ritratti e Disegni Storici*, Bari, 1937.
Saint-Evremond, *Réflexions sur les Divers Génies du Peuple Romain*, in *Oeuvres*, II, Amsterdam, 1739.
Sallust, *Coniuratio Catilinae, Bellum Jugurthinum*, Florence, Giunta, 1513.
Sanctis, F. de—
　Storia della Letteratura Italiana.
　Nuovi Saggi Critici, Napoli, 1872.
　Saggi Critici, vol. III, 1a ed., milanese.
Suetonius, *Vitae XII Caesarum*, Aldus, 1516.
Tacitus, *Opere Latino e volgare*, Florence, 1637.
Taine, H., *Essai sur Tite-Live*, 1860.
Texte, J., *L'Influence Italienne en France* in *Etudes de Littérature Européenne*, 1898.
Toffanin, G.—
　Machiavelli e il Tacitismo, Padova, 1921.
　Il Cinquecento, Milan, 1929.
Tommasini, O., *La Vita e gli Scritti di Niccolò Machiavelli*, 2 vols., Turin, 1883–1911.
Valerius Maximus, *Dictorum et factorum Memorabilium*, Aldus, 1502.
Vignal, L. Gautier, *Machiavel*, Paris, 1929.
Villari, P.—
　La Storia di Girolamo Savonarola e de' suoi tempi, 2 vols., Florence, 1887–8.
　The Life and Times of Niccolò Machiavelli, tr. Linda Villari, London, 1929.
Walpole, H., *Letters to the Countess of Ossory*, 3 vols., London, 1903.
Whitfield, J. H.—
　Petrarch and the Renascence, Oxford, 1943.
　New Views on the Borgias, in *History*, XXIX, 1944.
Zambelli, A., *v.* under Machiavelli, *Il Principe*.

INDEX